Straight to FIRST

Student's Book with Answers

Roy Norris

Contents

Unit	Language focus	Vocabulary	Writing
1 Influence Page 6	1 Present tenses 2 Past tenses	1 Influences 2 The weather	Part 1: Essay
2 Success! Page 14	Comparisons	Word formation: Adjectives Sport	Part 2: Article
Review Units 1 and 2 Page 22	Reading and Use of English Part 4: Transformations Reading and Use of English Part 3: Word formation		
3 Image and images Page 24	1 Modals of speculation and deduction 2 Relative clauses	Appearance	Part 2: Review
4 Going away Page 32	Gerunds and infinitives	Holidays and travel Word formation: Prefixes	Part 2: Email and letter
Review Units 3 and 4 Page 40	Reading and Use of English Part 4: Transformations Reading and Use of English Part 1: Multiple-choice cloze		
5 Fitting in Page 42	1 Time linkers with past tenses 2 The future	Word formation: Nouns 1 Personality	Part 2: Report
6 News and views Page 50	Reported speech Reported statements Reported questions Reporting verbs	Making decisions	Part 1: Essay
Review Units 5 and 6 Page 58	Reading and Use of English Part 4: Transformations Reading and Use of English Part 2: Open cloze		
7 Survival Page 60	1 Countable and uncountable nouns 2 Obligation, prohibition, advice and necessity	1 Surviving 2 Prepositions Word formation: Adverbs	Part 2: Report
8 Brain games Page 68	1 The passive 2 Passive of reporting verbs	1 Memory 2 Arts and culture	Part 2: Review
Review Units 7 and 8 Page 76	Reading and Use of English Part 4: Transformations Reading and Use of English Part 2: Open cloze		
9 A slave to routine Page 78	Conditionals	Time Word formation: Nouns 2	Part 2: Letter and email
10 Getting on Page 86	1 *Wish, if only* and *hope* *Should have/ought to have* 2 *have/get something done*	1 Relationships 2 Age	Part 2: Article
Review Units 9 and 10 Page 94	Reading and Use of English Part 4: Transformations Reading and Use of English Part 3: Word formation		
Additional Material Page 96	Grammar Reference Page 102	Writing Bank Page 116	Wordlist Page 124

Reading and Use of English		Listening	Speaking
Part 7: Multiple matching	Part 1: Multiple-choice cloze	Part 2: Sentence completion	Part 1: Personal questions
Part 6: Gapped text		Part 3: Multiple matching Part 4: Multiple choice	Part 2: Talking about photos
Part 5: Multiple choice		Part 3: Multiple matching Part 1: Multiple choice	Part 3: Collaborative task Part 4: Further discussion
Part 7: Multiple matching	Part 2: Open cloze	Part 2: Sentence completion	Part 2: Talking about photos
Part 5: Multiple choice	Part 3: Word formation	Part 3: Multiple matching Part 1: Multiple choice	Part 2: Talking about photos Part 3: Collaborative task Part 4: Further discussion
Part 6: Gapped text	Part 1: Multiple-choice cloze	Part 4: Multiple choice	Part 3: Collaborative task
Part 7: Multiple matching	Part 3: Word formation	Part 1: Multiple choice Part 2: Sentence completion	Part 3: Collaborative task Part 4: Further discussion
Part 5: Multiple choice	Part 1: Multiple-choice cloze	Part 4: Multiple choice	Part 2: Talking about photos
Part 5: Multiple choice	Part 2: Open cloze	Part 2: Sentence completion Part 3: Multiple matching	Part 3: Collaborative task Part 4: Further discussion
Part 6: Gapped text	Part 1: Multiple-choice cloze	Part 3: Multiple matching Part 4: Multiple choice	Part 2: Talking about photos Part 3: Collaborative task Part 4: Further discussion

Phrasal Verb list
Page 129

Listening scripts
Page 131

Answer key
Page 144

Introduction

About the course

Straight to First is a preparation course for students wishing to take the *Cambridge English: First (FCE)* examination, equivalent to level B2 in the Council of Europe's Common European Framework of Reference for Languages. The course is designed to improve your overall language level and help you develop the skills which are required for the *First* exam.

The Student's Book

The **Student's Book** comprises ten units which provide a range of interesting topics to help stimulate discussion. Each of these units contains thorough preparation and practice for the *First* exam, and you will find the following boxes to help you deal successfully with each task:

- In the early units there are regular **Help** boxes, which give advice on how to approach the various task types in the four papers of the *First* exam.
- In later units you will find **Remember** boxes, which provide reminders of the main points of the advice in the Help boxes.
- Throughout the book there are **Useful language** boxes, containing vocabulary and structures which you could use when doing speaking and writing tasks.

Reading, writing, listening and speaking **skills** are given comprehensive coverage in each unit, and to help you further with writing, there is a **Writing Bank** at the end of the book on pages 116–123. This includes a sample question and model answer for all the different writing types in the Writing paper, highlighting the most important features of each one. The Writing Bank also includes Useful language boxes and further writing tasks for you to do.

In order to help you increase your word store, each unit contains at least one **Vocabulary** section. In these sections, particular emphasis is placed on collocations (pairs or groups of words that are often found together) and these are highlighted in bold for you to record in your vocabulary notebook. In Units 2, 4, 5, 7 and 9 there are sections focusing on different aspects of **Word formation**, which are designed to help you build your vocabulary and prepare you for the Word formation task in the Reading and Use of English paper of the *First* exam.

There are also one or more **Language focus** sections in each unit, which help you revise and extend your knowledge of the main grammatical structures you are expected to be able to use at this level. Each section refers you to the relevant page of the **Grammar Reference** (which you can find on pages 102–115), but only after you have first been given the chance to show what you already know about the structures being dealt with.

After every two units there is a two-page **Review** section. These sections contain exercises which allow you to practise the vocabulary and structures you have covered in the previous two units. Each Review section also includes two Reading and Use of English tasks, one of which is always Part 4 of the Reading and Use of English paper, Key word transformations.

The Student's Resource Centre

On the **Student's Resource Centre**, which can be accessed using the code provided on the inside front cover of this book, there are videos of two candidates performing all four parts of the Speaking paper in the *First* exam. These, and the accompanying worksheets, allow you to see what an actual speaking test looks like as well as think about the best approach to answering questions in this paper. The Student's Resource Centre also contains extra language tasks for each unit, which give you further practice on grammar and vocabulary that is covered in the corresponding unit of the Student's Book. Finally, the **Wordlist**, which is at the end of the Student's Book on pages 124–128, is also available on the Student's Resource Centre with definitions, sample sentences and phonetic script for each word or phrase.

The Workbook

Accompanying the course is a **Workbook**, also with ten units. Every unit contains Vocabulary and Language focus sections, which provide further practice of the language from the corresponding unit of Student's Book. In every unit there is also one each of the following exam tasks: Reading, Use of English, Listening and Writing.

The Cambridge English: First (FCE) examination

The *First* examination consists of four papers. The Listening, Writing and Speaking papers are each worth 20% of the total marks; the Reading and Use of English paper is worth 40%. The scores from all four papers are averaged to give you an overall result for the examination. A summary of what each paper in the exam consists of is provided on the next page.

Reading and Use of English   1 hour 15 minutes

This paper has seven parts: Parts 1 to 4 are grammar and vocabulary tasks; Parts 5 to 7 are reading tasks. Each correct answer in Parts 1 to 3 receives one mark; each question in Part 4 carries up to two marks. For the reading comprehension tasks, each correct answer in Parts 5 and 6 receives two marks, and there is one mark for each question in Part 7.

Part	Task type	Number of questions	What you have to do
1	Multiple-choice cloze	8	There is a text with eight gaps. For each gap, decide on the best answer from a choice of four. The main focus is on vocabulary.
2	Open cloze	8	There is a text with eight gaps. Complete each gap with one word. The main focus is on grammar, with some focus on vocabulary.
3	Word formation	8	There is a text with eight gaps. Complete each gap with the correct form of a given word. The main focus is on vocabulary.
4	Key word transformations	6	Complete a gapped sentence with two to five words, one of which you are given. The completed sentence must have the same meaning as the lead-in sentence. The focus is on grammar and vocabulary.
5	Multiple choice	6	Decide on the best answer from a choice of four.
6	Gapped text	6	Replace sentences which have been removed from a text.
7	Multiple matching	10	Match questions or 'prompts' to the correct text or part of a text.

Writing   1 hour 20 minutes

This paper has two parts, each of which carries the same number of marks. There is one Part 1 question, which must be answered by all candidates, and in Part 2 you write an answer to one question from a choice of three. You are required to write between 140 and 190 words for each part.

Part	Task type	Number of tasks	What you have to do
1	Essay	1 (compulsory)	Write an essay. You are given a title and notes to guide your writing.
2	From the following: article, email/letter, report, review	3 (choose one)	Write your answer according to the task instructions.

Listening   approximately 40 minutes

This paper has four parts with a total of 30 questions. Each part contains one or more recorded text, which is heard twice. Recordings may be monologues, such as speeches, lectures or announcements, or they may be conversations, radio interviews or discussions. You are tested on your ability to understand, for example, opinions, attitudes, specific information, gist or detail. There is one mark for each correct answer.

Part	Task type	Number of questions	What you have to do
1	Multiple choice	8	Listen to eight short unrelated extracts, and answer one three-option multiple-choice question for each.
2	Sentence completion	10	Listen to one speaker for three to four minutes and complete gaps in sentences with words or phrases from the recording.
3	Multiple matching	5	Listen to five short related monologues and match each speaker to the correct option.
4	Multiple choice	7	Listen to an interview or an exchange between two speakers for three to four minutes and answer seven three-option multiple-choice questions.

Speaking   approximately 14 minutes

This paper has four parts. There are usually two candidates and two examiners, one of whom conducts the test and assesses, while the other assesses but does not take an active part in the test.

Part	Task type	Time	What you have to do
1	Personal questions	2 minutes	Respond to questions from the interviewer with information about yourself.
2	Talking about photos	4 minutes	Talk about two photographs for one minute, and comment for 30 seconds after the other candidate's turn.
3	Collaborative task	4 minutes	You are given instructions with written prompts which you use in a two-minute discussion, followed by a one-minute decision-making task.
4	Further discussion	4 minutes	Take part in a discussion which is related to the topic of Part 3.

1 Influence

Vocabulary 1
Influences

1 💬 The pictures below show different influences in our lives. Discuss these questions with a partner.

1. How can these people and things influence us?
2. Are these influences good or bad? Why?

2a Complete the phrases in **1–5** using the correct form of the verbs in the box.

| copy | encourage | have | look | set | shape |

1. My kids love his classes. He's clearly going to _____ **a big influence on their lives**.
2. Parents can _____ children **to** read by reading to them, but also by _____ **a good example** and reading themselves.
3. I always admired and _____ **up to** my older sister – I thought she was wonderful.
4. Some people believe everything they read and this can really _____ **their opinions**. It's quite worrying really.
5. This guy is a role model for a lot of youngsters. The kids idolise him and _____ **his every move**!

2b Match the comments in **2a** to pictures **A–E**.

3 💬 Discuss these questions with your partner.

1. Which teacher has had the biggest influence on you?
2. Did you idolise a celebrity when you were younger?
3. Which celebrity today do you think is a good role model? And a bad one?
4. Were/Are you encouraged to read by your parents?

Reading and Use of English Part 7

Multiple matching

1 Work in pairs. You are going to read a magazine article in which four people have written about the person who has influenced them the most. Look at the people (**A–D**). What influence do you think they had on the person writing?

2 Now look at the questions and read the texts again carefully. For questions **1–10**, choose from the people (**A–D**). The people may be chosen more than once.

Help

- Read through the questions and underline key words. Numbers **1** and **2** have been done for you.
- Read section **A** and answer any questions you can. Underline the relevant part of the text.
- Do the same for sections **B–D**.
- If you have any unanswered questions look at the texts again.

Which person who is described

gave advice to the writer when the writer was not at all receptive?	1
always remained calm?	2
changed the way a lot of people thought?	3
was the reason for the writer changing career?	4
is one of a number of people who have been important to the writer?	5
caused people to stop laughing at the writer?	6
influenced the writer more than the writer first realised?	7
only knew the writer for a short time?	8
was unselfish with their time?	9
achieved results by not giving up?	10

3 Work in pairs. Use the surrounding context to help you work out the meanings of the phrasal verbs in **bold** in the text. Then check your ideas on pages 129–130.

4 Have you or anyone you know been influenced in the same ways as the writers of the article? Apart from people, what other influences are there in your life?

People who have influenced us

You tell us about the person who has most influenced you in your life.

A MY FRENCH TEACHER

It's not easy to single out just one person from the many who have had a significant influence on my life, but if I have to make a choice, it would have to be my French teacher at secondary school. After all, it's because of her that I started out on my chosen career path and **ended up** where I am today. Her passion and enthusiasm for the subject touched everyone in the class and I knew from the very first moment she started teaching that languages were going to figure somewhere in my life. It's quite scary really, to see how significant a teacher's influence can be. He or she can bring a subject alive for the students – or totally kill it off! Miss Winters was with us for just one term but a lot of her passion for languages **rubbed off on** me and for that I will always be grateful.

B MY BIG SISTER

I used to worship my older sister, Ruby. She was my idol and I copied everything she did. Her favourite colour was my favourite colour – her favourite food was mine too. Even into our teenage years I followed her taste in clothes and music. Now, **looking back**, I think what I admired most about her was her patience with me. I must have been a complete pain but she never lost her temper. She devoted many hours to helping me with school work or sitting down with me and talking through any problems I had. Back then I copied her because I thought she was beautiful and clever and I wanted to be just like her, but now I understand that in fact her influence went a lot deeper. I hope I've developed into a caring, patient person and if so, then I certainly learnt it from her.

C A CHARACTER IN A FILM

I was a very shy ten-year-old boy when I first saw *Billy Elliot* on the big screen. I had always wanted to dance but had never been allowed to. It was my sister who went to the ballet classes and I tried to copy the steps in our living room. The kids at school heard about it and I was teased mercilessly. Where I came from, boys just didn't do dancing – like *Billy Elliot*! I still had this deep desire to dance – but I'd been **covering it up** for a long time. Then I saw the film. It gave me the confidence to ask for dancing classes and it also altered many other people's perception of boy dancers. There was no more teasing or making fun of me. I stayed at the dancing school until I left full-time education and now dancing is my career. I often wonder how many other lives *Billy Elliot* is responsible for changing.

D MY BEST FRIEND

When you get into trouble and think there's no way out, the last person you want to talk to is your family. You feel that you've **let** them all **down**. I'd got into a bad situation. I was going round with the wrong people and not exactly behaving myself, when my best friend, Boyd, realised what was happening and persuaded me to break away from them. It can't have been easy – I wasn't listening to anyone at the time. But he stayed with it and refused to abandon me. Boyd helped me see life in a completely different way and because of him I **gave up** my job in insurance and retrained to be a counsellor so that I could help other young people.

Unit 1 Influence

Listening Part 2
Sentence completion 🔊 1.01

1. 💬 Work in pairs. When you buy items such as clothing, technology, food and drink, what are your favourite brands? Why?

   To what extent do television or internet adverts influence what you buy?

2. 💬 Read the following dictionary entry and discuss the questions with your partner.

   product placement NOUN
   the use of a company's product in a film or television show as a way of advertising the product

   1. Does product placement exist on television in your country?
   2. Why do you think companies might choose this form of advertising?

3. 🔊 You will hear a man called Tim Lee talking on the radio about product placement. For questions 1–10, complete the sentences with a word or short phrase.

   Product placement

   One example of product placement Tim gives is that of an actor eating a (1) ....

   Tim says it is not product placement when a (2) .... appears on television by chance.

   Before 2011, product placement was permitted in the UK only in films or (3) .... programmes.

   Product placement is still not allowed in news or (4) .... programmes.

   For a product to be placed in a programme, the product must be (5) ....

   Tim gives the example of washing powder in a (6) .... scene to illustrate what would not be permitted.

   There should be no obvious (7) .... of a placed product in a programme.

   Advertisers cannot place products which have a negative effect on (8) ....

   A special symbol appears on screen at least (9) .... times during a programme containing a placed product.

   Tim suggests that product placement might be (10) .... for viewers.

Help

- Think about the kind of information you need for each sentence: is it, for example, a type of food, a number or a place?
- You will hear the exact words you need for the answer, but the other words in the sentences may not be exactly the same as the words in the recording.
- You may hear information which could fit the gap but does not answer the question.
  For number 4, for example, you will hear several different types of programme, but only one of them is relevant here.
- Write no more than three words for each answer.

4. 💬 Do you think we should be worried about product placement? Why/Why not?

   Tim says that
   'the very young are influenced by adverts and … they in turn influence their parents and what they buy.'

   How true do you think this is?

Language focus 1
Present tenses
Present simple and continuous

1 In the listening, Tim says the following about the example of the washing powder.

I think you understand the point I'm trying to make.

Why does he use the present continuous with the verb *try*, but the present simple with the verbs *think* and *understand*?

2 In sentences **1–5**, underline the examples of the present simple and circle the examples of the present continuous. Then match each use **a–e** to the underlined and circled verbs.

1 Something like this often occurs quite by chance.
2 I'm using my mum's telly for a couple of weeks.
3 They're always advertising something on this show!
4 Children influence their parents' buying decisions.
5 Product placement is becoming increasingly popular.

a a temporary situation
b a change or development
c a regular, habitual action
d a repeated action that annoys the speaker
e something the speaker considers to be a fact

⚙ Read more about the present simple and continuous in the Grammar Reference page 102.

Present perfect simple and continuous

1 Look at sentences **a** and **b** from the listening, then answer questions **1** and **2**.

a Product placement … <u>has existed</u> on UK television **for** many years.
b **Since** February 2011, we<u>'ve been</u> able to see it in a number of other programme types.

1 The underlined verbs are in the present perfect simple. Why is this tense used here?
2 The preposition *for* is used in **a**, but *since* is used in **b**. Why is this?

2 Use sentences **a–c** to complete explanations **1–3** for the <u>underlined</u> examples of the present perfect simple.

a The exact time of the event or events is not known by the speaker or not important.
b The time period in which the event or events occurred has not finished.
c The event or events have some relevance to the present.

1 To give news of a recent event or events.
  _____.
  <u>I've just broken my leg</u> so I can't drive at the moment.

2 To talk about an event or events that occurred in the past.
  _____.
  I know <u>they've won the cup twice</u>, but I couldn't tell you when.

3 To talk about an event or events that occurred in the past.
  _____.
  So far this week <u>we've had three exams</u> – and it's only Tuesday!

3 💬 Work in pairs. For questions **1–4**, compare the two sentences **a** and **b**, and explain why the present perfect simple is used in one and the present perfect continuous in the other.

1 a We've organised all our photos – each year, up to and including this one, is now on its own memory stick.
  b We've been organising all our photos – we've just got the last two years to go through.

2 a John's worked in the family business ever since he left school in 1982.
  b John's been working in the family business since July. He starts back at school next week.

3 a My sister has been going to a pilates class recently – it's helping her to relax.
  b My sister has gone to her pilates class – she should be back soon.

4 a I've been writing emails all evening. I'm going to turn off the computer now.
  b I've written twelve emails this evening. I'm going to turn off the computer now.

⚙ Read more about the present perfect simple and continuous in the Grammar Reference pages 102–103.

4 Complete the gaps with the correct form of the verb in brackets. Use one of the following tenses. More than one answer may be possible.

| present perfect continuous | present simple |
| present perfect simple | present continuous |

I **1** _____ (stay) at my friend Paul's flat in the city centre since last Friday – just as a temporary measure. I **2** _____ (just/start) a job here and I **3** _____ (not/have) anywhere to live yet. Paul and his wife, Sara, **4** _____ (own) the flat and they **5** _____ (live) there with their two children and Sara's mother, so it's a bit crowded. Paul **6** _____ (help) me to look for a place of my own and we **7** _____ (see) several places in the centre already. I **8** _____ (think) of trying a different area, though – a one-bedroomed flat here **9** _____ (cost) more than a three-bedroomed house in the south of the city.

Speaking Part 1
Personal questions

1 In Part 1 of the Speaking test, the examiner asks you and your partner questions about yourselves. Ask and answer these questions with a partner.

1 Where do you live?
2 How long have you lived there?
3 What do you like about living there?

Help

- Do not memorise whole sentences about yourself. Your language should sound natural.
- Always extend an answer if you can, giving reasons and examples.
- Make sure your answers are relevant to the questions you are asked.

2 After asking some simple questions about where you come from, the examiner will ask you about things like your family and friends, your interests and your plans for the future.

With a partner, take it in turns to ask and answer these questions about people in your family.

FAMILY
1 Who do you admire most in your family? Why?
2 Who in your family did you use to get on best with when you were young? Why?
3 Who do you think you are most similar to in your family? Why?
4 Do you like going on holiday with your family? Why/Why not?

3 Work in pairs. Student A turn to page 96. Student B turn to page 101. Follow the instructions.

Vocabulary 2
The weather

1 Work in pairs. Describe the weather in each of the photographs. How do you think the people in the pictures are feeling?

2 For sentences 1–5, underline the correct words in *italics* to complete the different word combinations in **bold**.

1 On our holiday, every day started *fine/right* **and sunny**, then it would *cover/cloud* **over** during the morning and *pour/fall* **with rain** in the afternoon.
2 It was a *hard/strong* **winter**, with **temperatures** *cutting/dropping* to minus fifteen degrees.
3 There was no wind, not even a *slim/light* **breeze**, and any movement was exhausting in the *firing/blazing* **sun** and *intense/cooked* **heat** of midday.
4 The **gale-force** *airs/winds* and **torrential** *rainfall/downfall* caused extensive damage and widespread flooding.
5 There was an unusually **cold** *spell/spend* in April, with *heavy/wide* **snow** falling in some parts of the country.

3a Work in pairs. Tell your partner which of the situations described in exercise 2 you have experienced or heard about in your country. Give details.

3b To what extent does the weather influence how you feel? Why?

Unit 1 Influence

Reading and Use of English Part 1
Multiple-choice cloze

1 Look at the title of the text from a magazine below. What do you think it's about?
  Read the text, ignoring the gaps, to check your answers.

2 Read the text again and for questions 1–8, decide which answer (A, B, C or D) best fits each gap.
  There is an example at the beginning (0).

3 💬 Work in pairs. Do you agree or disagree with the points made in the article? Why?

Slaves to the weather?

It's a fact that blue skies tend to lift the spirits and (0) _C_ the world seem a better place. It's also true that overcast rainy days can make us feel gloomy and depressed. Or is it? It may (1) ..... as a surprise to some of us to learn that there is, in fact, no hard evidence to (2) ..... the theory that the weather plays an important part in influencing our moods.

A recent internet survey in Germany, which involved (3) ..... more than a thousand people questions over a (4) ..... of eighteen months, came (5) ..... the conclusion that apart from a small number of people who suffer from SAD (Seasonal Affective Disorder), a real problem where doctors (6) ..... depression to the weather, most of us are not really influenced by the weather at all. Apparently we believe that weather can influence our mood simply because we have always been told it can. The survey even claims that (7) ..... experts believe that all SAD sufferers feel depressed in the darker winter months, there are in fact some who suffer depression in the summer and (8) ..... in the winter!

0	A get	B let	C make	D allow
1	A look	B find	C come	D seem
2	A reveal	B support	C allow	D base
3	A asking	B reporting	C discussing	D questioning
4	A season	B period	C length	D date
5	A to	B at	C for	D with
6	A put	B link	C cause	D add
7	A despite	B however	C when	D although
8	A look forward	B run down	C cheer up	D take off

Help

In the multiple-choice cloze, there are several reasons why only one of the four options fits the gap. For example:

1 *It is the only word with the correct meaning.*
  Several trees blew down during the recent ..... .
  A <u>gales</u> B blows C draughts D bursts

2 *It is part of a collocation or other common word combination.*
  A ..... breeze caused the high grass to move from side to side.
  A narrow B thin C <u>light</u> D pale

3 *It is the correct preposition or part of a phrasal verb.*
  My role model and the person I look ..... most is my father.
  A down on B <u>up to</u> C back on D forward to

4 *It is the only word which fits grammatically.*
  My parents always ..... me to do sport, but I was never very good.
  A suggested B said C tried D <u>encouraged</u>

Unit 1 Influence

Language focus 2
Past tenses

1 Look at these statements made by different people about the weather. Underline the correct verb forms.

1 While I *had been walking/was walking* home the wind suddenly *blew/was blowing* my umbrella inside out.

2 Not long after we *had finished/had been finishing* putting the tent up, it *started/has started* to pour with rain.

3 That morning there was thick snow on the ground. It *was snowing/had been snowing* since eight o'clock the previous evening.

2a Match the verb forms you underlined in exercise 1 to the names of the tenses a–d.

a past simple
b past continuous
c past perfect simple
d past perfect continuous

2b Work in pairs. Explain why each of the different tenses is used in sentences 1–3 in exercise 1.

Check your ideas and read more about past tenses in the Grammar Reference pages 103–104.

3 Complete each gap in this story with an appropriate past form of the verb in brackets.

When we 0 *got* (get) up on Sunday morning, the sun 1 _____ (shine) brightly and the sky was a beautiful clear blue. The night before, the weatherman 2 _____ (say) it would stay fine all day, so we 3 _____ (pack) our things into the car and 4 _____ (set) off for the coast. We 5 _____ (drive) for half an hour when we first 6 _____ (notice) the clouds. They were quite small then, but by the time we 7 _____ (get) to the beach, the sky 8 _____ (cloud) over completely and the temperature 9 _____ (drop) considerably. Nevertheless, we 10 _____ (decide) to have the swim that we 11 _____ (promise) ourselves. Then, just as we 12 _____ (change) into our swimming costumes and 13 _____ (get) ready to go into the water, the skies 14 _____ (open) up and it 15 _____ (begin) to pour with rain.

Writing Part 1
Essay

1 Read the following Part 1 task, a student's plan and the model answer, then answer these questions.

1 Which point appears in the model answer but not in the plan?
2 Which point appears in the plan but not in the model answer?

In your English class you have been talking about different influences on people's lives. Now, your English teacher has asked you to write an essay. Write an essay using **all** the notes and giving reasons for your point of view.

Do you think new technology has had a positive or a negative influence on our lives today?

Notes
Write about:
1 travel
2 education
3 .... (your own idea)

Essay plan
Introduction: general view vs my opinion – negative effect
Paragraph 2: education
Tablets, laptops in schools a distraction.
Students don't concentrate.
Paragraph 3: travel
Satnavs and mobile phones cause car accidents.
Internet tickets – too many people flying – bad for the environment.
Paragraph 4: shopping
Internet shopping – small shops close – causes unemployment
Automatic checkouts – cashiers redundant – makes shopping very impersonal.
Conclusion: repeat introduction (in a different way)

Unit 1 Influence

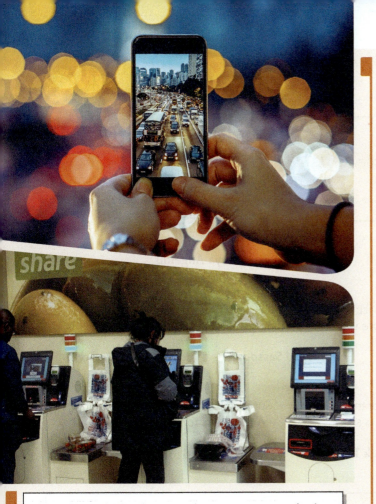

2 Read the model answer again and do the following tasks.

a Complete the table below with expressions from the model answer. The first one has been done for you.

Saying what others think	Expressing your own opinion
many people believe that	

b <u>Underline</u> examples of linking words and phrases in the model answer.
however, for example, ...

c Find words in the model answer which are used to avoid repeating the words *influence* and *cause*.
influence (noun): *effect*   cause (verb): *leads to*

3 Write an answer to the following Part 1 task in **140–190** words.

> In your English class you have been talking about different influences on people's lives. Now, your English teacher has asked you to write an essay. Write an essay using **all** the notes and giving reasons for your point of view.
>
> Do you think new technology has had a positive or a negative influence on our lives today?
> **Notes**
> Write about:
> 1 relationships
> 2 leisure time
> 3 .... (your own idea)

Help

- Decide how you will answer the question:
  Has technology had a positive or negative influence?
- Write your plan.
  Use the example in exercise **1** as a guide. Include relevant points for **relationships**, **leisure time** and one more category (**your own idea**). Further possible categories include: **work**, **health**, **professional sport** as well as **travel**, **education** or **shopping.**
- Write your essay. Make sure you:
  a organise your ideas into paragraphs and use a variety of linking words and phrases.
  b include a range of vocabulary and, where possible, avoid repeating words.
  c write in a consistently formal style.

More information in the Writing Bank pages 116–117.

Most of us in developed countries have access to new technology and many believe that it has improved the way we live. In my opinion, however, technology has had a negative effect on our lives.

In schools, for example, large numbers of pupils use tablets or laptops. Whilst many consider these to be excellent educational tools, I personally feel they are very distracting, as they prevent students from concentrating on their lessons. Furthermore, reference sites on the Internet discourage them from thinking for themselves.

Travel is another area in which technology has had a negative impact. For one thing, irresponsible use of satnavs and mobile phones in cars leads to thousands of accidents each year. In addition, cheap airline tickets bought online mean there are too many people flying every day with disastrous consequences for the environment.

Finally, technology is responsible for higher unemployment. Internet shopping has caused small shops to close because they cannot compete, and automatic checkouts in supermarkets have resulted in cashiers becoming redundant.

To sum up, although it is widely felt that new technology is a positive influence, there are many reasons to think the opposite.

2 Success!

Speaking
Success

1 Read the quotations about success and discuss these questions with your partner. Give reasons for your opinions.
   1 What is each quotation trying to say?
   2 Do you agree or disagree with it?
   3 Which is your favourite?

2 How would you define success?

> Success is liking yourself, liking what you do, and liking how you do it.
> **Maya Angelou**

> The only place where success comes before work is a dictionary.
> **Vidal Sassoon**

> If at first you don't succeed, try, try again.
> **Proverb**

> All you need in this life is ignorance and confidence; then success is sure.
> **Mark Twain**

> Success usually comes to those who are too busy to be looking for it.
> **Henry David Thoreau**

Listening Part 3
Multiple matching 1.02–1.06

1 You will hear five short extracts in which people are talking about success. For questions 1–5, choose from the list (A–H) what each speaker says. Use the letters only once. There are three extra letters which you do not need to use.

A I had to be patient for success to come.

B I enjoy the wealth associated with success.

C I listened to the advice of other experts.

D Good qualifications were the key to my success.

E A successful person is someone who accomplishes their goals.

F A combination of factors is required to become successful.

G It is important to anticipate potential problems.

H You need to have confidence in your own ability.

Speaker 1 [1]
Speaker 2 [2]
Speaker 3 [3]
Speaker 4 [4]
Speaker 5 [5]

Help

- On the recording you will not hear exactly the same words as those in sentences **A–H**. Before you listen, consider possible ways the speakers could express the ideas in the sentences. For example:
  A *It was a long time before I was successful, I needed to wait many years, I wasn't successful straight away.*
- You will hear all five speakers once, then the whole recording is played again. Listen both times very carefully to what each speaker says before making your decision.
- You will hear distractors – language or information in the script that may cause you to choose an incorrect answer. For example, although Speaker 1 mentions money, **B** may not be the correct answer.

2 Check your answers by reading the listening script on pages 131–132. <u>Underline</u> the parts of each extract which guide you to the correct answers. The first one has been done for you.

14

Word formation
Adjectives

1 Write the appropriate adjective form of the nouns in brackets to complete this extract from Speaker 1 in the Listening.

My career on the pitch lasted twenty years, and during that time I was _____ (luck) enough to play for three of the biggest clubs in the country, so I had plenty of _____ (value) experience. But of course, working with some of the players nowadays requires an _____ (addition) kind of skill.

2 Complete each gap with an adjective using the word in capital letters and one of the suffixes from the box. You may need to add the negative prefix *un-*. The words in **bold** will help you decide whether the adjective is positive or negative.

-y	able	-ant	-ed	-ful
-ing	-ive	-less	-ous	

0 In many parts of the world, children are **forced to work in dangerous and** _unhealthy_ **conditions**. HEALTH

1 Our staff are here to help you and ensure you **enjoy** a _____ **and relaxing** stay at our hotel. PLEASE

2 We **enjoyed** the film **but** the cinema seats were really _____ . COMFORT

3 The increase in the number of road accidents is **a** _____ **problem**. WORRY

4 After completing the 3,000-mile walk, Evans said **he felt** _____ and was looking forward to sleeping. EXHAUST

5 **Despite claims** that the drug has **no** _____ **effects**, many patients are **refusing to take it**. HARM

6 **I had to write my article again**: the teacher said there were **too many** _____ **mistakes**. CARE

7 In her autobiography, *How I made it*, the _____ **and determined** designer Amy Simon describes how she made it to the top of her profession. AMBITION

8 **No one will be sorry when they demolish** the office block – it's a very **dull, grey,** _____ building. ATTRACT

Speaking Part 2
Talking about photos

1 💬 Look at the photographs below. They show **people who have succeeded in something**.

Student A: Compare the photographs and say **how you think the people are feeling**.

Student B: When your partner has finished, answer the following question.

How do you normally celebrate success?

How are the people feeling?

2 💬 Now change roles. Look at the pictures on page 96 and follow the instructions.

Help

Student A
- Do not give detailed descriptions of each photo. Instead, comment on the similarities (*Both pictures show …*) and differences (*In the first picture … whereas in the second one …*).
- The second part of the task ('*and say …*') is always written as a question above the photos. Refer to this if you forget what you have to do.

Student B
- Develop your answer by giving examples of situations or reasons for your opinions.

Unit 2 Success!

Reading and Use of English Part 6
Gapped text

1 Many British children say they want to work in their own sweet shop when they grow up. What was your dream job when you were a young child?

2 The reading text is one of a series of articles entitled *How I made it*. Read the headline, introduction and first paragraph of the article, and predict what general points the article will mention.
I think it will say how Michael Parker got the money to start his business.

3 Read the base text (the main text with the gaps) and check the predictions you made in exercise 2. Do not read sentences **A–G** yet.

4 Six sentences have been removed from the article. Choose from the sentences **A–G** the one which fits each gap (**1–6**). There is one extra sentence which you do not need to use.

Help

- Before reading the missing sentences **A–G**, predict the type of information that could go in each gap, **1–6**. For example:
  1 *This will probably mention a job that Parker had between leaving university and starting his marketing company.*
- Read the missing sentences and decide where each one should go. When making your choices, make sure you read the information both *before* and *after* each gap in the text.
- Some parts of the base text have been highlighted to help you. Underline any words in the missing sentences **A–G** which help you make your choices. Note that in the *Cambridge English: First* exam none of the text is highlighted.
- When you have finished, read through the whole article again with the missing sentences in place to ensure that it makes sense. Check that the extra sentence does not fit into any of the gaps.

THE SWEET TASTE OF SUCCESS

Michael Parker, founder of 'A Quarter of', expects to sell £2.5m of old-fashioned sweets this year, writes Rachel Bridge.

When Michael Parker started his online old-fashioned sweet shop,
5 he had the advantage of one secret ingredient – nostalgia. He got
10 the inspiration for his business, 'A Quarter Of', from memories of the sweet shop at the end of the road where he grew up in Beaconsfield, Buckinghamshire.
15 Parker did well at school and later went on to study marketing and operational research at Lancaster University. ☐ **1** He eventually left there at the age of 33, to set
20 up a marketing company from his home using savings of £500.

He learnt everything he could about the Internet and soon found himself work helping firms to improve their position on search-engine sites.

But it was three years later that Parker came up with his winning idea. His brother had told him about a firm he had heard about on the radio. 2 Parker said: 'I thought if they could get ten orders a day by making people take a fixed selection, maybe I could get ten orders a day letting people choose what they wanted.'

He designed the website using a free demo disk from a magazine and then went to a local wholesale shop and spent £85 on sweets. 3 'I thought if it makes me £200 a month it will be an interesting thing to do and I will have learnt how to do websites for shops, which might come in handy for my marketing business.'

And for the first six months it was just that. 'I would get an order a day if I was lucky. I would have the sweets in the office with me and at about 3pm I would weigh them out and post them off.' 4

Things did not always go according to plan. Shortly before Christmas one year, two newspapers wrote articles about the firm. 5 He said: 'We had 5,000 e-mails and I worked out that if we worked absolutely flat out from 7am in the morning to 11pm at night every day in the run-up to Christmas, we might just be all right. We couldn't answer the phone. We just had a message on it saying, sorry, we are so busy we can't talk to you.' In the end, they managed to send out all the orders.

'A Quarter Of' now sells six hundred different varieties of sweets and turnover this year is expected to be about £2.5m. 6 'I will not compromise. If I think a sweet is not good enough for the site, we won't have it. You can get loads of cheaper versions of sherbet lemons, for example. They probably taste nice but the only ones that we sell on the website are the ones that I remember.'

He has this advice for budding entrepreneurs. 'Give it a go. So many people have emailed me to say they had the idea of starting an online sweet shop but didn't do anything about it. And learn as you go along. If you wait until you have got it absolutely perfect, you will never do it.'

A It put together boxes of traditional sweets to send to British people living abroad.

B Parker thinks the secret of his success has been having a strong vision of what he was trying to achieve, namely the sweet shop from his childhood.

C These created so much interest that Parker had to stop taking orders on 9 December.

D Fortunately, Parker succeeded in persuading them to continue production of their more traditional sweets.

E To begin with he imagined it would be a small operation.

F After graduating, he followed no particular career path, working first for a bank, then at Anglian Water and finally for a company that made automatic doors.

G However, after the first half-year Parker hired a PR company to advertise his website and as orders grew he took on staff to help him.

5 Underline the phrasal verbs 1–6 below in the text, then match them to their meanings a–f.
1 grow up (line 13)
2 go on + infinitive with to (line 16)
3 set up (lines 19–20)
4 come up with (line 25)
5 work out (line 44)
6 take on (sentence G)

a think of an idea or a plan
b start to employ someone
c change from being a child to being an adult
d calculate
e start a business or an organisation
f do something after you have finished doing something else

6 💬 Discuss these questions with a partner.
1 Read the last paragraph of the base text again. Do you think you would be a success as an entrepreneur? Why/Why not?
2 Do you know any famous entrepreneurs from your country? Why do you think they were successful?
3 Do you think you can learn to be an entrepreneur or does it depend on your personality?

Unit 2 Success!

Listening Part 4
Multiple choice 🔊 1.07

1 💬 Work in pairs. Imagine that you want to take part in a sporting activity to raise money for a local charity. Here are some of the activities you are thinking about.

> Cycle 100 kilometres
> Run a half-marathon
> Swim 40 lengths (2 kilometres) of an Olympic-size swimming pool
> Play table tennis non-stop for 8 hours
> Play basketball in a wheelchair for 4 hours

Talk to each other about what you would find easy or difficult about each activity, then decide which one you would both do together.

2 You will hear a radio interview with Mark Grant, who has just cycled round the world. Read question **1** then look at the highlighted part of the listening script on page 132 and choose the best option (**A**, **B** or **C**). Underline the part(s) of the script where you find the answer.

1 What motivated Mark to cycle round the world?
  A His grandfather encouraged him to do it.
  B He was trying to break the world record.
  C He wanted to collect money for an organisation.

3 Explain why the other options are wrong. Refer to the script on page 132.

4 🔊 Read questions 2–7. Then listen to the recording and choose the best answer (**A**, **B** or **C**).

Help

- Underline key words in the questions to help focus your attention on the important information when you listen to the recording. Question **2** has been done for you.
- The first time you listen to the interview, put a mark next to the option you think is correct. Listen carefully the second time before making your final decision.
- As with other parts of the listening paper, you will hear distractors.

2 What does Mark say about the <u>people</u> who came to <u>welcome</u> him home?
  A Some of them were crying.
  B Many were surprised by his appearance.
  C There were not as many as he had expected.

3 It was important for Mark each morning to
  A get up at exactly the same time.
  B have a large breakfast.
  C phone home.

4 While he was cycling, Mark frequently felt
  A fed up.
  B lonely.
  C tired.

5 Mark says that high winds caused him to
  A progress more slowly than planned.
  B lose confidence in his cycling ability.
  C fall off his bicycle and injure himself.

6 What does Mark say about the technological equipment he took?
  A It wasn't very heavy.
  B There was too much.
  C Some of it was stolen.

7 In some countries he visited, Mark was impressed with
  A the quality of the food.
  B the generosity of the people.
  C the size of the houses.

5 Look at the listening script on page 132. For questions 2–7 underline the part of the script that gives you the answer and explain why the other options are wrong.

6 💬 What qualities do you think Mark needed to succeed in achieving his goal?

Language focus
Comparisons

1 Complete each gap in these sentences from the listening with one word.

1 The record stands at 175 days and it took me quite a lot longer _____ that.
2 I wasn't quite _____ handsome as when I started out!
3 In fact the wind was by far the _____ difficult thing I had to deal with during the whole trip.
4 It seemed as if _____ harder I pedalled, _____ stronger the wind decided to blow.
5 I got to Australia a _____ later than I'd intended.

Check your answers in the script on page 132.

2 Work in pairs. What are the comparative and superlative forms of these adjectives and adverbs?

| ~~fast~~ | wet | white | early | slowly |
| gentle | reliable | good | bad | far |

fast: faster, the fastest

3a Match the structures and examples 1–5 to their functions a–e.
1 *a bit/a little/slightly* + comparative + *than*
  Alex is **slightly shorter than** Helen.
  not quite + *as/so* + adjective/adverb + *as*
  Alex is **not quite as tall as** Helen.
2 *(quite) a lot/much/far* + comparative + *than*
  The stage show is **far more enjoyable than** the film.
  not nearly + *as/so* + adjective/adverb + *as*
  The film is**n't nearly as enjoyable as** the stage show.
3 *by far/easily* + superlative
  This is **easily the most expensive** campsite we've ever stayed in.
4 *just/nearly* + *as* + adjective/adverb + *as*
  I'm **just as old as** Paul.
  just/nearly + *the same* (+ noun) + *as*
  I'm **just the same age as** Paul.
5 *the* + comparative, *the* + comparative
  The faster you work, **the less** time it will take.

a to show that two changes happen together; the second is often the result of the first
b to talk about people or things that are the same or almost the same in some way
c to describe big differences between two people or things
d to describe small differences between two people or things
e to emphasise the difference between one person or thing and all the others

3b Read sentences 1–5 in exercise 1 again and match them to functions a–e in exercise 3a.

Read more about comparisons in the Grammar Reference pages 104–105.

4a One word in each of these sentences is not correct. Change the incorrect word.
1 Books are many more interesting than films.
2 It's better to try and fail that never try at all.
3 The people in my country are among the friendliest of the world.
4 The more qualifications you have, the easilier you will find a job.
5 The *Hunger Games* films are by far the most entertaining films that have never been made.
6 Cats are not quiet as sociable as dogs.
7 English is probably the more difficult language of all to learn.
8 Many of the mistakes in this exercise are the same like the ones that I often make.

4b Do you agree with sentences 1–8? Tell your partner, giving reasons for your opinions.

Unit 2 Success!

Vocabulary
Sport

1a <u>Underline</u> the word in each group which is not normally associated with the sport in **bold**. Decide which of the sport(s) mentioned it is usually connected with.

a	**football**	boots	referee	track	match
b	**tennis**	racket	net	umpire	pitch
c	**basketball**	goggles	time out	referee	court
d	**athletics**	court	field event	meeting	starting blocks
e	**golf**	course	clubs	vest	tournament
f	**swimming**	lane	helmet	costume	pool
g	**skiing**	slope	poles	slalom	hole
h	**skating**	Rollerblades®	trunks	rink	knee pads

1b Copy the words from **1a**, including those you underlined, in their correct groups in your notebook. Organise the words into these columns.

Sport	Place	Clothes and equipment	Other words
football	*pitch*	*boots*	*referee, match*

2 For **a–e**, use the words in bold to help you complete each gap with the correct form of one of the words or phrases in blue. One of the words in each group is not needed.

a *take part   take place   take over   take up*
Sally has _____ **running** in order to keep fit, but also to raise money for charity. She wants to _____ **in** the London **marathon**, which usually _____ **in April**.

b *next   runner-up   silver   second*
It wasn't Trenkov's first time as an **Olympic** _____ **medallist**: he came _____ in the same event in Sydney, where he was also the _____ in the long jump.

c *spectators   viewers   public   crowd*
Over twenty-three million **television** _____ watched American star Serena Williams win the Women's US Open Tennis Final, in addition to the 22,500 _____ who filled the Arthur Ashe Stadium. The **home** _____ was clearly delighted with the result.

d *beat   win   draw   score*
In last night's Champions League matches, Real Madrid _____ FC Zürich **5–2**, Barcelona _____ **0–0** with Inter, and FC Sevilla _____ **2–0** against Belarusian opponents BATE Borisov.

e *practise   do   play   go*
I'm sorry, they're not here. Ellie has _____ **swimming** and Paul is _____ **football**. Well, not a whole game – he said he was going to the park with Steve to _____ taking penalties.

Writing Part 2
Article

1 💬 Read the following Part 2 question and tell your partner how you might answer it.

> You have seen this announcement in an international magazine.

> **Articles wanted**
> **The Importance of Sport**
> *What benefits do you get from doing sport?*
> Write and tell us why taking part in sport is important for you.
> The best articles will be published in next month's magazine.

Write your **article**.

2 Read the model answer and compare the benefits the writer mentions with those you discussed in exercise **1**.

> *A way to keep fit ... and much more*
>
> Can you think of a better way of keeping in shape than taking part in a team sport? Last year I took up volleyball, and as well as being the fittest I've ever been, I'm also a lot happier.
>
> In the past I'd tried going to the gym and I'd also been running, but I lost interest and gave them both up. Why? Because I was always on my own, and it wasn't nearly as enjoyable as doing something together with other people. Now I have a great time during practice sessions, and I've made lots of new friends.
>
> Playing volleyball has helped me with my exams, too. It gives me a break from my studies, clears my mind and makes me feel good. So after a game I'm much more able to sit at my desk and carry on with my revision.
>
> If you don't do any team sports, then sign up for one now — as well as keeping you physically and mentally fit, it's great fun and wonderful for your social life. What could be better?

3 Find examples of the following features of informal language in the model answer.
1. **Contractions:** *I've*
2. **Phrasal verbs:** *took up*
3. **Conjunctions at the beginning of sentences:** *Because*

4 Underline the structures which are used to make comparisons.

Can you think of <u>a better way</u> of keeping in shape <u>than</u> taking part in a team sport?

5a Read the following Writing Part 2 question.

> You see this announcement in your school English-language magazine.

> **Sports competition**
> Your school wants to organise a sports competition for its teachers and students. Football, tennis, basketball and swimming have all been suggested, but only one will be chosen. Write us an article:
> - telling us which one of these sports you like best for the competition and why
> - explaining why you are less keen on the other sports.

Write your **article**.

5b 💬 Tell your partner which sport you would choose and why. Consider, for example, which one would be:
- the easiest to organise
- the most popular
- the most enjoyable
- the best for teachers and students to do together.

6 Write your article in **140–190** words. Your article is for the school magazine: you can write in a formal or informal style, but it must be consistent.

Help

Read the following advice to help you plan your article.
- **Title:** This should give an idea of the article's general content. Write this when you have finished your article.
- **Introduction:** Interest your readers from the start. You could ask a question or make a surprising statement. For example:
Can you imagine the fun we'd have beating the teachers in a game of football?
- **Central paragraph(s):** Give your reasons. Try to use some of the sport vocabulary and/or structures for comparisons from this unit.
- **Conclusion:** End with a statement or question which summarises your opinions and/or leaves the reader something to think about. For example:
Clearly, then, the swimming competition would be the most popular choice. Who could fail to enjoy it?

More information in the Writing Bank page 118.

Review | Units 1 and 2

Reading and Use of English Part 4
Transformations

For questions **1–6**, complete the second sentence so that it has a similar meaning to the first sentence, using the word given. **Do not change the word given.** You must use between **two** and **five** words, including the word given. Here is an example **(0)**.

0	I haven't watched television for three weeks.
	LAST
	It's three weeks _SINCE I LAST WATCHED_ television.

Help

- The word given in capital letters might relate to a particular area of grammar or it could be part of a phrasal verb or an expression.
- When you rewrite the sentence, pay attention to the correct use of tenses, verb patterns, negatives, and prepositions.

1 I started to feel ill this morning and I'm still not very well.
  FEELING
  I .... ill all day.

2 I knew the song but was unable to think of the name of the singer.
  COME
  I knew the song but could .... the name of the singer.

3 I met Gary when we were at university together.
  KNOWN
  I .... we were at university together.

4 I have never seen such a dirty beach before!
  EVER
  This is the .... seen!

5 There are fewer students in the class than there were last week.
  AS
  There .... in the class as there were last week.

6 Elisa is slightly younger than Lara.
  QUITE
  Elisa .... as Lara.

Reading and Use of English Part 3
Word formation

For questions **1–8**, read the text below. Use the word given in capitals at the end of some of the lines to form a word that fits in the gap **in the same line**. There is an example at the beginning **(0)**.

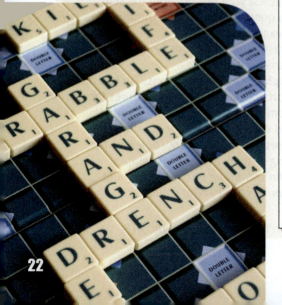

A Success Story

The popular family board game Scrabble™ is a truly
(0) _REMARKABLE_ success story. Over 100 million sets have   **REMARK**
been sold in 29 (1) .... languages and in 121 countries, **DIFFER**
making it (2) .... the world's best-selling word game.   **EASY**
It began life in 1931 during the Great Depression, when, like
so many other Americans, architect Alfred Butts found
himself without (3) .... His passion for words led him **EMPLOY**
to devise a game he called 'Lexico', in which players' scores
were determined by the (4) .... of the words they   **LONG**
formed. The board was incorporated in 1938, when Butts
changed the name to 'Criss-Crosswords'. Some of the
(5) .... features still appear in today's game, including **ORIGIN**
the values of the letters, which remain (6) ....   **CHANGE**
However, neither Lexico nor Criss-Crosswords was commercially
(7) .... and Butts went back to being an architect.   **SUCCEED**
Then, in 1948, James Brunot bought the manufacturing rights,
simplified the rules and came up with the new name of
'Scrabble'. In the first year of (8) .... , just 2,251   **PRODUCE**
sets were sold. Then, in 1952, Macy's department store
began stocking the game – and the rest is history.

Vocabulary

1 Complete each gap with a word from the box.

up (x 2)	down	out
on (x 2)	back	

1. Steven looks _____ to his older brother, James – he even tries to look like him.
2. When I was ill I let _____ a lot of people at work because I just couldn't finish the reports on time.
3. He started out as a messenger boy and went _____ to become managing director of the company.
4. You should give _____ your part-time job and apply to work at the department store – I hear they're taking _____ new staff.
5. When I look _____ I can see that I've done some really silly things over the years.
6. I've just worked _____ the total cost of our holiday – it's not cheap!

2 Complete each gap with a word from the box. Then match the sentence beginnings 1–6 with the sentence endings a–f.

breeze	heat	rainfall
snow	sun	winds

1. **Torrential** _____ flooded the main **tennis**
2. **Heavy** _____ fell, covering the **football**
3. **Gale-force** _____ swept across the **golf**
4. The cool, light _____ at today's **athletics**
5. **Intense** _____ on the outdoor **basketball**
6. The **blazing** _____ heated the **swimming**

a. **pool** so the water felt more like soup.
b. **court** and the match was abandoned.
c. **meeting** was perfect for the runners.
d. **court** melted the paint on the lines.
e. **pitch** in a very thick, white blanket.
f. **course**, making it impossible to play.

Language focus

1 <u>Underline</u> the correct word in *italics*.

I **1** *don't believe/'m not believing* in fate, but a couple of hours ago something amazing **2** *has happened/happened*. Normally, I **3** *walk/'m walking* to school every day, but I **4** *have just had/have just been having* an operation on my knee, so at the moment **5** *I'm going/I've gone* by bus. Anyway, I **6** *was coming/came* home this afternoon, when I **7** *noticed/had noticed* a notebook on the floor under the seat in front of me. I **8** *was picking/picked* it up and **9** *was realising/realised* that it **10** *was belonging/belonged* to Olga, a friend of mine from school. She's from Russia, originally, but she **11** *has been living/is living* here with her family for many years.

Anyway, Olga **12** *was writing/had written* her name on the inside cover, so I **13** *phoned/had phoned* her to tell her I **14** *had been finding/had found* it. She **15** *was walking/walked* her dog in the park so I **16** *went/had gone* there to meet her in order to give her the book. She was delighted and very relieved: she **17** *worried/had been worrying* about it for hours because it **18** *contains/is containing* all her exam notes. Apparently, she **19** *was dropping/had dropped* it on the bus on her way to the doctor's just after lunch. It was just so lucky that I **20** *had been choosing/had chosen* to sit in that seat on the bus!

2 Complete each gap with one word.

1. This is probably the _____ comfortable room _____ the building – it's _____ lot colder than any of the other classrooms, and with no natural light it's _____ far the darkest.
2. My grandad's _____ nearly as old _____ you might think. He's got grey hair and wrinkles, but he's about the same age _____ Cheryl's dad – perhaps a _____ older, but not much.
3. There weren't as _____ cars on the road _____ we expected, so it wasn't _____ a bad journey as last year. In fact, it took us _____ than four hours to get there – three hours fifty minutes to be precise.
4. They were lovely little cakes. 'Eat as _____ as you want,' they said to us. So we did, and I didn't feel very well after that. Annie felt much _____ than me, though, which was strange, because she had _____ cakes than anyone else – just two, in fact.
5. The _____ I think about it, _____ less I like the idea. Actually, it's probably one of the silliest ideas you've _____ had – maybe not _____ as silly as your plan to hitchhike to Japan, but almost.

3 Image and images

Vocabulary
Appearance

1 Complete each sentence with a word from the box that means the opposite of the word in **bold**.

| narrow | thick | straight | wrinkled |
| clear | slim | dull | full |

1 Her complexion isn't **spotty** now, it's _____ .
2 My gran's face used to be really **smooth** but these days it's quite _____ .
3 Harry used to be quite **tubby** but since he's been on the diet he's got very _____ .
4 Jan's parents spent a lot of money at the orthodontist's and her **crooked** teeth are now perfectly _____ !
5 You know you can have injections to make **thin** lips look _____ .
6 Hair transplants can make **thinning** hair _____ .
7 I'm going to have cosmetic surgery to change my nose. It's quite **broad** and I'd like it to be _____ .
8 When you're not well your eyes often change from **bright** and **sparkling** to **tired-looking** and _____ .

2 Match each group of adjectives **1–5** to the part of the body they describe **a–e**.

1 healthy/rotten/perfect   a complexion
2 piercing/hazel/almond-shaped   b teeth
3 pale/dark/freckled   c nose
4 shoulder-length/untidy/straight d eyes
5 hooked/sharp/upturned   e hair

3 Use the adjectives in exercises **1** and **2** to describe the people in the photographs at the top of the page.

Listening Part 3
Multiple matching 🔊 1.08–1.12

1a Read the extract from a magazine article about photo manipulation.

> **U**ntil relatively recently, we accepted that everything we saw in a photograph was true. We know now, of course, that this is not always the case. Most of us are aware of how photographs can be digitally altered, or 'retouched' and it can be fun to do ourselves. But when retouching is used for commercial purposes – to alter a model's appearance in a magazine advertisement, for example – many people feel cheated. The now common practice of photo manipulation to change features such as skin complexion, body shape or hair colour makes a lot of people angry.

1b 💬 Does photo manipulation make *you* angry? Why/Why not?

2 🔊 You will hear five short extracts in which people are giving their opinions about photo manipulation. For questions **1–5**, choose from the list (**A–H**) what each person says about the practice of retouching photographs. Use the letters only once. There are three extra letters which you do not need to use.

Help

- Underline the important words in the eight options **A–H** and think about what the speaker might talk about.
  It can be dangerous. (How? Who to?)
- You may hear words which distract you. For example 'healthy' might be said by one of the speakers but this does not necessarily make **E** the answer for that speaker.
- Listen to each speaker all the way through before you make a decision.

A	It can be dangerous.		
B	It is done in response to a demand.	Speaker 1	1
C	It does not improve a person's appearance.	Speaker 2	2
D	It is acceptable because people are aware of it.	Speaker 3	3
E	It encourages people to become healthier.	Speaker 4	4
F	It is something celebrities have a right to.	Speaker 5	5
G	It used to be a lot worse than it is now.		
H	It is fine if it doesn't go too far.		

3 Look at the listening script on page 133 and underline the information that helps you choose the right answers.

4 💬 Do you agree with the last speaker that *most people today are obsessed with appearance and how we all look*? Why/Why not?

Language focus 1
Modals of speculation and deduction

1 Read this dialogue between two people looking at a picture in a magazine, then underline the modal verbs and the infinitive forms which follow them. The first one has been done for you.

A: That <u>can't be</u> her real hair. She had it cut really short for her latest film.
B: I agree. It must be a wig. It can't have grown that quickly.
A: But, you know, it could be her own hair with extensions.
B: That's true. I hadn't thought of that.
A: And she must have had some dental work. Her teeth used to be crooked, don't you remember?
B: Another thing – she must be wearing coloured contact lenses! I'm convinced her eyes are brown!

2a Look at the dialogue again. Decide which modal verbs are used to express ideas **a–c** below.

a I think this is possible.
b I'm sure this is the case.
c I'm sure this is not the case.

Which two modal verbs can be used in the dialogue in place of *could* and have the same meaning?

2b Which of the following infinitive forms are used in the dialogue to refer to **1–3** below:
- simple infinitive *be*
- continuous infinitive *be wearing*
- perfect infinitive *have grown*

1 past situations
2 present actions
3 present states

⚙ Read more about modals of speculation and deduction in the Grammar Reference page 105.

3 Each of the following sentences contains one mistake. Correct the mistakes.
1 Jack mustn't have gone to work because his car is still outside.
2 This can't have been Bath already, can it? It hasn't taken us very long to get here.
3 I'm not sure where Ken is. Try the library – he can be there.
4 I didn't hear Chloe say she was getting married. I must have been done something else when she told you.
5 You seem certain that this painting is a fake, but it could not be – it's difficult to tell.

4 Write three replies and reasons for each of the questions **1–3**. Use modal verbs.

0 Are Ben and Sarah back from holiday yet?
  They must be back, there's a light on.
  They can't be back, their car isn't there.
  They might be back. Ben said they were going to try to get an earlier flight.

1 Do you think Lucy passed her exam?
2 Did your dad go shopping this morning?
3 Does Fred live near the college?

Unit 3 Image and images

Reading and Use of English Part 5
Multiple choice

1 Do you recognise the film in the poster?
If you have seen the film, did you enjoy it? Why/Why not?
If you haven't seen the film, do you think you would enjoy it? Why/Why not?

2 What type of film is *Up*? Think of one recent example of the other types of film in the box and tell your partner about them.

| thriller | science fiction | animation | horror | adventure |
| musical | period drama | comedy | romance | |

3 The film company that made *Up* is Pixar. What do you know about Pixar and the films they make?

4 Read the article quickly. Is it mainly about Pixar or *Up*?

5 Read the article carefully. For questions 1–6, choose the answer (**A**, **B**, **C** or **D**) which you think fits best according to the text.

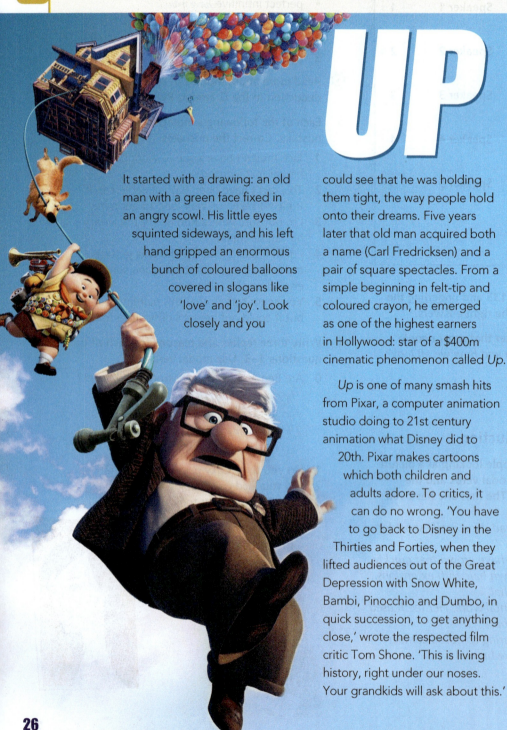

UP WITH PIXAR

It started with a drawing: an old man with a green face fixed in an angry scowl. His little eyes squinted sideways, and his left hand gripped an enormous bunch of coloured balloons covered in slogans like 'love' and 'joy'. Look closely and you could see that he was holding them tight, the way people hold onto their dreams. Five years later that old man acquired both a name (Carl Fredricksen) and a pair of square spectacles. From a simple beginning in felt-tip and coloured crayon, he emerged as one of the highest earners in Hollywood: star of a $400m cinematic phenomenon called *Up*.

Up is one of many smash hits from Pixar, a computer animation studio doing to 21st century animation what Disney did to 20th. Pixar makes cartoons which both children and adults adore. To critics, it can do no wrong. 'You have to go back to Disney in the Thirties and Forties, when they lifted audiences out of the Great Depression with Snow White, Bambi, Pinocchio and Dumbo, in quick succession, to get anything close,' wrote the respected film critic Tom Shone. 'This is living history, right under our noses. Your grandkids will ask about this.'

Pixar never sits still. When the firm takes risks, they get big results. The studio's 2008 film had been *Wall-E*, an odd love story about a garbage-eating robot. The film's hero communicated in bleeps and clicks. Its script contained barely a word of dialogue. On paper, it should never have worked. Instead, it made $521m, and won an Oscar for Best Animation. So then we had *Up*. The film is part action adventure, part about the meaning of happiness, love and loss. Critics, needless to say, adored it. They called it tender, thrilling, and very, very funny.

So, what is the secret of their success? Pixar Studios are near Oakland but spiritually, their home is more Silicon Valley. Round the office are pool, ping-pong and air hockey tables. Most of them are in use, throughout the working day. Grown men whizz down corridors on skateboards and scooters. Ask a guide why, and he'll shrug his shoulders and simply say: 'Because they're creative.'

What they mean is that Pixar is a professional playground for happy, inventive people.

'Most Hollywood studios are run by businessmen,' says *Up* director, Peter Docter. 'The problem with that is that if you start out on any film with the goal of simply making money, the chances are that you're not going to make a great movie.' Pixar approaches film-making from the opposite direction. They take talented people, allow them to enjoy themselves, and let that childish freedom rub off on films. As a result it encourages brave ideas that might, in a normal studio environment, end up on the cutting room floor. 'With *Up* people might have said, "You can't have an action adventure film that stars a 78-year-old man." But from the top, Pixar is different,' added Docter.

The film was one of the first major new products to be widely released in 3D in 2009. For film studios, 3D is a good investment. Tickets to 3D cinemas are expensive and their films are extremely difficult to pirate. But Pixar used the technology to add to *Up*'s narrative, creating a 'depth script' that varied the levels of contrast in the 3D according to the storyline. 'Carl, our main character, goes on an emotional journey,' said Bob Whitehill, the man responsible. 'When he's a boy, his life is very rich and full, so 3D in that section is pretty deep. When he loses his wife, his life is claustrophobic, so we reduce the depth, and make everything very shallow. Then when he lifts off to go on the adventure, things deepen again.' That pioneering way of thinking ensures that right now, the location where Silicon Valley meets Hollywood is an exciting place to be.

Unit 3 Image and images

Help
- Read the article first for an overall understanding.
- Then underline important words in the questions or stems. The first one has been done for you.
- Find the part of the text which is relevant to the question. Read it again with the question in mind.
- Eliminate the options which are clearly wrong. Decide on the best answer. If you are not sure, choose one. Marks will not be deducted for incorrect answers.

1 What do we learn about the <u>main character</u> in the <u>first paragraph</u>?
   A He was not a very pleasant person.
   B He had a lot of money.
   C He was easy to design.
   D He changed a little over the years.

2 What does the writer say about Pixar and Disney?
   A They have both had a big impact on audiences but at different times.
   B They have both had financial problems.
   C They both have a tradition of producing films very quickly.
   D They are both technically ahead of any other company.

3 The film *Wall-E* is mentioned to show
   A that Pixar has a lot of money to invest in the business.
   B that a good script is necessary for a successful film.
   C that Pixar does not always choose safe options.
   D that robots do not usually speak in films.

4 What is good about the working environment at Pixar?
   A It was designed by the people who work there themselves.
   B It suits the type of people who work there.
   C It encourages workers to take breaks from their work.
   D It is available for employees' families to enjoy too.

5 What does Peter Docter think about film-making?
   A The need for financial success can restrict creativity.
   B Filmmakers should sometimes listen more to children's ideas.
   C Statistics about films do not always tell the truth.
   D More money should be given to encourage new talent.

6 Why is 3D important to the film *Up*?
   A People are interested in new technology and will see the film for this reason.
   B It shows that Pixar is ahead of their competitors in this field.
   C The visual techniques help the development of the story.
   D Many cinemas today need 3D films to pay for their investment in equipment.

6 💬 Do you prefer watching films in 3D? Why/Why not?

Language focus 2
Relative clauses

1 Read sentences **a–f** and answer the questions which follow each pair.

a *Pixar makes cartoons <u>which</u> both children and adults adore.*
b *The film <u>which</u> won the Oscar for Best Animation in 2009 was 'Up'.*

1 Can the relative pronoun *which* be replaced by *that* in sentences **a** and **b**? Why/Why not?
2 *Which* can be omitted from sentence **a** but not from sentence **b**. Why not?

c *'Up' was also nominated for Best Picture, <u>which</u> was only the second time an animation film had received such a nomination.*
d *'Up', <u>which</u> opened the Cannes Film Festival in 2009, brought in over $731 million that year.*

3 What does the relative pronoun *which* refer to in sentences **c** and **d**?
4 *Which* cannot be replaced by *that* in either of sentences **c** or **d**. Why not?

e *It follows the story of an old man <u>whose</u> wife dies, leaving him lonely and irritable.*
f *It's a film in <u>which</u> lifelong dreams are fulfilled.*

5 Can the relative pronouns in sentences **e** and **f** be omitted or replaced by *that*? Why/Why not?

Read more about relative clauses in the Grammar Reference page 106.

2 Complete each gap with *who, which, whose, where, when, why* or *what*, adding commas where necessary. The first one has been done for you.

0 My father, <u>who</u> has always been a light sleeper, woke up when he heard a noise <u>which</u> sounded like a gunshot.
1 Last Saturday _____ she stayed at my house Sally slept in the attic _____ my parents have converted into a guestroom.
2 I got exactly _____ I wanted for my birthday – a new wallet. It was the only thing _____ I really needed.
3 I don't see any reason _____ my parents won't let me have a sleepover party for my birthday.
4 Our headteacher _____ is retiring at the end of the year has been at this school for over twenty years.
5 An equinox is one of two days during the year on _____ night and day are of equal length.
6 There's a prize for anyone _____ can tell me the name of the actor _____ was born in Los Angeles in 1974 and _____ films include *Titanic*, *The Aviator* and *The Wolf of Wall Street*.
7 I slept until half past nine this morning _____ is very unusual for me.
8 The only person _____ I really get on with at work is leaving next week. She's got a job at The Grand Hotel _____ her dad works as a doorman.

3 Look again at your answers in exercise **2**. Decide which of the words you have written:
a can be omitted.
b can be replaced by *that*.

In the example:
a *neither 'who' nor 'which' can be omitted.*
b *only 'which' can be replaced by 'that'.*

Unit 3 Image and images

Speaking Part 3
Collaborative task

1. Would you like to work in the film industry? Why/Why not?
2. Below are some jobs in the film industry. Before you do tasks a and b, read the information in the Help box below.

a Talk to each other about the good and bad points of doing these different jobs.

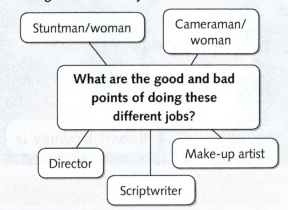

2b Now decide which of these jobs would be most difficult to do without help from other people.

Help

- In the exam you have two minutes for task **a** and one minute for task **b**. As this is the first time you have practised this task, allow yourself more time to complete the tasks.
- Talk to your partner (not the examiner) and respond to his or her comments as well as giving your own opinion.
- In task **b** you do not have to agree with your partner when making your final decision.
- Do not worry if the examiner has to stop you at the end of each task. This means that you have a lot to say, which is good.

Useful language

Make suggestions:
Let's start with this one …
Shall we move on to … ?
Ask for your partner's opinion/reaction:
What do you think about … ?
Don't you think that … ?
I think … How about you?
Agree/disagree with your partner:
Yes, I completely agree …
That's true. You've got a point …
No, I don't really think …

Speaking Part 4
Further discussion

In Part 4 of the Speaking test the examiner will ask you questions related to the topic you discussed in Part 3.

Work in pairs. Take turns to ask and answer the questions. Add a comment to your partner's answer.

Help

- The examiner will ask you and your partner questions in turns. You may both be asked the same question.
- If you have an opinion about a question your partner has been asked or want to comment on his/her opinion, you can.
- When you reply to a question, develop your answers giving reasons for your opinions.

1. What kind of films do you like best? Why?
2. Many people prefer seeing films at the cinema to watching them at home. Why do you think this is?
3. How important do you think it is to have age limits for watching some films? Why?
4. Some people say it's better for film-makers to show us more of the real world than to invent new ones. How far do you agree?
5. Do you think films that cost a lot of money to make are usually better films than those that cost less? Why/Why not?
6. What do you think are the disadvantages of being a famous film star?

Unit 3 Image and images

Listening Part 1
Multiple choice 🔊 1.13–1.20

🔊 You will hear people talking in eight different situations. For questions **1–8**, choose the best answer (**A, B or C**).

1. You hear a man talking on a radio phone-in about a quiz programme he saw during the week. Why is he phoning?
   - A He thinks the topic is not good for the quiz.
   - B He doesn't enjoy this quiz show.
   - C He disagrees with a few answers.

2. You overhear two friends talking about a film they've just seen. What sort of film was it?
   - A a horror film
   - B an action film
   - C a comedy film

3. You hear someone leaving a voicemail message. What does he want to do?
   - A change an arrangement
   - B ask for some advice
   - C make a complaint

4. You hear two mothers talking about their children's birthday parties. What did the magician do at both parties?
   - A card tricks
   - B an animal trick
   - C an egg trick

5. You hear part of a TV review programme. What is the reviewer's opinion of the first episode of the new series?
   - A It made a good impression.
   - B It was disappointing.
   - C It showed promise.

6. You hear a man phoning his friend. Why is he phoning her?
   - A to invite her to a live concert
   - B to make travel arrangements
   - C to check whether she's going to see a film

7. You hear a newscaster talking about an art exhibition at a local gallery. Why won't one painting be in the exhibition?
   - A It could be a fake.
   - B It has been stolen.
   - C It wasn't allowed out of the USA.

8. You hear a writer talking about her work. What does she feel about writing?
   - A It is lonely.
   - B It is unpredictable.
   - C It is exhausting.

Coldplay

Robert Downey Jr

Help

- You will hear eight short extracts. These are either monologues or conversations.
- Before each extract is played, the introductory sentence is read out. For question **1**, for example, you will hear the sentence beginning *You hear a man talking,* but not the question *Why is he phoning?* or the three options **A–C**.
- You will hear distractors. Always listen carefully both times to the whole extract before you decide which option to choose.

Writing Part 2
Review

1. 💬 Work in pairs. Discuss these questions.
   1. Have you watched a TV drama series recently? What did you like/not like about it?
   2. Do you usually read reviews for films or TV programmes? Why/Why not?
   3. What was the last review you read? Was it good/bad? Did you agree with it?
   4. What information do you expect a film or TV drama review to include?

2. Read these comments from reviews. Then write down an example of a film or TV drama they could be describing.
   - 0 The actor who plays the lead **role** gives an excellent **performance**.
     Eddie Redmayne in 'The Theory of Everything'
   1 The **special effects** are stunning.
   2 The **acting** was very convincing.
   3 The **plot** is quite complex and confusing.
   4 The first film was excellent but the **sequel** was disappointing.
   5 The action **scenes** were really gripping.

Unit 3 Image and images

3 Read this short review of a TV drama series. What does it say about the following?

1. the plot
2. the actors
3. the setting
4. the special effects
5. the writer's opinion

Merlin

Do you like TV series that are exciting and dramatic, <u>set</u> in a historical period but with a very modern interpretation? Then 'Merlin' is definitely for you. It's <u>based</u> on the legends of King Arthur but written to <u>appeal</u> to a 21st century audience.

The series <u>tells</u> the story of Merlin the wizard and King Arthur when they were both young. In each <u>episode</u> they have a new adventure, often fighting magical monsters. The plots are especially clever and bring in characters from the old legends in new situations.

Leading the <u>cast</u> are Bradley James as Arthur and Colin Morgan, whose acting in the title role is superb. The programmes are also visually stunning. It was filmed on <u>location</u> in a spectacular French castle and the Welsh forests, and there is also excellent use of special effects to create the monsters.

I bought the complete box set on Blu-ray last year and have watched all five series – twice! It's well acted, cleverly written and directed, and totally addictive! I guarantee that if you watch one episode, you'll want to watch the rest.

---

4 Complete each gap in **1–6** using the underlined words from the review of *Merlin*.

0. The series was filmed entirely on ___location___ in Sweden.
1. This story of young love will _____ mainly to teenagers.
2. If you thought the first _____ of the series was scary, wait till you see the second!
3. It _____ the story of a group of pioneers who get lost on their journey west.
4. There is not a single adult in sight; the _____ is made up entirely of children.
5. It is _____ on the true story of a man who was wrongly imprisoned for murder.
6. This gripping new drama is _____ in Liverpool in the late 19th century.

5 Summarise the purpose of each of the four paragraphs in the review opposite.

Paragraph 1: We are told the name of the series and generally what it's about.

6 Write an answer to the following Part 2 task in 140–190 words.

> You recently saw this notice on an English-language website called *TV World*.

> **Reviews wanted!**
> What's your favourite TV series? We'd love you to send us a review telling us about it. Include information on the setting, the characters and the plots, and say why you think other viewers would enjoy it.
> The best reviews will be posted on the website next month.

Write your **review**.

Help

- <u>Underline</u> key words in the question to ensure you include all the points.
- Plan your review well and divide it into clear paragraphs. See exercise **5** above.
- You could begin your review with a question to attract your readers' attention, for example: *Do you like TV series that are exciting and dramatic?*
- Express your opinion in each paragraph, using a range of adjectives, such as *stunning, gripping, convincing*, etc.
- Use relative pronouns and words such as *but, because* and *so* to link ideas.

More information in the Writing Bank page 119.

4 Going away

Vocabulary and Speaking
Holidays and travel

1 💬 Which of the following types of holiday have you been on? Tell your partner, giving details.

| package | adventure | camping |
| skiing | working | sailing |

Would you like to go on any of those you haven't yet experienced? Why/ Why not?

2 💬 Discuss these questions with your partner.
1 Where do you usually **spend** your **summer holiday**?
2 Do you prefer **going on holiday** with your family or your friends? Why?
3 Do you enjoy, or think you would enjoy, going to **seaside holiday resorts**? Which one(s)?
4 What did you do on the last **public holiday**? Did you **go away**?

3 For sentences **1–6**, complete the gaps with two of the answers **A–D**.
0 When we used to take the caravan to Wales, my dad would _drive_ and my mum used to _navigate_. Now she doesn't need to, because we've got a satnav.
   (A) navigate   B ride   C pilot   (D) drive
1 Charlie watched as Lucy's plane _____ along the runway, _____ and disappeared into the cloudless sky.
   A landed   B took off   C taxied   D touched down
2 I can _____ to London on Friday – I'm going there for the day. And when you come back on Sunday, phone me from the train and I'll _____ at the station.
   A see you off   B drop you off   C pick you up   D give you a lift
3 I'm going to have a _____ when I'm on holiday, but I also want to _____ myself.
   A relax   B enjoy   C unwind   D rest
4 Tim's just called from the airport; his flight's been _____ by three hours so he hasn't _____ the plane yet.
   A delayed   B booked   C boarded   D cancelled
5 I spent the long weekend in Dublin. My brother _____ me up for two nights and I _____ at Jane's house on Sunday.
   A lived   B put   C accommodated   D stayed
6 Cerys and Jim have just got back from their _____ to California. When they were there, they went on a _____ of all the movie stars' homes in Beverly Hills.
   A travel   B journey   C tour   D trip

4 💬 What are your favourite and least favourite forms of transport? Why?

How good is the public transport system in your local area? What, if anything, could be done to improve it?

Unit 4 Going away

Reading and Use of English Part 2
Open cloze

1 This is a text with eight gaps to fill. Here are some examples of the types of words which are tested in Part 2. Most are grammatical, though some are vocabulary items, such as phrasal verbs or fixed phrases.

Complete each gap with one word.

1 **Phrasal verbs:** I'm much fitter now that I've given _____ smoking.
2 **Prepositions:** Rosie had spent all her pocket money _____ sweets.
3 **Pronouns:** I can't drink coffee because _____ gives me a headache.
4 **Relative pronouns:** We only employ people _____ have some experience.
5 **Linkers:** I wore my coat _____ it was cold when I got up this morning.
6 **Auxiliary verbs:** This is the worst snow we _____ had for a long time.
7 **Negatives:** The hotel staff were rude and _____ at all helpful.
8 **Articles:** It was _____ first time Lionel had been to Paris.
9 **Determiners:** Then add the herbs and a _____ salt to the mixture.
10 **Fixed phrases:** We would like to wish Harry _____ the best in his new job.

2 Now do an exercise like the one in the exam. First, read the text below, ignoring the gaps, and answer these questions.
1 What was the 'mistake' mentioned in the title?
2 What caused it?
3 What did the victim of the error have to do?

3 Now read the text again and think of the word which best fits each gap. Use only **one** word in each gap. There is an example at the beginning (0).

Help
Read the whole sentence carefully before you decide which word to put in a gap. Adverbs such as *very, quite, rather, fairly* seem to fit into the following gap.
We enjoyed the holiday, but sometimes it was _____ windy by the seaside …
However, when you read to the end of the sentence, you see that the answer is *so*.
We enjoyed the holiday, but sometimes it was __so__ *windy by the seaside that we could hardly walk.*

4 Match the answers in exercise 3 to the categories in exercise 1.

0 *of – preposition and part of a fixed phrase*

5 💬 Have you or anyone you know been the victim of a mistake on holiday? What happened?

An expensive mistake

Holidaymaker Samantha Lazzaris booked a trip (0) ..*OF*.. a lifetime to Costa Rica, in Central America, but ended (1) .... 1,300 miles away in the US territory of Puerto Rico. Miss Lazzaris realised the mistake when she got into a taxi at the airport. "I asked the taxi driver to take me to the hotel I (2) .... pre-booked. He looked in amazement at me, then laughed and said, 'This is not Costa Rica. It's Puerto Rico'."
(3) .... a result of the mix-up, Miss Lazzaris had to spend £800 on three extra flights to get (4) .... her intended destination, losing four days of her holiday. (5) .... seems the travel agent had used the booking code for San Juan, capital of Puerto Rico, (6) .... of the code for San José, capital of Costa Rica. The airport codes are similar to each (7) ....: SJO for San José and SJU for the airport in San Juan. A spokesman for the travel agent promised it (8) .... fully investigate the complaint as soon as possible.

Unit 4 Going away

Reading and Use of English Part 7
Multiple matching

1. 💬 Apart from clothes and other essential items, what things do you usually take with you when you go on holiday? Give details.

   I always take three or four books in case it rains and we can't go anywhere. They're nearly always crime novels because ...

2. You are going to read a magazine article about parents of young children and what they take on holiday with them. For questions **1–10**, choose from the parents (**A–D**). The parents may be chosen more than once.

Help

As with other Reading tasks in the *First* exam, the multiple matching task contains distractors. For example, section A includes the words *first aid kit*, *medicines*, *plasters* and *fall ill*, but this does not necessarily mean that **A** is the answer for question **6**.

Which parents

do not allow their children to do certain activities when travelling?	1
are generally pleased at their children's growing desire for independence?	2
have children who grow tired of each other's company on holiday?	3
have avoided one problem but created another?	4
accept that they are sometimes over cautious?	5
have experience of their children being unwell as the result of an activity?	6
keep something secret from their children until it is needed?	7
are amused by the results of their children's activities?	8
have no objections to the repetitive nature of a particular activity?	9
have not needed to make use of something they always take on holiday?	10

3. 💬 Ask and answer the questions in pairs.
   1. Where did you use to go on holiday as a young child?
   2. How did you spend your time there?
   3. What types of things did you take with you?

A Robbie and Trudi Jones

When we go away we always take a first aid kit, with all the usual children's medicines and plasters and so on. Amazingly, we've never once had to get it out on holiday, but I bet that if we didn't take it, the kids would fall ill and we'd regret not having it with us. It's the same with their clothes. We always pack something for every type of weather and they end up wearing the same three or four t-shirts all fortnight because, despite our fears to the contrary, it doesn't rain or snow or blow a gale. I guess for some things we're guilty of worrying a little too much about what might go wrong. Maybe we should relax a bit more. After all, that's what holidays are all about.

B Tanya and Steve Simpson

We usually spend our summer holiday camping in the south of France, so the main challenge for us is keeping the children entertained during the long journey down. Reading is not an option because it makes them carsick, as we've learnt to our cost in the past! And we don't believe in letting them watch videos or play computer games when we go away, especially not when there are so many more interesting things to see out of the window. So we always take loads of music and audiobooks with us. The children have their favourites of course, and we often have to listen to the same ones again and again, but it's a small price to pay and we don't mind it. In fact, we rather enjoy the stories, so it's really not a problem.

C Dale and Paula Lambert

My wife and I are interested in photography and we own expensive camera equipment. Our young daughters have now reached an age where they want to do things for themselves, which we both think is great, of course. But for a while they kept asking us to let them take their own photos with our cameras. We did sometimes, but to prevent costly accidents we now buy them each a disposable camera before we go on holiday. They're cheap to buy, so we don't have to worry about them being dropped or broken and the girls have stopped asking to use our cameras. The only thing now is that when we're in the car, they keep wanting us to stop to take photos every five minutes, which can be very irritating. Having said that, we always enjoy looking at their photos when we get back home. My wife and I have a private laugh when we see the images of headless people or little girls' fingers, but our daughters are proud of their efforts and that's the main thing.

D Gerry and Hannah Naylor

Our boys generally get on quite well, but after a few days on holiday, they get fed up with being together all the time and tempers are often lost. So we always make a point just before we go of buying a few new toys and games to take with us. They give us a chance to calm things down at moments of high tension and help restore the peace between them. We don't tell the boys we've bought these things, so it comes as a pleasant surprise for them when we suddenly produce them. That's part of the trick, of course. The other thing is that because these disputes are quite frequent when we're away, we only buy fairly cheap things – otherwise we couldn't afford to have a holiday!

Unit 4 Going away

Language focus
Gerunds and infinitives

1a Sentences **1–3** below are taken from the reading text on pages 34–35. Complete each gap using either the infinitive with *to*, the infinitive without *to* or the gerund of the verb in brackets.

0 If we didn't take it … we'd regret not _having_ (have) it with us.   (Section A)
1 We don't believe in _____ (let) them _____ (watch) videos.   (Section B)
2 They give us a chance _____ (calm) things down at moments of high tension.   (Section D)
3 … otherwise we couldn't _____ (afford) _____ (have) a holiday.   (Section D)

1b Check your answers in the relevant sections of the reading text.

2 Match each of the answers in exercise **1** to one of the explanations **a–f** below.
'having': (b) a gerund after the verb 'regret'

A gerund is used:
a after prepositions.
   *They get fed up with **being** together all the time.*
b after certain verbs.
   *Paul suggested **staying** in a campsite.*

An infinitive with *to* is used:
c after certain nouns.
   *I admire her ability **to keep** calm.*
d after certain verbs.
   *We've decided not **to go** abroad this year.*

An infinitive without *to* is used:
e after modal verbs.
   *It means we can **get** a bit of peace and quiet.*
f after *help, let, make, would rather, had better*.
   *I'd rather **go** on holiday with my friends.*

 Read more about the different uses of gerunds and infinitives in the Grammar Reference pages 106–108.

3 Work in pairs. Underline all the examples of gerunds and infinitives (with and without *to*) in Section C of the reading text on page 35. In each case, explain why the gerund or infinitive is used.
… they want to do things for themselves …
infinitive with 'to' after the verb 'want'

4 Two of the sentences **1–10** below are grammatically correct. The others each contain one mistake. Find the mistakes and correct them. There is an example at the beginning.

TOP 10 TIPS Staying safe in the sun

0 Failure ~~following~~ *to follow* the advice below can result in serious damage to your skin.
1 Always use a high-factor sun cream for protect your skin.
2 Apply sun cream to your skin at least 30 minutes before go to the beach or pool.
3 80% of ultraviolet radiation can pass through clouds, so you still need put on sun cream on cloudy days.
4 Avoid to go out in the sun between 12 noon and 3pm.
5 Never sunbathe for more than 30 minutes at a time and do not let your skin to burn.
6 Remember to take water with you when travelling – and don't forget drinking it!
7 You should avoid alcohol, tea, coffee and fizzy drinks as they dehydrate you.
8 Choose light-coloured, loose-fitting clothing and get used to wear a hat.
9 It is essential to wear sunglasses that block ultraviolet rays.
10 Spend time on sunbeds can be just as dangerous as overexposure to the sun, and should be avoided.

5 Which of the above advice do you normally follow? Do you disagree with any of the advice?

Unit 4 Going away

Listening Part 2
Sentence completion 🔊 1.21

1 💬 You will hear a man called Mark Mitchell talking on the radio about 'food miles'.

What do you think 'food miles' are?

2 🔊 Listen to the recording and for questions **1–10**, complete the sentences with a word or short phrase.

Food miles

Mark Mitchell says that food miles measure how far food travels from 'field to **(1)** _____'.

The UK imports **(2)** _____ per cent of its fruit.

Some consumers are worried that food transported by air is contributing to rising **(3)** _____.

Some UK supermarkets used a **(4)** _____ showing an aeroplane to help shoppers make informed buying decisions.

'Locavores' are people who buy **(5)** _____ fruit and vegetables if they can.

Critics of the concept of food miles say it is too **(6)** _____ and does not help shoppers.

From the month of **(7)** _____ it is more environmentally-friendly to import apples from New Zealand to the UK.

As well as food miles, we need to consider the time of year food travels and the **(8)** _____ used.

There are **(9)** _____ million Africans working in the business of supplying fruit and vegetables to the UK.

Kenyan farming methods do not include the use of **(10)** _____ or chemical fertilisers for growing green beans.

Remember

- You may hear *distractors* – information which could fit the gap but does not answer the question.
- For questions **2**, **7** and **9** in this particular task, you will hear more than one mention of a percentage, a month and a figure in millions. Listen carefully to ensure you choose the right one for each.

3 💬 Consumers are used to having a wide choice and eating fruit and vegetables when they are out of season. Do you think this is a good thing? Why/Why not?

Word formation
Prefixes

1 Write the correct negative form of the adjectives in brackets to complete these extracts from the recording.
   a 'Environmentally _____ (friendly),' say some. 'Not at all,' say others.
   b The concept of food miles, then, is not wrong; it is simply _____ (complete).

2 A number of prefixes can be used to make words negative. For 1–6, make each adjective negative using an appropriate prefix from the box.

un-	in-	dis-	im-	ir-	il-

1 honest   4 practical
2 lucky   5 correct
3 legal   6 rational

3 Now do the exercise on page 97.

37

Unit 4 Going away

What would it be like to live and work in places like these?

1

2

Speaking Part 2
Talking about photos

1 Look at photographs 1 and 2. They show places where people live.

> **Student A:** Compare the photographs and say **what you think it would be like to live and work in places like these.**
> **Student B:** When your partner has finished, answer the following question.
> **Where would you prefer to live?**

Useful language

Structures: The language of comparisons and modal verbs of speculation and deduction will be useful in Speaking Part 2.

Vocabulary: Use your dictionary to help you match the words below to photographs **1–2** above and **3–4** on page 97. You may use some words more than once and others not at all.

exciting   inhospitable   overcrowded
appealing   bleak   bustling   dreary
unhurried   dull   vibrant   pleasant
stressful   monotonous   relaxed
depressing tough

2 Now change roles. Look at the pictures on page 97 and follow the instructions in exercise **1**.

Writing Part 2
Email and letter

In Part 2 of the Writing paper, one of the options might be a letter or an email. The requirements are the same for both. Answers must be written in a style which is relevant to the situation and the target reader. The abbreviated language of textspeak is not acceptable.

1 Read the following Part 1 question. Which place would you recommend?

> You have received this email from your English-speaking friend Paul.

> **From:** Paul
>
> **Subject:** Beach holiday
>
> Alicia and I are planning on having a foreign beach holiday this summer. I'd be happy to spend every day swimming and sunbathing, but Alicia says she'd get bored and wants to travel around and see the local area.
>
> You've had lots of seaside holidays – do you know anywhere with good beaches and an interesting local area that would keep us both happy? A decent nightlife is important, too.
>
> Thanks
> Paul

Write your **email**.

Unit 4 Going away

2 Read the following answer to the question in exercise 1. Which part of the question has the writer, Sam, forgotten to mention?

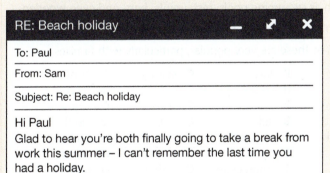

RE: Beach holiday

To: Paul
From: Sam
Subject: Re: Beach holiday

Hi Paul
Glad to hear you're both finally going to take a break from work this summer – I can't remember the last time you had a holiday.
If it's good beaches you're looking for, then I'd recommend those in the south–east of this country. There are many to choose from, and they're all top quality.
As well as having lovely soft sand, they're extremely clean and the water is so clear you can see hundreds of colourful fish as you swim in the warm sea. What could be better than that?
There's also plenty to see and do in the surrounding area. One idea is to hire a car and drive up into the nearby mountains, where there are lots of pretty medieval villages to visit. Make sure you go on a day when there's a craft market – the local pottery is fantastic. Or else you could take a boat trip round one of the islands and see the seals and seabirds – I'm sure Alicia would love that.
I hope that's helpful. Let me know if you decide to go there and I'll give you more information.
Best wishes
Sam

3 Read the answer in exercise 2 again. What is the purpose of each paragraph?
Paragraph 1: general reference to Paul's email

4 Find examples of the following features of informal letters and emails in the answer in exercise 2.
a linking words and phrases: *If ... then, and*
b expressions for making recommendations and giving advice: *I'd recommend*
c a range of language to talk about the beaches, the sea and the local area: *top quality*

5 Either
a write your own answer to the question in exercise 1. The area you choose does not necessarily have to be in your own country.
or
b write an answer to the following question.

You have received this email from your Australian friend, Susi.

From: Susi
Subject: Travelling holiday

A couple of friends of mine are going to be travelling around your country during the first two weeks of May. They want to see some beautiful countryside but they also enjoy visiting historical buildings.

Could you recommend two or three areas they could visit where there wouldn't be too many tourists? What's the weather like at that time of year?

Thanks
Susi

Write your **email**.

Help

- Write a plan. Make sure you address all the points in the question, otherwise you will lose marks.
- Write your email. Make sure you:
  a organise your ideas into paragraphs
  b use a variety of suitable linking words and phrases
  c include a range of vocabulary and structures
  d write in an appropriate style.

More information in the Writing Bank page 120.

Review | Units 3 and 4

Reading and Use of English Part 4
Transformations

For questions **1–6**, complete the second sentence so that it has a similar meaning to the first sentence, using the word given. **Do not change the word given.** You must use between **two** and **five** words, including the word given.

1 It's possible I threw the magazine away when I was tidying up.

   MIGHT

   I .... the magazine away when I was tidying up.

2 He's asleep already so I'm sure he was tired.

   MUST

   He .... he's asleep already.

3 It's nearly midnight, so I think I ought to go home now.

   BETTER

   It's nearly midnight, so I think I .... home now.

4 It was so hot yesterday that we didn't want to do anything.

   FEEL

   We didn't .... yesterday because it was so hot.

5 Amy broke her sister's glasses by accident.

   MEAN

   Amy .... break her sister's glasses.

6 I have always admired the work of Woody Allen.

   SOMEBODY

   Woody Allen .... work I have always admired.

Reading and Use of English Part 1
Multiple-choice cloze

For questions **1–8**, read the text below and decide which answer (**A, B, C or D**) best fits each gap. There is an example at the beginning (**0**).

Camping holidays

Every summer we load up the car with our tent, cooking equipment and sleeping bags and drive off in (**0**) _C_ of adventure. At home or abroad, camping is our preferred way of (**1**) ..... the summer holidays, away from the crowds of the city, sleeping under canvas and surrounded by nature. It's the perfect way to (**2**) ..... and unwind. The smaller, two- or three-star campsites have all we need in terms of facilities and are usually (**3**) ..... in beautiful countryside locations, where we can enjoy a quieter, (**4**) ..... pace of life.

Of course, camping does not (**5**) ..... to everyone; many would (**6**) ..... sit by a hotel pool all day or sunbathe on a beach. But for a little more comfort, there are always the more expensive five-star campsites, which have (**7**) ..... of amenities such as swimming pools, restaurants, bars, and even wooden cabins if you don't want to sleep in a tent. Make (**8**) ..... you book in advance though, as these are very popular, particularly with families.

0	A	seek	B	look	C	search	D	hunt
1	A	bringing	B	spending	C	going	D	staying
2	A	ease	B	slow	C	relax	D	enjoy
3	A	put	B	set	C	left	D	fixed
4	A	unhurried	B	delayed	C	rested	D	braked
5	A	interest	B	appeal	C	please	D	attract
6	A	consider	B	appreciate	C	rather	D	prefer
7	A	number	B	full	C	several	D	plenty
8	A	plain	B	clear	C	sure	D	safe

Vocabulary

Underline the correct alternative in *italics*.

1 She's had *hooked/crooked/upturned* teeth since she was a child.
2 The adverts promise that this cream will give you a *straight/slim/clear* complexion.
3 In the sunlight, you can see his hair is *sparkling/thinning/piercing*; he'll be completely bald in a few years.
4 Old age has left his skin *wrinkled/freckled/spotty*; a new line seems to appear each year, rather like the rings on a tree.
5 Ms Taylor is away on a business *travel/journey/trip*. She'll be back in the office on Friday.
6 My friend has offered to *bring/put/let* me up at his place for the night when I go to London for my interview.
7 I really enjoyed *with/all/myself* those family camping holidays we went on when I was growing up.

Language focus

1 Complete each gap in these short dialogues using a modal verb and the verb in brackets.

0   A: Do you think Rex invited Helen to the party?
    B: He ___*must have invited*___ her because she was telling everyone about it this morning! (invite)
1   A: Jack _____ at work because his car's still outside his house. (be)
    B: He _____ in bed! I know he was out late last night and his curtains are still closed. (be)
2   A: You _____ much time on this work Rose. It's terrible. (spend)
    B: You're right. I did it really quickly.
3   A: I'm going to check my messages. I'm meeting Ted later and he _____ while I was in class. (phone)
    B: I don't think so. He's been in a lecture for the last two hours.
4   A: You _____ Spanish really well. You lived in Spain for five years didn't you? (speak)
    B: Yes, but I've forgotten it all now.

2 In each of the following sentences one word is incorrect. Find the word and change it. The first one has been done for you.

0   James walks to school every day with his sister, ~~which~~ *who* is five years old.
1   The last bus leaves at half past nine, what seems quite early to me.
2   I lent my sleeping bag to my friend Tony, that was going camping with his friends.
3   Jake took a sleeping pill it had been prescribed by his doctor.
4   The regulations state that any worker who's working day is longer than six hours is entitled to a break of at least 20 minutes.
5   He's a terrible manager: it's a clear example of someone being promoted to a position for that they're not qualified.
6   Do you have any idea of the reason for he decided to resign?
7   After school on Fridays we usually go to the café where is next to the bus station.
8   They met on 14 December, which it snowed all day.

3 Complete each gap with the correct form of the verb in brackets.

Amsterdam

There is no city I enjoy **1** _____ (visit) more than Amsterdam. If you ever get the chance **2** _____ (go), don't hesitate **3** _____ (do) so!

There are some great parks and fascinating museums, and even if you don't normally like **4** _____ (look) at paintings, I'd still recommend you **5** _____ (go) to the Van Gogh museum. It's well worth **6** _____ (see) and you'd be sorry **7** _____ (miss) it. If you want to avoid **8** _____ (have) to wait for hours in a long queue, don't forget **9** _____ (buy) your tickets on the Internet before **10** _____ (leave) home.

11 _____ (travel) within the city is easy. If you'd rather **12** _____ (not walk), the best way **13** _____ (get) around is by bike. Everywhere is flat so it's easy **14** _____ (cycle). But I couldn't **15** _____ (imagine) anyone **16** _____ (go) to Amsterdam without **17** _____ (have) a ride on a canal boat. They're clean, dry and comfortable and they enable you **18** _____ (get) the best views of the beautiful buildings which line the canals.

If you feel like **19** _____ (get) out of the city, then why not take the train and bus to Keukenhof **20** _____ (see) the tulips? Go in April and May, when the flowers are in full bloom. It's an experience you won't forget!

5 Fitting in

Speaking Part 2
Talking about photos

1. Look at the two photographs below. They show young people together.
   Student A: Compare the photographs and say why you think one of the people is unhappy.
   Student B: When your partner has finished, answer the following question.

   Which person do you think will be unhappy longer?

2. Now change roles. Look at the pictures on page 98 and follow the instructions.

3. What advice would you give to the young people who said the following?

   I don't enjoy going to parties because I never know what to say to people.

   I'm a bit nervous because I'm changing to a different school and I won't know anyone there.

   I'm going abroad to study and I'll be staying with a family. I'm worried because I don't speak their language very well.

   I live with my parents in the city, but we're moving to a house in the countryside soon. How will I make friends?

Help

Student A
You have one minute to do this task in the exam. You should have time to comment on at least two or three similarities and differences *before* you answer the question in the box.

Student B
You have 30 seconds to answer your question. Make sure you develop your answers fully.

Useful language

- Use modal verbs to speculate about what happened to make the person unhappy.
  *They **might/could/may have had** an argument.*
- Avoid repetition of *unhappy* by using alternatives.
  *She is **sad/miserable/fed up/upset/in a bad mood/feeling down**.*
  *She/He is **feeling sorry for herself/himself**.*

Why do you think one of the people in each photograph is unhappy?

Listening Part 3
Multiple matching 1.22–1.26

1 You will hear five short extracts in which people are talking about experiences they have had while settling in to a new situation. For questions 1–5, choose from the list (A–H) what each speaker says. Use the letters only once. There are three extra letters which you do not need to use.

A	All the time I was there I didn't make any friends.
B	I regretted my decision to ignore people's advice.
C	I felt self-conscious in the clothes I had to wear.
D	Some people laughed at the way I spoke.
E	It was a long time before I felt accepted by the others.
F	A recent experience has made me consider leaving.
G	I began to have trouble sleeping at night.
H	I wasn't looking forward to the new situation.

Speaker 1	1
Speaker 2	2
Speaker 3	3
Speaker 4	4
Speaker 5	5

2 Have you been in any situations similar to those of the speakers? Tell your partner about them and say how you felt.

Language focus 1
Time linkers with past tenses

1a Complete each gap in these extracts from the listening with a word from the box.

after	~~at~~	at	before	soon	for	for	for
by		eventually	until	when	while	whenever	

Speaker 1
0 I often laugh about it now, but _at_ the time it was quite hurtful.
1 They'd all been working together _____ years.
2 _____ someone had a birthday, they would all go out for a drink after work.
3 It wasn't _____ I'd been in the job _____ about nine months that I began to feel like I was one of the crowd.

Speaker 2
4 _____ my dad got his promotion, we had to move to a different part of the country.
5 It wasn't long _____ I'd settled in, though.
6 _____ the end of the first week I'd got in with a group of lads from my class.

Speaker 3
7 _____ first it used to get me down.

Speaker 4
8 I stuck with it _____ a while, but I left _____ , not long _____ my mum and dad had bought the uniform.

Speaker 5
9 Almost as _____ as I'd moved in, I made a really good group of friends.
10 _____ I was sleeping upstairs, someone broke into my cottage.

1b Check your answers in the listening script on page 135.

2 Identify the tenses or forms of the verbs in exercise 1.
I often laugh – present simple   *it was – past simple*

Read more about time linkers in the Grammar Reference page 108.

3 In each sentence there is one mistake in the use of time linkers or tenses. Correct the mistakes.
1 Not long time after I started at this school I made lots of new friends.
2 It wasn't until I have been studying English for about three years that I began to feel comfortable speaking it.
3 I watched a little bit of television before of leaving the house this morning.
4 I wasn't paying very much attention whenever I was reading the Grammar Reference just now.
5 As soon as I was getting up this morning I had a shower.
6 I spoke to one of my friends during over half an hour on my mobile yesterday.
7 Last night I lay awake for more than an hour after that I'd gone to bed.
8 I wasn't sure what to do last Saturday evening: at first I thought about going to the cinema, but at last I decided to stay at home and play on the computer.

4 Work in pairs. Discuss how true the sentences in exercise 3 are for you.

Unit 5 Fitting in

Reading and Use of English Part 5
Multiple choice

1 💬 Imagine a member of a small tribe on an island in the Pacific Ocean came to visit your country for the first time. What aspects of your society and its way of life would he or she find strangest and/or most difficult to adapt to?

2 Read the text quite quickly. Were any of your ideas from exercise 1 mentioned?

Help
- In most *Cambridge English: First* reading texts you should be able to guess the meaning of words you are unfamiliar with.
- In paragraph 4, use the surrounding context to help you decide on the approximate meaning of *hurly-burly* and *caught on*.

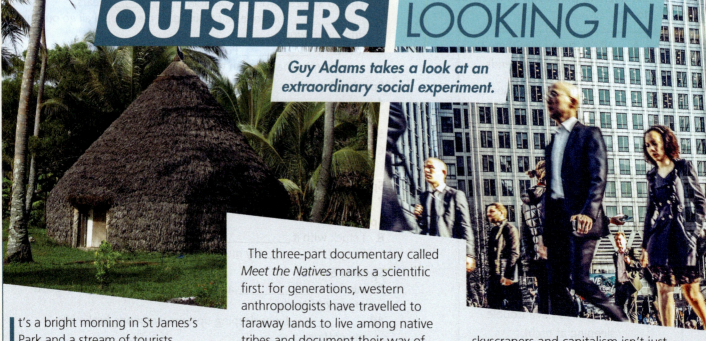

OUTSIDERS LOOKING IN

Guy Adams takes a look at an extraordinary social experiment.

It's a bright morning in St James's Park and a stream of tourists approaches Buckingham Palace. In the middle of the crowd walk five very short, very unusual-looking men. They carry camcorders, gesticulate wildly, and talk in a language no one can understand. In the heart of picture-postcard London, this group of people stands out like a sore thumb.

Further investigation reveals that a film crew is following the party, at a discreet distance. For not so long ago, a British TV company invited a small tribe called the Kastam, from the tiny South Pacific island of Tanna, to send a delegation to England, a country none of its people had ever visited before. They spent a month living here, learning the customs, and making a film about the way the strange and alien inhabitants of a modern western democracy live. The five men walking up The Mall are this delegation.

The three-part documentary called *Meet the Natives* marks a scientific first: for generations, western anthropologists have travelled to faraway lands to live among native tribes and document their way of life. But, until now, anthropology has always been a one-way street; alien cultures have never 'gone native' over here. The project was an experiment in what one might call reverse anthropology.

The five men, whose names are Yapa, Joel, JJ, Posen and Albi, come from a small hillside village on Tanna, which is the southern tip of the archipelago that makes up the island nation of Vanuatu. At home, they live in mud huts, and spend their time growing crops, looking after their animals and sitting contentedly in the shade of the banyan tree. The **hurly-burly** of central London couldn't be more different. For men who grew up in a place where the only form of currency is animals, and innovations like electricity, television and the internal combustion engine never **caught on**, the land of skyscrapers and capitalism isn't just another country. It might as well be another planet.

In a strange way, however, the five visitors from Tanna were ideally equipped to study our frenetic society: as the ultimate outsiders, their opinion of everything from household gadgets to domestic relations and workplace convention promised to be unique. Over the three episodes of *Meet the Natives* the group lives amongst the three great English tribes: the middle-class, upper-class and working-class. They spend a week on a Norfolk farm, a week on a Manchester housing estate, and a week at Chillingham Castle in Northumberland. 'We had four weeks to give them a sense of the enormous diversity of England, and decided this was the best way to show them a snapshot of what was here,' says Will Anderson, the series producer.

Most surprising is what Yapa, Joel, JJ, Posen and Albi find either enjoyable, or shocking. In Manchester they were amazed by the phenomenon of homelessness (in Tanna, your family provides a home, whatever happens), but felt relatively at home in a nightclub, since ritual dancing is an important part of their culture. They learnt to love fish and chips, but were left cold by the hustle and bustle of city living. They are astonished at the amount of time Britons spend cleaning and washing up, which is regarded as a waste of time and effort. They are also amazed at the fact we spend most of our lives working.

'One of the problems of our modern world is that for too long we've regarded these cultures as a sort of exotic creature, thinking how primitive they are,' says anthropologist Kirk Huffman, who acted as a consultant to the project. 'But I've spent 18 years living with them, and there's a lot we can learn. They are much more open-minded, and interested in the big questions. In the West, we are obsessed by little things. Our culture is all about *how*: to travel faster, to live longer, and make more money. Smart cultures are more about *why*. They are more reflective. That's what they can teach us.'

3 For questions 1–6, choose the answer (**A**, **B**, **C** or **D**) which you think fits best according to the text.

1 What do we learn about the visitors from Tanna in the first paragraph?
   A They are not at all like the other tourists.
   B They are very excited to be visiting London.
   C They would prefer to keep away from other tourists.
   D They have problems communicating with each other.

2 What does the writer say in the third paragraph about *Meet the Natives*?
   A It questions the methods used by western anthropologists.
   B It introduces a new area of anthropology.
   C It aims to compare life under two political systems.
   D It forms part of a series of films on different western cultures.

3 In lines 56–57, the writer says 'It might as well be another planet' to highlight
   A the enormous distance that separates England from Tanna.
   B the great lack of open spaces in London compared to Tanna.
   C the high cost of living in London compared with Tanna.
   D the huge differences between life in England and life on Tanna.

4 What does the writer say about the five visitors from Tanna in paragraph 5?
   A They have no class system in Tanna.
   B They were surprised at the size of England.
   C They were the right people for the project.
   D They were reluctant to express their opinions.

5 The writer is surprised by
   A the Kastam's mistrust of homeless people.
   B the Kastam's style of dancing.
   C how easily the Kastam find somewhere to live.
   D how comfortable the Kastam felt in a nightclub.

6 What does Kirk Huffman say in the last paragraph about people like the Kastam?
   A They are unwilling to adopt a more western lifestyle.
   B They have been undervalued by western cultures.
   C They pay a great deal of attention to their appearance.
   D They are incapable of making quick decisions.

4 💬 Discuss the following question.

Kirk Huffman says that people in the West *are obsessed by little things*. How true is that for people in your country? And you?

Unit 5 Fitting in

Word formation
Nouns 1

1 Write the correct noun form of the words in brackets to complete the extracts from the text on pages 44 and 45. Use the suffixes in the box. Check your answers in the text.

-ance	-ant	~~-ist~~	-ity
-ion (x 2)	-ing	-ness	

0 A stream of _tourists_ (tour) approaches Buckingham Palace.
1 … a film about the way the strange and alien _____ (inhabit) of a modern western democracy live.
2 Further _____ (investigate) reveals that a film crew is following the party, at a discreet _____ (distant).
3 … a place where _____ (innovate) like _____ (electric) and television never caught on.
4 In Manchester they were amazed by the phenomenon of _____ (homeless).
5 They were left cold by the hustle and bustle of city _____ (live).

2 Use the suffixes in exercise **1** to form nouns from these pairs of words. Use the same suffix for both words in each pair.

able/generous – *ability, generosity*

~~able/generous~~	appear/perform	assist/participate
build/meet	cycle/science	predict/reduce
tired/weak		

3a In the following text there is one spelling mistake. Find the mistake and correct it.

Margaret took great pleasure working as a librarian in her local neighbourhood and had considerable difficulty adapting to retirement when it came. She sorely missed the many friendships she had formed. Her absence was felt as well; the new arrival, Margaret's replacement, did not have the same personal warmth and unlimited patients.

3b Underline all the nouns in **3a**, then write down the word from which each noun is formed.

pleasure – *please*

3c Use the same suffixes that appear in **3a** to form nouns from these pairs of words. Use the same suffix for both words in each pair.

honest/discover – *honesty, discovery*

~~honest/discover~~	differ/exist	argue/equip
music/politics	depart/fail	approve/propose
long/wide	child/likely	member/champion

Reading and Use of English Part 3
Word formation

For questions **1–8**, read the text below. Use the word given in capitals at the end of some of the lines to form a word that fits in the gap in the same line. There is an example at the beginning (**0**).

Ring-necked parakeets

Originally from India, the ring-necked parakeet has become a common (0) _SIGHT_ in recent years in a number of European cities. In the UK alone there are currently over 8,600 pairs breeding annually. Three factors have contributed to the (1) _____ of this exotic outsider: a (2) _____ food supply, a tolerable climate and a distinct lack of (3) _____ from other species. Parakeets feed on a wide variety of seeds, berries, fruit and nuts, which are all (4) _____ available in urban parks and gardens. As a native of the Himalayan foothills, they can live (5) _____ in the cold winters of northern Europe, where they have been reproducing in the wild for over forty years. And as they begin nesting in holes in trees as early as January, they normally get first choice of nesting sites. These (6) _____ but very noisy birds receive mixed (7) _____ in those countries where they settle: loved by some, they are considered (8) _____ visitors by others, who see them as a threat to native species of birds that share similar habitats.

SEE
SURVIVE
RELY
COMPETE
FREE
COMFORT
COLOUR
REACT
WELCOME

Writing Part 2
Report

1 Read the following Part 2 task and the model answer. For numbers **1–10** in the model answer, cross out **one** word or phrase which does not fit in the sentence for reasons of either meaning, grammar or register. There is an example at the beginning (**0**).

The word 'reason' does not fit grammatically: it would be followed by the preposition 'for', not 'of'.

> In recent months, the school where you study English has received a number of negative comments from students about the atmosphere in the school. The director of the school has asked you to write a report, giving suggestions on how to create a more friendly atmosphere in the school and make it a more welcoming place for students.
>
> Write your **report**.

> *Creating the right environment*
>
> *Introduction*
> The (0) aim/purpose/~~reason~~ of this report is to (1) consider/look/ suggest ways to make this school a more friendly and welcoming place for students.
>
> *Reception area*
> (2) Firstly/To begin with/At first, a few improvements to the reception area would help to create the right impression (3) as soon as/during/ when students walk into the building. I suggest (4) putting/to put/ we put some paintings on the wall and plants in the entrance (5) for/ in order/so as to make it more cheerful. (6) However/Moreover/In addition, comfortable armchairs would encourage students to sit and chat before lessons, creating a more relaxed atmosphere.
>
> *Social events*
> It would also be a good idea to organise (7) a number of/loads of/ several social events throughout the year so students and teachers can get to know (8) each other/one another/themselves in more informal situations. These could include day trips to local places, meals in restaurants, or even sporting competitions.
>
> *Student committee*
> (9) Finally/At last/Lastly, I recommend setting up a student committee, which could meet regularly and continue to suggest ideas for improvements.
>
> *Final comments*
> I am confident that these (10) paces/measures/changes will make this school a much more pleasant place for students to learn English in.

2 Reports should have a main heading and a heading for each section. Find examples of the following features of reports in the model answer.

a structures and phrases for making suggestions and recommendations
'I suggest putting' or 'I suggest we put'

b a variety of appropriate linking words and phrases
Firstly, To begin with

3 Write an answer to the following Part 2 task in 140–190 words.

> You have a part-time job in a local library. The manager feels that not enough young people are using the library and has asked you to write a report, giving suggestions on how to make the library more popular with young people.

Write your **report**.

Help

Plan what you are going to write. Make a list of ideas, then organise the best ones into logical paragraphs. When you write your report:
- Include a brief introduction and conclusion and give each of your paragraphs a heading.
- Use a variety of linking words and phrases.
- Include a range of verbs and phrases for making suggestions.
- The report is for the library manager so you should write it in a consistently formal style.
- Check your answer for grammar and spelling mistakes.

More information in the Writing Bank page 121.

Unit 5 Fitting in

Vocabulary
Personality

1   For 1–8, underline the adjective in each group which is very different in meaning to the other three. In each case say in what way it is different. Use a dictionary to help you.

cheerful   fussy   enthusiastic   lively

A fussy person is someone who worries too much about small details. The other three are all positive adjectives describing happy, keen or energetic people.

1 friendly	outgoing	reserved	sociable
2 patient	grumpy	moody	bad-tempered
3 responsible	sensible	irritable	reliable
4 tough	brave	adventurous	sensitive
5 easy-going	relaxed	nervous	even-tempered
6 confident	tolerant	decisive	self-assured
7 kind	caring	thoughtful	lazy
8 rude	practical	impolite	bad-mannered

2   Which of the adjectives in exercise 1 would you use to describe the following people?

yourself   a relative   a friend   a fictional character

Speaking Part 3
Collaborative task

1a   Work in pairs. Here are some people whose jobs are in isolated places. Talk to each other about the personal qualities people need to do these jobs.

Deep-sea fisherman   Wildlife photographer

What personal qualities do people need to do these jobs?

Astronaut   Shepherd   Safari guide

1b   Now decide which job would be the most difficult to do.

Useful language

- Use different structures to talk about the qualities needed. For example:
  You need/have to be patient.
  It's important/essential to have a cheerful personality.
  You should never lose your temper with others.
  You can't afford to be sensitive.
- Decide which adjectives you could use when talking about the different jobs.
  Think about the qualities you need (e.g. a <u>cheerful</u> personality) and those which might not be helpful (e.g. a <u>sensitive</u> nature).
- Give reasons for your opinions.
  that's because … in order (not) to …
  the (main) reason for this is …

2   Now do the Speaking Part 4 task on page 99.

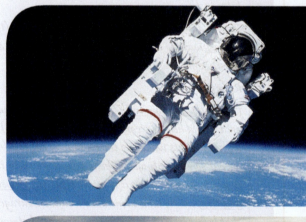

Listening Part 1
Multiple choice 1.27–1.34

You will hear people talking in eight different situations. For questions **1–8**, choose the best answer (**A, B or C**).

1 You hear a teenager talking to a friend about becoming a firefighter. What has prevented her from making an application?
   A her age
   B her eyesight
   C her height

2 You hear a wildlife cameraman talking on the radio about his work. What aspect of his work does he particularly enjoy?
   A the solitude
   B the danger
   C the unpredictability

3 You hear a woman talking about a walking holiday she is going on soon with some friends.
   Why are they going without a guide?
   A They will have more freedom to do what they want.
   B They cannot find a guide for the place they are going to.
   C They have had a bad experience with a guide in the past.

4 You hear a commercial fisherman being interviewed on the radio. How does he feel about life at sea?
   A He often misses his family.
   B He dislikes the lack of privacy.
   C He doesn't get on with the crew.

5 You hear a British woman talking about travelling to Mongolia. What advice does she give to tourists who visit Mongolia?
   A They should be tolerant of discomfort.
   B They should avoid some of the local food.
   C They should take gifts for the nomads.

6 You hear an elderly man talking about retirement. How does he say he sometimes feels now that he has retired?
   A isolated
   B bad-tempered
   C anxious

7 You overhear a woman talking about her husband. What is her husband's job?
   A an army officer
   B a prison officer
   C a police officer

8 You hear an extract from a radio play. What is the man's relationship with the teenage girl?
   A He is her father.
   B He is her employer.
   C He is one of her teachers.

Language focus 2
The future

1 The following sentences from the listening each contain a different verb form to talk about the future. Match each sentence **1–5** with an explanation for the choice of the underlined form.

> ~~a personal opinion~~   a personal intention
> an arrangement   a possibility
> an action in progress at a particular moment

1 I don't think it'll be a problem.
   a personal opinion
2 Next month I'll be trying to film pumas in the Andes.
3 I may not succeed.
4 We're spending another week in the Lake District next month.
5 I'm not going to apply for it.

⚙ Read more about ways of expressing the future in the Grammar Reference page 109.

2 Underline the correct alternative in *italics*.
   1 I'm probably *about/going/thinking* to spend a fortnight camping in France next year.
   2 Charlotte's not feeling too well, but she *should/hope/can* be better in a few days.
   3 I may *well/be/try* get in touch with Lucy this weekend.
   4 Tom and I *will play/be playing/are playing* tennis tomorrow. We've booked a court.
   5 I'm going straight home as soon as this class *will finish/has finished/is finishing*.
   6 My dad is *certainly/possibly/likely* to get angry if I don't get home before midnight tonight.
   7 I'll *learn/be learning/have been learning* English for three years by the end of this year.
   8 I *hope/expect/want* that Steve goes to the party on Saturday.

3 Write five sentences, each including a different way of expressing the future from exercise **2**. Your sentences should be true.

I'm probably going to stay in and watch a film tonight.

4 💬 Work in pairs. Compare and discuss your sentences from exercise **3**.

6 News and views

Reading and Use of English Part 6
Gapped text

1 **Work in pairs. Discuss these questions with your partner.**
  1 Do you and the rest of your family keep up to date with national and world news? Why/Why not?
  2 Which way of getting the news do you (or your family) prefer? Why?

2 **Look at these photographs and answer the questions.**
  1 What do you think the story might be behind each one?
  2 Which story would interest you the most? And the least?

3a You are going to read about the life of a breakfast radio news presenter. What do you think he likes and doesn't like about his job? What sort of problems might he have?

3b Read the article, ignoring the gaps, and check your ideas.

Unit 6 News and views

4 Read the article again. Six sentences have been removed. Choose from the sentences **A–G** the one which fits each gap (**1–6**). There is one extra sentence which you do not need to use.

A DAY IN THE LIFE OF A RADIO NEWS PRESENTER

Without doubt, the worst part of my job is the unearthly hour that I have to get up at every day. This puts me in a foul mood for at least two hours as I am not, nor have I ever been, a morning person!

'Why, then?' people ask me, 'Why do you have a job that means you have to get up at 3.45 in the morning?' The simple answer is that the job of presenting the breakfast news programme on a radio station is what I have always wanted to do. **1** But there are no two ways about it – I am still not a morning person!

Having hauled myself out of bed, I get a taxi to the radio station (I wouldn't trust myself driving at that hour), and when we arrive, it is still dark with only a few brave birds daring to break the silence. Singing is the last thing I feel like doing. **2**

In much better spirits now, I sit in on the news conference, which is where the news editors make the big decisions on which news stories we are going to run with and in which order. They discuss events that have happened overnight and developments in any stories we ran yesterday. **3** You can feel the excitement in the air on mornings like these, particularly if it's an event with important national or international implications.

The discussions are fierce. Which stories do we report and in how much depth? Then the big question – which stories get priority? We may have five big stories but which do we lead with? Is it the celebrity who has been caught for dangerous driving or is it yet another political scandal? Is it the murder of a homeless person or the fact that Australia has just won another gold medal?

People in the meeting pull in different directions. **4** Others think that local crimes need to be top of the list. The team thrashes out the possibilities and eventually I am nearly ready to go on air.

This is when the adrenalin really kicks in. It is a buzz presenting a show live but there is not much room for mistakes and things do not always go smoothly. My job is to appear to be in control and I have to be alert and able to think on my feet. **5** Or else I get connected to the wrong reporter – that can be very confusing!

Of course, there are also those callers on the phone-in sections who see it as an opportunity to go way off topic and complain about everything from taxation to the quality of the burgers in the restaurant down the road! There's a lot of mental gymnastics that goes on and afterwards I always feel completely exhausted. **6**

Before leaving the studio there's another meeting to discuss items for tomorrow's show. Then I'm out of the door, determined to enjoy the rest of the day before I go to bed at the obscenely early time of 8.30!

A There may even be a breaking news story happening at the time.

B Of course, I realise there's a contradiction here, and I shouldn't be moaning about getting up early when my job is the envy of hundreds of other 'would-be' presenters in Australia.

C When you're talking on the radio, you have to imagine that you're talking to one person face to face.

D Sometimes sound links with correspondents in the field can go wrong and I'm left talking to complete silence.

E Some want to win the popular vote – celebrity stories attract listeners, the more sensational the better.

F However, that's all part of the job and the unpredictability is one of the reasons I love it so much.

G A couple of strong coffees later, however, I feel better able to face the day and my grumpiness begins to lift.

5a Work in pairs. Look at the newspaper headlines below. Imagine you are going to plan a radio news bulletin and discuss these questions. Give reasons.
  • Which story would you lead with?
  • What order would you present the other items in?

1 Celebrity arrested for dangerous driving
2 Government reduces money for hospitals
3 Airport strike
4 Murder of homeless man
5 Politician fails to pay his taxes
6 Outbreak of dangerous spiders
7 Dog saves its master from freezing river
8 Small country wins big sports trophy

5b Compare your list with that of another pair of students.

Unit 6 News and views

Reading and Use of English Part 1
Multiple-choice cloze

1 Work in pairs. These pictures show people getting the news in different ways. Compare the pictures and say what the advantages and disadvantages are of getting the news in these ways.

2 Read the text below, ignoring the gaps. Choose the best title for the article.
a The importance of keeping informed
b The death of the newspaper?
c A career in journalism
d Which newspaper is best?

3 For questions **1–8**, read the text below and decide which answer (**A, B, C** or **D**) best fits each gap. There is an example at the beginning (**0**).

The future of the daily newspaper is in (0) _B_ . More and more of us are turning (1) ..... from the traditional daily newspaper as a means of getting our information and going online or to TV news for the (2) ..... and main stories instead. Does this mean that newspapers will (3) ..... become a thing of the past?

Newspapers may well survive in some form in the future (4) ..... the convenience of the Internet, their main rival. Many people read newspapers not simply for getting the information about (5) ..... events but as part of a traditional routine. For them, catching up with the main stories electronically from news websites or TV news (6) ..... will never be a real substitute for turning the pages of a paper on the train or at the table.

However, the main competition for newspapers (7) ..... from their own online versions. A (8) ..... of newspaper corporations have been charging for access to these for some time, convinced that this is the only way forward.

0	A	problems	B	danger	C	fear	D	worry
1	A	out	B	over	C	away	D	forward
2	A	titles	B	signs	C	descriptions	D	headlines
3	A	shortly	B	next	C	lately	D	early
4	A	although	B	however	C	despite	D	but
5	A	modern	B	current	C	late	D	ultimate
6	A	emissions	B	sendings	C	hearings	D	broadcasts
7	A	gets	B	goes	C	gives	D	comes
8	A	collection	B	set	C	number	D	quantity

4 Would you be willing to pay for online access to news websites? Why/Why not?

Will newspapers continue to survive in print form?

Vocabulary
Making decisions

1. Look at these comments people have made about making decisions. <u>Underline</u> the correct word in *italics*.

    1. I usually take a long time to make decisions because I like to **take** everything **into** *mind/account/view*.
    2. I agree. It's not a good idea to *rush/speed/force* **into a decision**; you need to *look/stand/weigh* **up the pros and the cons**.
    3. Once I've decided something, I rarely **change my** *mind/head/thought*. I don't like *giving/going/looking* **back on a decision** once I've made it.
    4. My problem is that I can never *make/take/work* **up my mind**! I usually *give/set/put* **off making a decision** until the last possible moment.
    5. It takes me no time at all to *come/arrive/reach* **to a decision** – I'm known for being *decided/decisive/deciding*.
    6. I always **leave it** *in for/up to/out of* **someone else to decide** things like where to go on holiday or what to do at the weekend.
    7. I usually **let my heart** *decide/rule/work* **my head**, and that's not always a good thing! I should think more about decisions and not get too emotional.

2. Work in pairs. Tell your partner how similar you are to each of the people who made comments **1–7**. Give reasons and examples.

    I'm a bit like the people in sentences 1 and 2. For example, if I'm buying something like a new smartphone or tablet, I spend ages comparing different models on the Internet.

Speaking Part 3
Collaborative task

1. Here are some decisions people often have to make and a question for you to discuss.

    a. Talk to each other about what people need to consider when making these decisions.

    b. Now decide which is the most difficult decision to make.

    #### Useful language

    Avoid repeating the words *consider* and *difficult*. Here are some alternatives:

    You need to **think about/bear in mind/take into account** a number of factors.
    It's a **hard/complicated/tricky/tough** decision to make.
    It **isn't a/an easy/simple/straightforward** decision.
    Deciding what to do **is no easy matter**.

    #### Remember

    - In **a**, don't rush through the five decisions. Spend some time talking about each one before you move on to the next.
    - In **b**, you do not have to agree with your partner about which is the most difficult decision.

Unit 6 News and views

Listening Part 4
Multiple choice 2.01

1. Look at the photographs below, which were taken at an International Session of the EYP, the European Youth Parliament. Then discuss these questions with a partner.
   1. What do you think happens at an International Session?
   2. What do you think the aims of the International Sessions are?

2. Read the following text about the International Sessions and check your ideas from exercise 1.

EYP

International Sessions of the EYP bring together young people from all over Europe to discuss current topics in European politics. The aim of the sessions is to promote European values, strengthen intercultural skills and create a sense of European citizenship. After an initial team-building stage, participants work together in groups, or '**committees**', in an attempt to come up with solutions to some of Europe's most urgent problems. Each committee puts its ideas together in a written document called a **resolution**, which it then presents for debate in a parliamentary **assembly** at the end of the session.

3. You will hear an interview with a student called Emma Baines, who participated in an International Session of the European Youth Parliament. For questions 1–7, choose the best answer (A, B or C).

   1. How did Emma's family react when she was selected for the International Session?
      A Her sister was jealous of her.
      B Her mother was not surprised.
      C Her father did not want to discuss it.

   2. Emma thinks the teacher in charge of the school debating society was impressed by
      A her self-confidence.
      B her passion for politics.
      C her natural enthusiasm.

   3. What did Emma like most about the team-building stage in Barcelona?
      A The groups were multinational.
      B The activities were enjoyable.
      C The language spoken was English.

   4. What did Emma find difficult about the committee work?
      A the lack of sufficient time to debate each issue
      B the complexity of the problem they had to discuss
      C the need to give careful consideration to everyone's ideas

   5. After the General Assembly, Emma says she felt very
      A relieved.
      B anxious.
      C satisfied.

   6. What does Emma say about Europe?
      A Its future is positive.
      B Its people are friendly.
      C Its languages are difficult.

   7. What does Emma say about her future career plans?
      A She wants to take her time to decide.
      B She wants to become a local politician.
      C She wants to travel to a number of countries.

4. Discuss these questions in small groups.
   1. Would you be interested in participating in a youth parliament? Why/Why not?
   2. In the listening, Emma says, '*I came away with a greater understanding of Europe and what it means to be European.*' If you are from Europe, what does it mean to you to be European? Do you feel part of Europe? Why/Why not? If you are not from Europe, how important is it to you that you are a citizen of your continent? Why?

Language focus

Reported speech
Reported statements

1a Sentences **1–3** are reported versions of what Emma said in the listening. Rewrite the sentences with the actual words she used.

1 Emma said her mum was in local politics and she had always encouraged her to take an interest in what was going on in the world.
  'My mum's in local politics and she …'
2 She said that the previous year, the teacher in charge of the school debating society had decided to take a team to the regional meeting.
3 She said she would probably go abroad the following year to do voluntary work and after that, she wanted to go to university.

1b Listen again to check your answers.

2a Compare the tenses actually used by Emma with those in the reported statements in exercise **1**. How do the tenses in the box change in reported speech?

present simple	present perfect
present continuous	past simple
will future	

present simple → past simple

2b How do the following words used by Emma change when they are reported?

| my | me | I | last year | next year |

2c What changes, if any, would be made to the following words if they were reported?

now	today	tomorrow	yesterday
here	this	can	may
could	would	should	might

Check your answers to **2c** and read more about reported statements in the Grammar Reference page 110.

3 Report the following statements.

1 'I need to go shopping this morning,' my brother told me.
  My brother told me …
2 'We're both going out for a meal tomorrow evening,' said Mike.
3 'Yesterday afternoon I went to see the film you recommended to me,' Helena told me.
4 'I've been looking forward to coming here,' Elisa said.
5 'I know I should go to the doctor's today, but I'll probably go next week instead,' said Amy.

Reported questions

1a Compare these two questions, which the interviewer asked Emma, with their reported versions. Then answer the question in **1b**.
'How did you become involved in the European Youth Parliament?'
The interviewer asked Emma how she had become involved in the European Youth Parliament.

'Did you stay with the same group for the rest of your time in Barcelona?'
He asked her if she had stayed with the same group for the rest of her time in Barcelona.

1b What happens to the following when questions are reported?

auxiliary verbs *do, does, did*	verb tenses
yes/no questions	word order
punctuation	

Check your answers and read more about reported questions in the Grammar Reference pages 110–111.

2 Report the following questions which the interviewer asked Emma.

1 'What was it like when you got to Barcelona?'
  He asked Emma what …
2 'Did you and your group share your solutions with the other committees?'
3 'What do you think you gained from going to Barcelona?'
4 'What are your plans for the future?'

3 Work with a partner and follow these instructions.

1 Ask your partner four questions about himself/herself. Note down the answers.
  'Lara, are you interested in politics?' 'Yes, I find it fascinating.'
2 Work with a different partner and report the questions and answers from **1**.
  However, you should report **one** of the answers incorrectly.
  I asked Lara if she was interested in politics and she told me she found it boring.
3 Your new partner should guess which answer you have reported incorrectly.

Unit 6 News and views

Reporting verbs

1 Complete each gap with one of the reporting verbs.

| admitted | congratulated |
| ~~invited~~ | offered suggested |

0 My teacher ___invited___ me to join the school team going to the Regional Forum.
1 She _____ to give us all coaching in public speaking.
2 During the lessons she _____ that we should all stand up straighter.
3 At one point, she _____ thinking that we didn't have much chance of success.
4 She _____ the team on being selected for the National Session.

2a Look at the verb patterns after the reporting verbs you wrote in exercise **1**. Then add the reporting verbs to the correct groups **a–e**.

Verbs followed by
a infinitive (… *to do something*)
b object + infinitive (… *someone to do something*) *invite*
c gerund (… *doing something*)
d object + preposition + gerund (… *someone on/for/of/against doing something*)
e (that) + clause (… *(that) someone should do something*)

2b Now add these verbs to the correct groups **a–e**. Some verbs can go in more than one group.

accuse	ask	recommend
blame	warn	encourage
advise	insist	promise
refuse	deny	persuade
remind	tell	threaten

 Check your answers and read more about reporting verbs in the Grammar Reference page 111.

3 Complete the second sentence so that it has a similar meaning to the first sentence, using the word given. **Do not change the word given**. You must use between **two** and **five** words, including the word given.

1 'It was Jim who left the light on,' said Rosie.
   ACCUSED
   Rosie ………………………… the light on.

2 Sean said he would not take care of my cat while I was on holiday.
   REFUSED
   Sean ………………………… after my cat while I was on holiday.

3 'I think you should come to a decision soon, Robin,' said his Mum.
   MAKE
   Robin's Mum suggested ………………………… his mind soon.

4 'Please don't put your feet on the table, Liz,' said her Dad.
   ASKED
   Liz's Dad ………………………… put her feet on the table.

5 'I'm sorry I didn't make my bed,' said Jack.
   NOT
   Jack apologised ………………………… his bed.

6 'I demand to see the manager,' insisted the customer.
   INSISTED
   The customer ………………………… the manager.

Writing Part 1
Essay

1 Read the following Part 1 task and the model answer. The writer is asked to give their 'own idea'. What is the writer's 'own idea' in the model answer?

In your English class you have been talking about the work of politicians. Now, your English teacher has asked you to write an essay.
Write an essay using **all** the notes and giving reasons for your point of view.

Do you think that politicians should be paid higher salaries?

Notes
Write about:
1 the use of public money
2 the nature of politicians' work
3 ……………… (your own idea)

Unit 6 News and views

2. The model answer in exercise **1** is sometimes called a 'balanced' essay. In what way is the essay 'balanced'? What is the purpose of each paragraph?

3. In the Writing Paper, it is important to use a range of language and avoid repetition. Look at the model answer again and find words and phrases which include the idea of paying or earning money.

receive (much lower) salaries

4a You should include a variety of appropriate linking words and phrases in your answer. Add the underlined words and phrases from the model answer to this table.

Giving your opinion	
Introducing one side of the argument	*Some people believe that ...*
Introducing the other side of the argument	
Making additional points	
Concluding	

4b Now add the following words and phrases to the table.

On the one hand	My personal view is that
On balance	In addition (to this)
Furthermore	On the other hand
Moreover	I partly/fully agree that

5. Write an answer to the following Part 1 task in 140–190 words.

> In your English class you have been talking about the large sums of money earned by some sportspeople. Now, your English teacher has asked you to write an essay.
>
> Write an essay using **all** the notes and giving reasons for your point of view.

> Is it right that some sportspeople earn such large sums of money?
>
> **Notes**
> Write about:
> 1. the nature of their work
> 2. the entertainment they give
> 3. .... (your own idea)

Remember

- Organise your ideas into logical paragraphs.
- Include a range of language.
- Use a variety of linking words and phrases.
- Write your answer in a consistently formal or neutral style.

Politicians in my country receive much lower salaries than most executives and managers in large private companies. Should they be paid the same amount?

<u>Some people believe that</u> this would not be a good use of taxpayers' money. After all, politicians are civil servants and, unlike executives in private companies, it is not their job to make profits so that they can give themselves large salaries. <u>Besides</u>, many of them receive income from other sources, and it is almost impossible to find a poor politician.

<u>However, others argue that</u> politicians deserve to earn more because they do a very important job. They have a great deal of responsibility and make decisions which can affect millions of people, in areas like education, health and transport. <u>What is more</u>, there is a danger that if they are not paid enough, they might decide to look for work in the private sector, and we would lose our best politicians.

<u>In conclusion, I personally feel that</u> politicians deserve more money. It is unreasonable to expect them to work hard for us and then not reward them.

Review | Units 5 and 6

Reading and Use of English Part 4
Transformations

For questions 1–6, complete the second sentence so that it has a similar meaning to the first sentence, using the word given. **Do not change the word given**. You must use between **two** and **five** words, including the word given.

1. John ate a big meal shortly before he went swimming.

   LONG

   John went swimming .... eaten a big meal.

2. 'I'm postponing the party until next week, Jane,' said Anna.

   TOLD

   Anna .... off the party until the following week.

3. 'Did you take the book back to the library?' Alicia asked me.

   TAKEN

   Alicia wanted to know .... the book back to the library.

4. United probably won't beat City on Saturday.

   UNLIKELY

   United is .... against City on Saturday.

5. The government lost the election because it had completely failed to reduce unemployment.

   ITS

   The government lost the election because of .... reduce unemployment.

6. You need to consider the cost of your meals when planning the journey.

   ACCOUNT

   You should .... the cost of your meals when planning the journey.

Reading and Use of English Part 2
Open cloze

For questions 1–8, read the text below and think of the word which best fits each gap. Use only **one** word in each gap. There is an example at the beginning (0).

Judging the judges!

Everyone is (0) *AN* armchair critic these days. A quick look (1) .... any TV schedule shows that reality TV programmes dominate our screens and most of these ask the viewers to vote on which contestant or participant should (2) .... eliminated from the show and which should progress to the next level. But (3) .... do we make our choice? Often we rely (4) .... guidance from the professional judges on the show.

So, what makes a good professional judge? Many of them comment on the contestant's performance without giving detailed reasons (5) .... it was good or poor. A good professional judge needs to be (6) .... to give constructive criticism and articulate his or her opinions about the strength or weakness of a performance. They need to be an expert in their field, (7) .... it is music or cookery, and also (8) .... be afraid of telling the truth as they see it. It is definitely not the judge's job to be popular.

Vocabulary

1 Complete the compound adjectives so that they have a similar meaning to the word in brackets. The first letter has been given to you.
1. He's such a bad-m_____ (rude) child – he never says 'please' or 'thank you'.
2. They're like chalk and cheese: Lina is very shy, whereas her sister is extremely self-a_____ (confident).
3. Helen never gets angry or upset – she's so even-t_____ (calm).
4. Paul is very open-m_____ (tolerant) and wouldn't criticise anyone for their religious beliefs.
5. Our last teacher was very strict – the new one is so much more easy-g_____ (relaxed).

2 Write the opposite of each of the following adjectives. In each group of three, one adjective requires a different prefix or suffix to the other two.

0	enthusiastic	adventurous	decisive
	unenthusiastic	*unadventurous*	*indecisive*
1	sociable	responsible	reliable
2	friendly	patient	polite
3	thoughtful	tolerant	sensitive
4	kind	caring	practical

3 Match each sentence beginning **1–8** with an appropriate ending **a–h**.
1. It's almost July and I still haven't **made**
2. It took the judges a long time to **come**
3. My parents bought the dog, but it was **left**
4. My dad said I could go, but then he **went**
5. A local man has been arrested and **accused**
6. Actor, Jeremy Duggan, was **congratulated**
7. Sally drives fast, but she wasn't to **blame**
8. It's his own silly fault. He's been **warned**

a **back on** his decision after speaking to my mum.
b **for** the accident – it was the cyclist's fault.
c **to** a decision – the quality of entries was so high.
d **on** his 90th birthday by the Minister of Culture.
e **up** my mind where to go on holiday in August.
f **of** stealing ten left shoes from outside a shoe shop.
g **against** cycling in the dark without any lights.
h **up to** me and my brother to choose a name for it.

Language focus

1 Complete each gap with an appropriate form of the verb in brackets. There may be more than one possible answer.

a
I **1** _____ (go) into town with my mum to get some shoes this afternoon. I hope it **2** _____ (not take) too long – Colleen **3** _____ (come) round at seven and I want to do a few things before she **4** _____ (get) here.

b
Claire: Where **5** _____ (we/go) on Saturday? Any ideas what we can do?
Paul: Sorry Claire but I **6** _____ (stay) at home and work on Saturday. My exams **7** _____ (start) on Monday so I **8** _____ (revise) all weekend.
Claire: Alright then. I **9** _____ (phone) Tony later and see if he wants to do anything.
Paul: Don't call him between eight and ten – he **10** _____ (watch) the football then.

c
I'm just about **11** _____ (start) packing for our holiday. We're planning on **12** _____ (set off) at about five on Sunday morning. There isn't likely **13** _____ (be) much traffic around at that time so we **14** _____ (probably/get) to the coast by midday. I **15** _____ (give) you a ring when we **16** _____ (get) to the hotel, if you like.

2 Read this voicemail message from Paul to Helen.

Hi Helen! I've just got back from the Climate Change protest march. I was expecting to see you on the train but I couldn't find you. Did you go? It was amazing. I'm sitting here watching the march on TV. Are you watching it too? It looks really impressive! Well, it's been a long day so I'm going to bed early. I'll give you a ring soon. Bye!

The next day, Helen told her friend, Andy, what Paul had said in his message. Complete her words using reported speech.

Hi Andy. Paul phoned last night and left a message. He told me he'd just got back from the Climate Change protest march and said that he …

59

7 Survival

Speaking Part 3
Collaborative task

1 💬 Work in pairs. Here are some things which some people think may not survive for very long. Match them to the photos 1–5.

- Books
- Tropical rainforests
- What aspects of the modern world threaten the survival of these things?
- Cinemas
- Board games
- Small shops

2a 💬 Talk to each other about what aspects of the modern world threaten the survival of these things.

2b 💬 Now decide which **two** of these things it is most important to save.

3 Now do the Speaking Part 4 on page 99.

Useful language

(Board games) **may not survive much longer** if/unless/because …
(Tropical rainforests) **are in danger of disappearing** if/unless/because …
The biggest threat to (books) **is the fact that** (people don't read enough).
(Small shops) **are under threat from** (hypermarkets).
(Illegal downloading) **is putting the survival of** (cinemas) **at risk**.

Vocabulary 1
Surviving

1 Complete each gap with a word from the box.

| get | get | live | make | stay |

1 I don't need a powerful computer; I can _____ **by with** just a tablet.
2 My grandparents receive a very small pension and **find it hard to** _____ **ends meet**.
3 I never work during the summer holidays; I can _____ **on** the money my parents give me.
4 If I was lost in the mountains or a forest, I'd know what plants, berries and other food I could eat in order to _____ **alive**.
5 I need at least three cups of coffee to help me _____ **through the day**.

2 Match the **bold** phrasal verbs and expressions which you completed in exercise **1** to a definition **a–e**.

a continue to live when you are in a dangerous situation *stay alive*
b have enough of something (e.g. equipment, knowledge) to be able to do what you need to do
c have a particular amount of money to pay for the things you need to live
d manage to deal with the situations you encounter during the day
e have trouble paying for the things you need in order to live

3 💬 Look again at the sentences in exercise **1** and say how true each one is for you, giving reasons and examples.

1 2

Unit 7 Survival

Listening Part 1
Multiple choice 2.03–2.10

You will hear people talking in eight different situations. For questions **1–8**, choose the best answer (**A**, **B** or **C**).

1. You hear a man talking about a documentary he saw on television.
   What aspect of the documentary's location surprised him?
   A the beauty of the scenery
   B the variety of the wildlife
   C the severity of the climate

2. You hear a shop owner being interviewed on the radio.
   What does she say is the main threat to her business?
   A the current economic situation
   B the competition from large stores
   C the import of cheap foreign goods

3. You hear a teacher being interviewed on the radio.
   Why is his school celebrating Tiger Day?
   A to make children aware of the tiger's situation
   B to collect money to help with tiger conservation
   C to protest against keeping tigers in zoos

4. You hear a woman talking about books and e-readers.
   Why does she prefer books to e-readers?
   A They will last longer than e-readers.
   B They are easier to keep clean than e-readers.
   C They are more pleasant to hold than e-readers.

5. You overhear a man speaking on his mobile phone.
   Who is he talking to?
   A his boss
   B his brother
   C his neighbour

6. You overhear a student speaking about her financial situation.
   What is she complaining about?
   A She gets no help from her parents.
   B She is having trouble finding a job.
   C She has to repay money she borrows.

7. You hear a man speaking on the radio.
   What is his occupation?
   A a professor
   B an author
   C a reporter

8. You hear a woman talking to a friend about her first week as a teacher.
   What has she found most tiring about it?
   A planning her lessons
   B the length of her teaching day
   C maintaining discipline

Unit 7 Survival

Language focus 1
Countable and uncountable nouns

> A **countable** noun has a plural form and can be used after *a/an* when it is singular. For example:
> book   letter   shop   match
> An **uncountable** noun has no plural form and is not used after *a/an*. For example:
> furniture   health   progress

1 In sentences 1–10, which are taken from the listening on page 61, some of the nouns have been underlined. Write C if the noun is countable, and U if it is uncountable.

0   **Many** small <u>businesses</u> are having to close.   *C*
1   **A large number of** <u>hypermarkets</u> seem to be popping up everywhere.   __
2   There are **very few** <u>tigers</u> left in the wild.   __
3   **Several** <u>schools</u> in the area are hoping to raise **a large amount of** <u>money</u>.   __ __
4   My son downloaded **some** <u>eBooks</u> onto it for me.   __
5   There wasn't **much** <u>damage</u> at all in our <u>street</u>.   __
6   **A lot of** <u>trees</u> were blown down.   __
7   I think the <u>house</u> next door lost **a couple of** <u>roof tiles</u>.   __
8   Clearly I had to have **some** <u>knowledge</u> of the subject and I did **a great deal of** <u>research</u>.   __ __
9   A <u>journalist</u> on a Welsh language newspaper gave me **a lot of** <u>help</u> and <u>advice</u>.   __ __
10 I did think I might have **a few** <u>problems</u> with bad <u>behaviour</u>.   __ __

2 Put the words and phrases in **bold** in exercise **1** into the correct columns in the table below. The first one has been done for you.

Before [U] nouns	Before plural [C] nouns	Before [U] and plural [C] nouns
	many	

⚙ Read more about countable and uncountable nouns in the Grammar Reference pages 111–112.

3 For **1–4** <u>underline</u> the correct alternative in *italics*.

1   *Any/Several/Every* sections of the art gallery were destroyed in the fire, but a surprisingly large *number/deal/amount* of works survived.
2   There weren't *no/much/many* people on the flight out and there were *plenty/most/lot* of free seats on the plane home, too. I don't know how that airline survives.
3   *All/Each/Some* time I go to Greece, I manage to get by with a *few/little/lot* words of Greek, a *few/little/lot* English and a *few/little/lot* of gestures.
4   A small *number/deal/amount* of salt each day is fine, but too *more/most/much* salt in your diet increases your chances of developing high blood pressure.

Reading and Use of English Part 7
Multiple matching

1 💬 Look at the website advertisement at the top of page 63. Would you be interested in going on a course like this? Why/Why not?

2 You are going to read an article in which four people describe their experiences on a weekend survival course for families. For questions **1–10**, choose from the people (**A–D**). The people may be chosen more than once.

Which course participant	
was not discouraged by the bad weather?	1
found one activity particularly satisfying?	2
had not been keen to go on the course?	3
was pleasantly surprised to make new friends?	4
has learnt to appreciate the relative comfort of their life?	5
felt there was the right mixture of informative and practical sessions?	6
shared the same positive opinion as all the other participants?	7
felt accepted by the other people on the course?	8
appreciated not being criticised for doing something wrong?	9
was disappointed at not being allowed to do a particular activity?	10

3 💬 What do you think would be your favourite and least favourite activities on a survival course like this? Why?

WEEKEND SURVIVAL COURSES FOR FAMILIES

COULD YOU SURVIVE ALONE IN THE WILD? WOULD YOU BE ABLE TO KEEP WARM, FIND FOOD AND WATER, AND NAVIGATE YOUR WAY TO SAFETY?

With the emphasis on fun, our qualified instructors will teach you and your family the essential skills needed to stay alive in remote woodlands.

You'll get hands-on experience of building a shelter and lighting a fire, using only natural materials. You'll also learn how to purify water, identify edible plants, track animals and cook your own bread. And there are sessions on navigation skills and using knives and axes.

Click here for information on dates and prices.

SURVIVAL COURSE

A JACK, 16 years old

I expected to see more people of my age on the course, but there were a lot of really small kids there. I didn't do it to make friends, though, so it didn't matter much. Besides, the adults in the group were very friendly and they made me feel like I was one of them. I did get a bit fed up with the rain, especially during the night, when it started coming in through the shelter my dad and I had built. And to be honest, I don't think I'd be able to survive for very long in the wild after doing the course, but it did make me realise how easy we have it compared to people who used to live like that, or in some cases, still do. My dad wants to do another one, but he'll have to go by himself next time – once is enough!

B MIKE, 41 years old

My daughter was desperate to do this for her sixteenth birthday. It wasn't my idea of fun and I'd have happily let her go on her own or with her friends, but there were no places left on the courses for teenagers, so I didn't have much choice. I have to say, though, I was pleasantly surprised by the whole thing. I enjoyed learning all about plants in the wild – which ones you can eat and which ones to avoid – and also how to light a fire with two bits of wood. What made the course though, were the two instructors, who were extremely professional, and always helpful and encouraging if we made a mistake. It was obvious our shelter was a disaster, but instead of putting us down in front of the group, Ian and Joe focused on the positives and told us we should feel proud of our effort. Everyone on the course gave them excellent feedback and I was no exception.

C AMY, 15 years old

It was my dad's idea for the whole family to do the course. My mum wasn't too keen on going, but I thought it would be a bit of a laugh. And it was. For one thing, there were quite a few other people my age there. We all got on really well and some of us have stayed in touch, which was an unexpected bonus. The activities were enjoyable too, especially the fire-lighting – it was a great feeling being able to light a fire without using matches. I felt really pleased with myself. I thought it was really unfair, though, that the adults went off with the instructors for a class on using knives and axes, while we had to do an animal tracking game. They said it wasn't safe for anyone under eighteen, but not all teenagers are incapable or irresponsible. It was definitely worth going, though.

D CLAIRE, 38 years old

On the first day it poured down all morning, but we didn't mind. My son, Paul, and I had good waterproof clothing, and for most of that time we were under a type of tent, learning how to purify water and talking about knife safety. Then it cleared up around midday, just in time for the fire-lighting class. Paul got his grass to catch fire really quickly, but I was obviously doing something wrong. I couldn't even get any smoke, so I had to cook my fish over Paul's fire in the end. Despite my failure, I really enjoyed that activity, as well as all the others where we actually made things, like the shelter or the bread. Of course, there were times where we just had to listen and learn, but I think the instructors achieved a good balance of the two types of class.

Unit 7 Survival

Vocabulary 2
Prepositions

1a Complete each gap in these sentences from the reading text on page 63 with a preposition.
1 … he'll have to go _____ himself next time – once is enough! **(A)**
2 … I'd have happily let her go _____ her own … **(B)**
3 … some of us have stayed _____ touch … **(C)**
4 … I had to cook my fish over Paul's fire _____ the end. **(D)**

1b Check your answers in the relevant sections of the reading text, shown by the letters in brackets.

2a Complete each gap with a preposition which can be used after all four verbs. There is an example at the beginning.

about	at	for	~~in~~	on	to

0 invest   believe   participate   result _in_ something
1 belong   listen   object   respond ____ something/somebody
2 pay   apologise   save up   apply ____ something
3 depend   concentrate   insist   agree ____ something
4 worry   dream   complain   forget ____ something/somebody
5 smile   look   shout   stare ____ somebody

2b Complete each gap with a preposition which can be used before all four nouns.

at	by	in	on	out of

1 _____ purpose   fire   average   offer
2 _____ home   risk   work   fault
3 _____ heart   bus   accident   chance
4 _____ date   breath   order   sight
5 _____ theory   practice   danger   charge

3 Complete each gap with a noun or the appropriate form of a verb from exercise 2.
1 The fire chief **in** _____ of the operation said that the whole area was **on** _____ , putting over two hundred homes **at** _____ and the lives of residents **in** _____ .
2 I broke a chair at school **by** _____ . I kept telling them I hadn't done it **on** _____ but they still made me _____ **for** a new one.
3 The hand dryer in the toilet is always **out of** _____ . I keep _____ **about** it to the caretaker but he just _____ politely **at** me and shrugs his shoulders.
4 Over 150 countries _____ **in** last month's conference, which _____ **in** a decision to reduce carbon emissions by 15–20%. Representatives could not, however, _____ **on** an exact figure.

Listening Part 2
Sentence completion 🔊 2.11

1 💬 Work in pairs. Tell your partner about the last time you visited a museum. Did you enjoy it? Why/Why not?

2 🔊 You will hear a man called John Taylor talking about an exhibition he went to. For questions **1–10**, complete the sentences with a word or short phrase.

The Maritime Museum

John's favourite exhibition at the Maritime Museum was entitled **(1)** _____ .

On display was the boat in which Ernest Shackleton and **(2)** _____ members of his crew sailed to South Georgia in search of help.

Shackleton's ship, *Endurance*, became trapped in Antarctic ice in the month of **(3)** _____ 1915.

In 1972, the Robertson family's yacht sank after an attack by **(4)** _____ .

Initially, all the Robertsons had to eat were biscuits, sweets, fruit and a **(5)** _____ .

The Robertsons were rescued by a **(6)** _____ fishing boat.

One part of the exhibition focused on the skills and personal qualities needed to sail **(7)** _____ .

The Maritime Museum has a large number of **(8)** _____ exhibits.

John's son was particularly interested in the display of **(9)** _____ .

Entry to the exhibition is free for **(10)** _____ .

---

3 💬 Tell the class about any other 'tales of endurance and survival against the odds' that you know.

64

Word formation
Adverbs

1 Read the spelling rules and complete the gaps with the correct adverb form.

a Many adverbs are formed by adding -ly to the corresponding adjective.
slow _slowly_   careful _____
If the adjective ends in -ll, add only -y to form the adverb.
full _____   dull _____

b For adjectives ending in a consonant + -le, omit the -e and add -y.
reasonable _____   gentle _____
Omit the final -e and add -ly in these two cases:
true _____   whole _____
In all other cases, the final -e is kept.
immediate _____   brave _____

c For adjectives ending in -y, change the -y to -i and add -ly.
happy _____   noisy _____

d It is usually necessary to add -ally to adjectives ending in -ic.
automatic _____   scientific _____
A common exception to this is:
public _____

2a Complete each gap in these sentences from the listening with the adverb form of the words in brackets.

Adverbs can be used:

with verbs.
0 … that was when his interest in boats and the sea _really_ (real) **began**.
1 And did everyone **get back** _____ (safe)?
2 They were _____ (eventual) **picked up** 300 miles west of Costa Rica.
3 … there are always plenty of sections which _____ (specific) **cater** for children.

with adjectives.
4 … I saw the _____ (enormous) **popular** *Surf's Up* exhibition …
5 I would be _____ (extreme) **foolish** even to think of doing it!

on their own at the beginning of a clause or sentence.
6 _____ (surprise), perhaps, given that I'm not a sailing enthusiast, one of my favourites is the National Maritime Museum in Cornwall.
7 _____ (incredible), Shackleton and all those who'd sailed on the *Endurance* lived to tell the tale.

2b Check your answers in the listening script on page 139.

Reading and Use of English Part 3
Word formation

1 For questions 1–8, read the text opposite. Use the word given in capitals at the end of some of the lines to form a word that fits in the gap **in the same line**. There is an example at the beginning **(0)**.

2 Would you be interested in reading *Touching the Void*? Why/Why not?

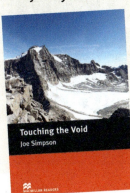

Touching the Void

Perhaps the best non-fiction book I have read **(0)** _RECENTLY_ is *Touching the Void* by Joe Simpson. It is a **(1)** _____ remarkable tale of courage and **(2)** _____ in extreme conditions, and is **(3)** _____ well written.

RECENT
TRUE
SURVIVE
EXCEPTION

The author describes in chilling detail what happened in 1985 on a mountaineering expedition in the Peruvian Andes after he and his friend Simon Yates had **(4)** _____ climbed the previously unconquered West Face of Siula Grande. During their descent from the summit, the weather changed **(5)** _____ and, blinded by snowstorms, Simpson fell badly and broke his leg. **(6)** _____ to walk, he had to be lowered by Yates down the mountain using their rope.

SUCCEED
DRAMA
ABLE

Disaster struck again when Simpson was left hanging over a precipice and could not communicate his situation to his climbing partner.

Yates made the only **(7)** _____ available to him and cut the rope, sending Simpson plunging into a deep crevasse. **(8)** _____, Simpson managed to crawl his way out and back to camp, where he met up again with Yates.

DECIDE
AMAZE

Unit 7 Survival

Language focus 2
Obligation, prohibition, advice and necessity

1a Complete each gap in these sentences from the listening with one of the items from the box. Use the same words that the speakers used.

| have to | had to | don't have to | mustn't |
| must | ought | need | should |

1 They _____ leave the rest of the crew behind on a small island in order to go and look for help.
2 This is not one of those museums where you _____ touch anything.
3 So anyone with even the slightest interest in the sea really _____ to pay a visit.
4 And how much do you _____ pay to get in?
5 Children under five _____ pay …
6 Students _____ to show their student card, of course …
7 … and senior citizens _____ take some proof of their age, just in case they're asked to provide it.
8 Now, if you get the chance, you really _____ go along and see the latest exhibition there.

1b Check your answers in the listening script on page 139.

⚙ Read more about obligation, prohibition, advice and necessity in the Grammar Reference pages 112–113.

2 There is a mistake in each sentence **1–8**. Correct the mistakes. You may need to delete a word or change one or more words.
0 I think you should ~~to~~ stop now – you've been in front of that screen for too long.
1 You can touch and stroke them if you want to but you don't be allowed to feed them.
2 We would better clear this up before she gets back or she'll be really angry.
3 He made me to stay in during the break just because I was talking.
4 We mustn't wear a tie if we don't want to, but I think our customers prefer it if we do.
5 I needn't having spent so much time worrying – it was really easy.
6 Steve lent me his pair the last time I went birdwatching, but I dropped them and did must buy him some new ones.
7 It broke down on the way to work on Monday, so now I must walk or get the bus everywhere while it's being repaired.
8 We've got plenty here in the flat for you to use, whether in the bathroom or on the beach, so there's no need to you for bring your own.

3a 💬 Work in pairs. Discuss the possible context for each of the sentences in exercise **2**. Consider:
• who might be talking
• who they might be talking to
• what or who they might be talking about.
0 *This might be a parent telling their child to stop playing on the computer or watching television.*

3b Work in pairs. Write a six-line dialogue. The first or last line of the dialogue must be one of the sentences in exercise **2**.

3c 💬 Read your dialogue to another pair of students, but do not read out the sentence from exercise **2**. Can the other students guess which sentence you chose?

Writing Part 2
Report

1 💬 Read the following Part 2 task. Which places would you recommend in your town and why?

> A group of foreign students is going to be staying in your town for a fortnight this summer. You have been asked to write a report for the group leader suggesting ways in which the students might spend their free time in your town without having to spend much money. Give advice on cheap places to go for entertainment and say why you think they would be suitable for the students.

Write your **report**.

2 Read the model answer on page 67 and write these paragraph headings on the appropriate lines.

The sea is free	Going dancing
Introduction	Indoor water fun
Conclusion	

Unit 7 Survival

<u>Compton: surviving on a low budget and having fun</u>

1 ....

The aim of this report is to suggest things to do in Compton which do not involve spending a great deal of money.

2 ....

Compton is noted for its large number of discos, including many which are specifically aimed at under-16s, so are ideally suited to your younger group members. Most town centre discos are not cheap so I would advise students to go to those on the seafront, where admission is inexpensive and drinks are affordably priced.

3 ....

There is of course no charge for entry to the beach, a must for all your students, who will love its fine sand and clean water. There are also plenty of amusements here which appeal to every age group, such as crazy golf, trampolines and even bungee jumping, and prices are reasonable.

4 ....

I would also recommend a visit to the indoor Aqua Park, which has two wave pools and several water slides. It is highly popular with young people and there are generous student discounts.

5 ....

It is clear that your students will be able to enjoy themselves in Compton without having to spend a fortune.

3 Read the report again. Who is it written for (the target reader) and has the writer used a formal or informal style?

4 Find examples in the model of:
a words and phrases for showing the amount or number of people and things. For example:
a great deal of money
b words and phrases for talking about price. For example:
town centre discos are **not cheap**
c phrases for making recommendations. For example:
I would advise students to go to those on the seafront

5 Apart from the price, what other reasons does the writer give for recommending the different places to the students?

6 Now do the following task.

A group of foreign students is going to be staying in your area for a fortnight this summer. You have been asked to write a report for the group leader about eating out both cheaply and healthily. Give advice on the best places for the students to eat healthy food in your area without having to spend a lot of money, and say why you would recommend them.

Write your **report**.

Remember

- <u>Underline</u> key words in the question to ensure that you include all the points in your answer.
- Write a plan. You might consider the following places:
  fast food restaurants with healthy options
  salad bars
  cheap seafood restaurants
  restaurants with healthy national dishes
  foreign restaurants
- Organise your ideas into paragraphs, including a brief introduction and conclusion.
- Give the report and each of the paragraphs a heading.
- Use a variety of linking words and phrases.
- Include a range of vocabulary.
- Write in a consistently formal style.

8 Brain games

Vocabulary 1
Memory

1 **Complete each gap with a word from the box.**

| memory | faces | heart |
| memories | figures | |

1 How easy do you find it to **remember names and** _____ ?
2 Do you **have a good memory for facts and** _____ ?
3 Can you write down five people's phone numbers **from** _____ ?
4 What are the most recent song lyrics you have **learnt by** _____ ?
5 Is there any particular song that **brings back** special _____ for you?

2 Discuss the questions in exercise 1 with your partner.

3 Tell your partner about:
a a **memorable** moment or event from your last holiday.
b an **unforgettable** film you've seen.
c someone you know who is quite **forgetful**.
d a technique you use to help you **memorise** information.
e a word in English you **keep forgetting**.
f a person you know who **reminds** you **of** someone famous.

Reading and Use of English Part 1
Multiple-choice cloze

1a You are going to read a short text about the World Memory Championships. What do you think the competition involves?

1b Read the text quickly, ignoring the gaps, to check your ideas in **1a**.

2 For questions **1–8**, read the text again and decide which answer (**A, B, C or D**) best fits each gap. There is an example at the beginning (**0**).

The World Memory Championships

Every year, over 150 mental athletes from around the world come together for three days to take (0) _B_ in the World Memory Championships.

The ten different disciplines which (1) ..... up the competition are not designed to test an individual's knowledge on a particular subject. Instead, contestants are (2) ..... with previously unseen information, including lists of numbers, words, dates and playing cards, which they have to memorise over a (3) ..... period of time and then recall accurately against the clock. Top competitors are (4) ..... of memorising the exact order of over 1,400 playing cards from twenty-seven complete (5) ..... in just one hour, or four thousand binary digits – a long series of zeros and ones – in thirty minutes.

Organisers of the event (6) ..... that competitors were not born with a particularly good memory. It is a skill they have (7) ..... by learning the techniques and putting in endless hours of practice. It takes a considerable (8) ..... of dedication, but in theory, anyone could become a memory champion.

0	A place	B part	C position	D post
1	A form	B make	C contain	D consist
2	A shown	B presented	C offered	D demonstrated
3	A set	B flat	C fast	D straight
4	A possible	B skilled	C capable	D competent
5	A bricks	B packs	C stocks	D chunks
6	A tell	B advise	C insist	D remind
7	A grown	B progressed	C increased	D developed
8	A quantity	B amount	C number	D sum

3 Do you think you could become a memory champion? Why/Why not?

68

Unit 8 Brain games

Listening Part 4
Multiple choice 2.12

1 You will hear part of a radio interview about memory. Look at the photo. What do you think the connection is with memory?

2 Listen to the interview. For questions 1–7, choose the best answer (A, B or C).

1 What does the presenter say about his memory?
   A It is usually extremely good.
   B It used to be better.
   C It is improving with practice.
2 How did Roberta remember the appointment?
   A She associated it with an important event.
   B She kept a written record of it.
   C She needed to be reminded of it.
3 Roberta says that one way to remember something is
   A to create an unusual mental image of it.
   B to make an amusing sentence about it.
   C to relax and think about something else.
4 According to Roberta, actors often learn their lines
   A immediately after rehearsals.
   B by repeating them.
   C extremely quickly.
5 When he was younger, the presenter says
   A he did well because of his photographic memory.
   B he always wanted a photographic memory.
   C he was irritated by someone else's photographic memory.
6 What did the chimps have to do?
   A type their name on the computer
   B do several mathematical problems
   C remember the location of numbers
7 What does Roberta think might be true?
   A Only chimps have a photographic memory.
   B A photographic memory is more common in young people.
   C A photographic memory stays with you for life.

3 Work in pairs. Look at this list of things you have to buy. Make a memorable picture in your head involving all the items. Describe it to your partner. Are your pictures very different?

eggs
fish
tomatoes
stamps
book
shampoo
a cucumber

4 Discuss these questions with your partner.
1 Do you think some animals are as intelligent as human beings?
2 Is having a good memory the same as being intelligent? Why/Why not?
3 Some people say that technology such as smartphones, tablets and satnavs have had a negative effect on our ability to remember information. Why do you think they say this?

69

Unit 8 Brain games

Speaking Part 2
Talking about photos

1 💬 Look at photographs 1 and 2. They show people who are remembering different things.

> What sort of things are the people remembering?

Student A: Compare the photographs and say **what sort of things you think the people are remembering**.
Student B: When your partner has finished, answer the following question.
How do you think the people are feeling?

2 💬 Now change roles. Look at photographs 3 and 4. They show people who need to remember things for their work.

> What sort of things do the people need to remember?

Student A: Compare the photographs and say **what sort of things the people need to remember**.
Student B: When your partner has finished, answer the following question.
Which job would you prefer to have?

Useful language

Talking about people's feelings
They look pleased/enthusiastic/fed up.
I think they must be exhausted/worried/bored.
They might be depressed/nervous/emotional.

Talking about job preferences
I'd prefer to work as a (tour guide).
I'd much rather be a (tour guide) than a (taxi driver).

Language focus 1
The passive

1 These are comments made by people in the photographs on page 70. Decide which of the four photographs the speaker appears in.

a *End of year exams <u>are always held</u> in the hall.*
b *I have often been asked how I learnt the names of all the roads.*
c *I don't remember this one being taken!*
d *The ruins were discovered 200 years ago.*
e *We had to stay in our seats until all the papers had been handed in.*
f *These should definitely be stored somewhere safe – we don't want to lose them.*
g *The results will be posted to us on 16 May.*
h *Some people want to be driven to other cities. That's good money!*
i *We are being supervised by Miss Langton.*

2 <u>Underline</u> the passive forms in exercise **1**. Then match the forms to the tenses below.

Present simple: *are (always) held*
Present continuous: _____
Present perfect: _____
Past simple: _____
Past perfect: _____
Future simple: _____
Gerund: _____
Infinitive with *to*: _____
Infinitive without *to*: _____

3 Complete this text about the passive.

To form the passive, we use the correct tense of the verb _____ and the _____ participle. To talk about the agent (the person or thing doing the action) in a passive construction we use the preposition _____ .

4 Reasons 1–4 below explain why the agent is often *not* mentioned in sentences containing the passive. Match each reason to a sentence a–d.

1 to avoid the use of 'you' in official notices
2 it is obvious who or what the agent is
3 the agent is unknown or unimportant
4 the agent is 'people in general'

a Three men have been arrested in connection with the theft of the painting.
b Dogs must be kept under control at all times.
c Photographic memory is also known as eidetic memory, from the Greek *eidos* meaning 'form' or 'shape'.
d The vase was probably made in Italy in the sixteenth or seventeenth century.

⚙ Read more about the passive in the Grammar Reference pages 113–114.

5 Rewrite sentences 1–6 using the passive. Begin with the word(s) in brackets and omit the agent if it is not needed.

1 Dominic O'Brien wrote *How to Develop a Perfect Memory* in 1993. (*How to Develop a Perfect Memory* …)
2 People will still remember this artist's work two hundred years from now. (This artist's work …)
3 The teacher was giving us a vocabulary test when the fire alarm went off. (We …)
4 You must switch off mobile phones before the start of the exam. (Mobile phones …)
5 They regularly hold memory competitions all round the world. (Memory competitions …)
6 My neighbour has asked me not to play my music so loud. (I …)

6 Rewrite the following notice using the passive and omitting the agents where appropriate.

Notice for Teachers

We have found a smartphone in the sports hall. A cleaner discovered it early this morning and someone must have left it there after yesterday's exam. At the moment we are keeping it in the head teacher's office. We will send a message about the smartphone to all those students who were in the sports hall yesterday, asking the owner to go to the head teacher. We will then ask the owner's parents to come to the school to collect their child's smartphone. Teachers should remind all students that we do not permit phones in exam rooms.

Unit 8 Brain games

Reading and Use of English Part 5
Multiple choice

1 Work in small groups. If you enjoy playing video games, tell your group which ones you play and why you like playing them.

If you do not enjoy playing video games, tell your group why not.

2 Look at the man in the photo. Which of the following adjectives do you think might describe his personality?

aggressive	attention-seeking	modest	moody	placid
rebellious	respectful	polite	timid	vain

3 The man in the photo is Shigeru Miyamoto, a Japanese designer of video games. Read the text about Shigeru Miyamoto quite quickly and check your ideas for exercise 2.

THE BRAINS BEHIND THE GAMES

Shigeru Miyamoto was in London to collect his Bafta Fellowship, the British Academy of Film and Television Arts, lifetime achievement award. His name now sits proudly alongside the likes of Alfred Hitchcock, Stanley Kubrick and Woody Allen as a master of the arts.

SHIGERU MIYAMOTO is the most successful artist of the last 50 years. He has single-handedly laid the foundations for the world's largest entertainment industry. Sales of his video games, from Super Mario Bros to Wii Sports, have topped an incredible 500 million, and show no signs of slowing down. Miyamoto, who joined Nintendo in 1977, has created 8 of the top-10-selling video games of all time. His smash, Wii Fit, became the second biggest-selling game in history. It made video games a daily part of life for a huge demographic of people who previously dismissed them as child's play.

Yet over and above his phenomenal sales success, what really sets Miyamoto apart from anyone else in any creative field is his marrying of genius with astonishing modesty. He cuts an unimposing, diminutive figure, sitting obediently in his chair. A Beatles T-shirt and moptop haircut are the only signs of cultural rebellion, smoothed at the edges by a quiet reverence and politeness. It's immediately apparent that unlike many of the Bafta Fellows to whose club he now rightly belongs, impassioned tantrums and theatrical outbursts are not his style.

Neither, as it turns out, are the glitz and glamour to which some may suggest he is entitled. 'I'm not envious of the attention of movie stars. I enjoy not being recognised,' he says. 'It allows me to get on with my life. All I want is to be recognised through my work. It's funny – in America and the UK, they say I'm famous in Japan. In Japan, they say I'm famous in America and the UK.' Miyamoto's placid temperament and genial timidity form a perfect fit with the universally loveable nature of his work. Miyamoto has never produced a title that wasn't suitable for families to play together, even in the days when video games were the unique preserve of teens in darkened bedrooms.

So what does he make of the more violent end of video games? His respectful nature, it seems, stretches even to peers who incorporate aggression into their gaming narrative. 'When it comes to the question of how each designer creates their games, I don't think we should intervene in how they express themselves,' he says. 'However, our marketing people must be very careful as to how they promote which types of products to which audiences, especially children.'

72

Unit 8 Brain games

4 Match the highlighted nouns in the text to their meanings in this context a–h.

a an activity that only one type of person does
b a strong feeling of respect and admiration for someone or something
c the situation in which there is not very much of something
d something that is extremely successful
e public attention and interest
f sudden short periods of unreasonable childish anger
g a group of people that a company wants to sell its products to
h the state of being rich and successful

5 Read the article again. For questions 1–6, choose the answer (**A, B, C or D**) which you think fits best according to the text.

Remember

- <u>Underline</u> important words in the questions.
- Find the part of the text which is relevant to the question.
  The questions are in the same order as the information in the text.
- Eliminate the options which are clearly wrong.
- Decide on the best answer. If you are not sure, choose one.

1 What does the writer say in the first paragraph about the games Miyamoto has created?
  A The sales figures have been exaggerated.
  B It looks as if they will continue to sell well.
  C They are more popular with children than adults.
  D The majority of people do not take them seriously.

2 According to the writer, Miyamoto's personality
  A can be irritating to those meeting him for the first time.
  B has led the artist to feel isolated within his profession.
  C is unusual for someone so talented working in the arts.
  D has caused him to reject some of his fellow artists.

3 When talking about the artist's work, the writer suggests that
  A Miyamoto's love of nature is incorporated into many of his games.
  B Miyamoto's games are more suited to individuals than families.
  C Miyamoto's early work was designed specifically for teenagers.
  D Miyamoto's personality is reflected in the games he creates.

4 What does Miyamoto say about violence in video games?
  A He believes it should be illegal to sell games with violence to children.
  B He recognises the right of designers to include violence if they wish.
  C He criticises companies which advertise games with violent content.
  D He admires designers who can create stories that contain no violence.

5 What do we learn about Miyamoto's childhood?
  A He did not like the commercially available toys.
  B His family could not afford to buy him many toys.
  C He gave away the toys he made to other children.
  D He did not have any other children to play with.

6 The writer suggests that on the evening that Miyamoto receives his Bafta Fellowship the artist
  A has secret thoughts of changing his career.
  B dislikes the physical contact at the ceremony.
  C questions whether he deserves the award.
  D would be happier if he were somewhere else.

All of today's hottest developers cite Miyamoto as an inspiration. But growing up in the mountainous Kyoto, and with no video game industry in existence, how was Miyamoto himself inspired? 'I have often taken inspiration from my childhood memories,' he reveals. 'It was a happy time for me, even though I had less around me in terms of material prosperity than others, certainly far less than children today. Wealthy families tended to have a lot of stuff, while all the others of us had a scarcity when it came to toys. But because of that, I used to make toys for myself with my own hands. A lot of the encounters and experiences I had and my conversations with other children still influence the way I make games today.'

The next evening, Miyamoto excitedly skips along the red carpet of the Park Lane Hilton Hotel before collecting his Bafta Fellowship. A huge smile doesn't leave his face all evening. It no doubt masks a desire to escape the limelight he's reluctant to embrace; to return home to his wife, two children and his true out-of-work passion, playing and appreciating bluegrass music.

6a Imagine you had to design a video game which reflected your personality and your interests. Decide what type of game you would design. Make brief notes of the **general idea** for your game.

6b Work in small groups. Share your ideas with the other students in your group. Explain in what ways the game reflects your personality and your interests.

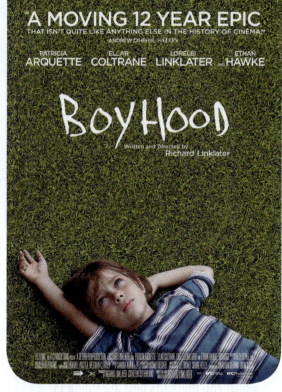

Language focus 2
Passive of reporting verbs

1 Some reporting verbs can be used with passive constructions to introduce generalised opinions and facts.

It + passive + that clause
It is said that Miyamoto dislikes being in the limelight.

Subject + passive + infinitive
Miyamoto is said to dislike being in the limelight.

Underline the infinitives in sentences **1–3** below. Then write each one next to its name in **a–c**.

1 Alfred Hitchcock is known to have appeared in most of his films.
2 The human brain is thought to be getting bigger.
3 Memory is said to improve the more often we use it.

a continuous infinitive _____
b simple infinitive _____
c perfect infinitive _____

2 Rewrite sentences **1–3** using *It + passive + that* clause.
It is known that Alfred Hitchcock ...

Read more about the passive of reporting verbs in the Grammar Reference page 114.

3a Rewrite these sentences using the two passive structures from exercise **1**.

0 People expect that video games will become even more complex in the future.
It is expected that video games will become even more complex in the future.
Video games are expected to become even more complex in the future.

1 People expect that climate change will get much worse over the next few years.
2 People say that eating fish improves brain performance.
3 People think that social networking has made people more isolated.
4 People consider that English and Spanish are easy languages to learn.
5 People say that daily life is getting much faster for most of us.

3b Work in pairs. Do you agree with the statements in **3a**?

Vocabulary 2
Arts and culture

1a For each of the words below, write down the first example you think of.

a novel	a ballet	an opera
a painting	a play	a poem

a novel: The Fault in our Stars

1b Compare your answers in small groups. Are there any possible explanations for any of your choices? Explain why you think you chose these examples.

I probably chose this novel because it brings back memories of my holiday last year, when I read it.

2 For each group of words, underline the one that doesn't fit. Give reasons for your choices.

0 biography   paperback   <u>soap opera</u>   best-seller
You watch a soap opera on television: the other three are things you read.

1 studio   gallery   concert hall   performance
2 cast   choir   ballerina   orchestra
3 exhibition   abstract   graffiti   portrait
4 novelist   musician   instrument   choreographer
5 classical   jazz   lyrics   hip hop
6 playwright   composer   poet   sculpture
7 comic   graphic novel   stage   cartoon

3 Work in pairs. Take turns to choose one of the words from exercise **2** and describe it to your partner, without saying the word. Your partner must guess which word you have chosen.

It's a person who dances classical ballet ...

Unit 8 Brain games

4a Complete each gap with a word from exercise 2.

1 I've never acted on _____ before. I think I'd be too nervous!
2 When I buy a book, I usually choose a _____ because I know other people have enjoyed it.
3 Some people think that _____ is vandalism but I don't. I think it brightens up dull areas.
4 I prefer to listen to music in small venues rather than in a great big _____ .
5 I can remember the _____ to songs I listened to when I was really young.

4b Are these sentences true for you? Explain why/why not.

Writing Part 2
Review

1 Read the Writing Part 2 questions **A–C** and tell your partner which one you would find it easiest to write an answer for.

A You recently saw this notice in a computer magazine.
   Reviews wanted
   Write us a review of a **computer game** that you enjoy playing. Describe the game's good and bad points and say who you would recommend it to.

B You see this announcement on a music website.
   Reviews wanted
   Write us a review of a **concert** you've been to recently. Include information on the music and the performers and say whether you would recommend others to go and see it.

C You recently saw the following announcement in an arts magazine.
   Reviews wanted
   Have you been to an **exhibition** recently? If so, could you write us a review telling us what you did and didn't enjoy about it and say whether you would recommend it to other people.

Write your **review**.

2 In **A–C** below, match the sentence beginnings 1–4 with the endings a–d.

A **Computer game**
1 One of its main   a get the 3D version.
2 I was more than a   b buy for fans of superheroes.
3 Make sure you   c strengths is the storyline.
4 This is a must   d little disappointed by the graphics.

B **Concert**
1 What made it for me was   a by the lead singer.
2 I wasn't very impressed   b for the evening performance.
3 It's better to get a ticket c the drum solo at the end.
4 Jazz lovers are sure   d to enjoy this.

C **Exhibition**
1 What I enjoyed most   a will appeal to children.
2 There were too many   b little extra for a guide.
3 It's worth paying a   c self-portraits for my liking.
4 The hands-on exhibits   d was the display of jewellery.

3 Write an answer to one of the questions **A–C** in exercise 1. You should write **140–190** words.

Remember

- Write a plan, including all the points in the question.
- Use a range of vocabulary and structures.
- Include a variety of linking words and phrases.
- Give your review a title.
- Check your answer for grammar and spelling mistakes.

More information in the Writing Bank page 119.

Review | Units 7 and 8

Reading and Use of English Part 4
Transformations

For questions **1–6**, complete the second sentence so that it has a similar meaning to the first sentence, using the word given. **Do not change the word given.** You must use between **two** and **five** words, including the word given.

1. Sarah's parents did not allow her to participate in the event.
   LET
   Sarah's parents did .... part in the event.

2. Ryan had to tidy his room before his mother gave him his pocket money.
   MADE
   Ryan's mother .... his room before she gave him his pocket money.

3. You don't need to phone John about the party because I emailed him yesterday.
   YOU
   There's .... phone John about the party because I emailed him yesterday.

4. Candidates are not allowed to remove question papers from the examination room.
   MUST
   Question papers .... candidates from the examination room.

5. Police are currently questioning a 30-year-old man in relation to the incident.
   QUESTIONED
   A 30-year-old man .... the moment in relation to the incident.

6. They think young people's hearing is getting worse because of too much loud music.
   THOUGHT
   Young people's hearing .... worse because of too much loud music.

Reading and Use of English Part 2
Open cloze

For questions **1–8**, read the text below and think of the word which best fits each gap. Use only **one** word in each gap. There is an example at the beginning (**0**).

The survival of Welsh

Welsh is **(0)** _ONE_ of the oldest surviving languages **(1)** .... Europe, with a history going back over fifteen centuries. In Wales itself it **(2)** .... now spoken by over half a million people. Street signs there are written in both English and Welsh, all official documents in English must also be available in Welsh, and **(3)** .... child in Wales learns Welsh in school up to the age of 16.

The Welsh Language Acts of 1967 and 1993 put an end to the dominance of English, **(4)** .... began in 1536, when Wales was united politically with its larger neighbour and English became the only official language.

Welsh was preserved thanks in great part **(5)** .... the translation of the Bible into Welsh and the continued use of the language in churches. Its general use, however, declined in the twentieth century: with very **(6)** .... job opportunities in the post-war depression of the 1920s and 1930s, many young Welsh speakers left Wales in search of work elsewhere.

(7) .... this decline has been reversed and Welsh is currently enjoying a revival, **(8)** .... number of children being brought up with Welsh as their mother tongue is falling.

Vocabulary

1 Complete each gap with the correct preposition.

1. John insisted .... paying .... the drinks.
2. My dad apologised .... shouting .... me.
3. We're saving up .... a new car, so I've been putting in some extra hours .... work.
4. When I complained to the neighbours .... the noise, they just laughed .... me.
5. The panda is .... danger of extinction and is on the World Conservation Union's Red List, which identifies all animals, birds and plants which are .... risk.
6. I've been staring .... this poem for ages – I'll never be able to learn it .... heart!
7. .... theory we should win this match, but what happens .... practice is another matter entirely.
8. Listen .... the recording again and concentrate .... finding the answers you missed the first time.

2 Underline the correct word in *italics*.

1 It helps if you can speak the local language, but you should be able to *get/pass/talk* by with just a few words.
2 I lost my job, and we're finding it hard to make ends *match/join/meet* each month.
3 This café *takes/brings/gives* back many memories for me – I used to come here as a teenager.
4 I'm getting quite *unforgettable/ forgetful/forgetting* – I can never remember where I put things.
5 My cousin wants to be an actor; he loves being in the *lamplight/ limelight/highlight*.
6 Dave's popstar sister is very *vain/ placid/modest* about her success, and rarely talks about herself.
7 The tune's good, but I don't understand the *letters/lyrics/ texts* – I have no idea what the song's about.
8 I normally love his films, but I wasn't very impressed by his *representation/rehearsal/ performance* in this latest one.

Language focus

1 Complete each gap with one word.

1 If _____ student in the school gave us three euros, just think how _____ money we would raise!
2 I'm really stressed: I've got so _____ things to do, but very _____ time to do them.
3 A rather disappointing exam: you made quite a _____ mistakes in Part 1 and you had very _____ correct answers in Part 2.
4 I've got _____ of paper: I can give you a _____ of sheets if you want. Will two be enough?
5 We've received a large _____ of emails from customers congratulating us on the speed of our service and there haven't been _____ complaints – none at all.
6 I've got _____ good news; you'll be pleased to hear there's _____ homework tonight.

2 Complete each gap in the text below with one item from the box. There may be more than one possible answer, but you must use each item only once. There is an example at the beginning (0).

| needn't | ~~had to~~ | have to | mustn't | don't have to |
| need to | ought | should | shouldn't | |

DESERT DRIVING IN CALIFORNIA

In the past, if you wanted to cross a Californian desert such as the Mojave or Death Valley, you **0** *had to* do so on horseback or in a covered wagon. Now, of course, there's no **1** _____ rely on your four-legged friend and, provided you stay on the roads, you **2** _____ go out and buy a special type of car either. But you do **3** _____ be aware of the dangers, take the necessary precautions and follow certain advice. For example, you **4** _____ always carry enough water to enable you and your passengers to survive in the desert if your car breaks down. And you always **5** _____ to take additional water for your car's radiator, too: some highways have water tanks at the roadside but you can't count on it. Fill up with gas and water whenever you can; you **6** _____ assume that the next filling station is open, nor indeed that there will be one in the next settlement, particularly when you're travelling off the major routes. If you do run out of gas or break down and you're in a remote area, you **7** _____ under any circumstances go off in search of help: try to find some shade near your car and wait for assistance to arrive. Of course, you **8** _____ take the car to see the desert if you don't want to – there are other options, such as coach tours or even hiking and camping. But that's another story.

3 Rewrite these sentences using the passive. Omit the agent when appropriate. Begin the sentence with the underlined word(s).

1 Two members of the paparazzi photographed <u>the celebrity</u> as he was leaving his house this morning.
2 You should take <u>these tablets</u> with food.
3 They say that <u>memory</u> gets worse with age.
4 Television presenter Mervyn Bagg was interviewing <u>the writer</u> when the lights suddenly went out in the studio.
5 They had chosen <u>Pat</u> to join the orchestra, so he was celebrating last night.
6 The decorators must finish <u>the decorating</u> before we go on holiday.
7 Most critics have given <u>the play</u> positive reviews.
8 They will hold <u>the elections</u> on 20 June.

9 A slave to routine

Reading and Use of English Part 5
Multiple choice

1. 💬 Ask and answer these questions with a partner.
   1. How do you usually feel when you wake up on a weekday?
   2. What is your normal morning routine at home before you go to school, college or work?
   3. Are things calm in your house in the morning or is everything done in a rush?
   4. How do you normally get to school, college or work?
   5. How do you spend your time on the journey?

2. 💬 The text below is an extract from a novel. The main characters are Polly, an overworked single mother and immigration lawyer, and her two children, Tania and Robbie. Read the extract quite quickly. Then discuss these questions with your partner, giving reasons for your answers.
   1. Do you recognise yourself in any of the characters?
   2. Who do you think Iryna is?

'Wake up!' she calls, going into each child's room and switching on their lights. Now the hour-long struggle begins. Tania slumbers on, her skin covered with sweat as Polly kisses her, but Robbie stirs and burrows deeper into his duvet. Polly notices with annoyance that Iryna has not put out his school clothes for him.

'Time to get up, my angel.'

'I hate school,' says Robbie, lashing out as his mother pulls the duvet off him.

'I hate Mondays,' says Tania, in turn. 'And I hate you.'

'Tough,' says Polly. 'Get dressed, or you'll be going to school in pyjamas.'

Each weekday morning, she has to make sure the children are dressed, fed, clean, have done their homework and get to school on time before going to her office. It does not sound like much, but there are days when she feels like she can't stand another minute of it.

'Robbie, you *still* haven't got your shoes on! Put them on, or you're going to school in your socks.'

'Why do I have to go to school? Why can't I stay with you?'

Polly sighs. She is trying to cram a full working day into eight hours, and she keeps her watch five minutes fast in order to get to any appointment, tricking herself into tiny panic attacks that are like the miniature muffled explosions in a combustion engine.

'Outside this country, and also in it, are millions and millions of people who would kill to have what you do here,' she says. 'They are clever, fantastically hard-working and they are all learning English. When you grow up, you're going to be competing with them for places at university, and for jobs.'

'Yeah, yeah,' says Tania rudely.

'You *have* to do this stuff,' said Polly. 'If you don't get good marks, you'll never go to university, and if you don't go to university you'll end up flipping burgers and –'. Then her heart jumps with the clock, for they have just forty-eight seconds left to get out of the door.

Where are their coats?

'How should I know?' Robbie answers, calmly.

'You *must* have them! It's freezing, it's January, you can't go out today without a coat. Look, I'm wearing my heaviest one again.'

'I can't find my school tie,' Polly's son complains. 'Iryna's hidden it.'

'Iryna!' Polly calls up the stairs. The girl is supposed to be down by now. No answer, and Robbie will be punished if he turns up without a school tie. She races upstairs to fish one out of the laundry basket, already nauseous with stress.

'I hate you!' Tania screams. 'I'm going to miss the school bus, and it's *all your fault!*'

Outside, Polly takes off like a rocket. They have only three minutes as a margin of error, never enough.

3 Match the infinitives of the highlighted verbs in the text to their meanings in this context a–j.

Phrasal verbs
a pull something out of a bag or other container
b suddenly try to hit someone
c arrive
d arrive and stop (in a vehicle)
e do many things in a short period of time

Other verbs
f push yourself under something so as to feel warmer or more comfortable
g move quickly and powerfully
h move slowly and with difficulty
i turn something over quickly (so as to cook it on both sides)
j sleep

4 Read the text again. For questions **1–6**, choose the answer (**A, B, C or D**) which you think fits best according to the text.

1 In the first paragraph we learn that Polly
  A normally finds it easy to wake her children up.
  B is irritated by somebody's failure to do something.
  C loves one of her two children more than the other.
  D usually asks somebody else to take her children to school.

2 How does Polly react to her children's anger at having to get up?
  A She threatens to leave the house without them.
  B She shows no sympathy towards them.
  C She complains to them about her routine.
  D She refuses to help them get ready.

3 The writer mentions a combustion engine to give an idea of
  A the complex nature of Polly's work.
  B the problems Polly has with technology.
  C how Polly's work sometimes affects her.
  D how Polly feels if she thinks she will be late.

4 Why does Polly talk to her children about 'millions and millions of people' who are learning English?
  A to show them how easily many people learn English
  B to convince them of the need to learn a foreign language
  C to encourage them to take their schoolwork seriously
  D to make them aware of the unemployment problem

5 When Robbie cannot find his school tie,
  A he appears to be unconcerned.
  B he blames somebody else.
  C Polly gets him a clean one.
  D Polly criticises him.

6 What do we learn about Polly in the last paragraph?
  A She is pleased her children do not go to a city centre school.
  B She is amused at the sight of Tania's friends in uniform.
  C She is sad that Tania does not return her love.
  D She is relieved that she does not live in a dangerous area.

'Oh, damn and blast!' she says, trying to text Iryna at a traffic light. 'I wonder where she is?'

The car surges forward. It is only a momentary release of frustration because a second later her undercarriage hits a speed cushion with a bang. Polly dreams long tedious dreams in which she does the school run, endlessly grinding up Highgate Hill to the bus stop for Tania's school. But now, at last, she is passing Highgate Cemetery and Karl Marx's tomb, racing past the ornate iron gates of Waterlow Park, out of Pond Square and then, just in time, she stops in front of the school bus.

'Love you,' Polly says, drawing up.

'Huh!' says Tania, slipping off to join the gaggle of other girls in uniform. Every day, when she goes back into the heart of London, Polly thinks how glad she is that her children will be out in the suburbs, where it is leafy and safe.

5 💬 If you are not a parent: how well would you cope if you had to get one or more children ready for school each day?

If you are a parent already: how well do/did you cope with getting your child or children ready for school?

Unit 9 A slave to routine

Language focus
Conditionals

1. **Identify the verb forms in bold in the following conditional sentences.**
   a If Tania **misses** the bus, Polly **has to** take her to school in the car.
   misses *present simple*
   has to *present simple*
   b Robbie **will be punished** if he **turns up** without a school tie.
   c Everything **would be** much easier if Iryna **were** here.
   d If Polly **had known** last night that Iryna wasn't in the house, she **would have put out** Robbie's clothes herself.
   e If we **had got up** earlier, we **might not be** in such a hurry now.

2. **Match each explanation 1–5 to sentences a–e in exercise 1.**
   1 an imaginary situation entirely in the past
   2 an imaginary situation in the past and its possible result in the present
   3 an imaginary situation in the present
   4 a situation which is always or generally true; *if* means *whenever* or *every time*
   5 the predicted result of a possible future situation

3. **Rewrite the following sentence from the text using *as long as* and *unless* instead of *if*.**
   If you don't get good marks, you'll never go to university.
   a You'll go to university **as long as** _____ .
   b You'll never go to university **unless** _____ .

4. **Complete this sentence from the text with one word. In this context the word has the same meaning as *if you don't* or *otherwise*.**
   Get dressed, _____ you'll be going to school in pyjamas.

   ⚙ Read more about conditionals in the Grammar Reference pages 114–115.

5. **Each of the following sentences contains one mistake. Correct the mistakes.**
   1 We'd better hurry up: Carla will be angry if we'll be late.
   2 I'll hate it if I had to work during the night, like nurses or firefighters.
   3 If we'd known the bus was going to take so long, Anita and I would walk home last night.
   4 You're going to fail these exams unless you don't study more.
   5 A good pair of shoes will last for years, as far as you look after them properly.
   6 If we'd taking the motorway, we'd probably be at home by now.

6. **Complete each gap with an appropriate form of the verb in brackets.**
   0 I *won't speak* (not/speak) to Mike again unless he *apologises* (apologise) for what happened the other night.
   1 If I _____ (not/have) an exam tomorrow, I _____ (go) to the match with you tonight, but I really must stay in and study.
   2 Paul should slow down at work, otherwise he _____ (make) himself ill.
   3 I'm sweating. If I _____ (know) it was going to be as warm as this, I _____ (not/bring) this coat with me.
   4 Julie's taking the jumper back to the shop. I'm sure they _____ (change) it for her, as long as she _____ (show) them the receipt.
   5 Stop complaining! If you _____ (have) a bigger breakfast this morning, you _____ (not/be) so hungry now.
   6 I _____ (stay) away from Sue this morning if I _____ (be) you – she's in a really bad mood.

7. 💬 **Work in pairs. You are going to complete some conditional sentences and then read out the sentences to your partner.**
   Student A: Turn to page 98 for your sentence beginnings.
   Student B: Turn to page 101 for your sentence beginnings.

80

Unit 9 A slave to routine

Vocabulary
Time

1a These extracts from the reading text on pages 78–79 contain expressions with the word *time*. Complete each gap with one word. The meaning of each expression is given in brackets.
  1 '[It is] Time _____ get up, my angel.'
    (= *it is the moment that something should happen*)
  2 … she has to make sure the children … get to school _____ **time**.
    (= *at the correct time, not late*)
  3 … just _____ **time**, she stops in front of the school bus. (= *early enough* [to catch the bus])

1b Complete each gap in these extracts from the text with one word.
  1 … there are days when **she can't stand another _____ of it**.
  2 … **she keeps her watch five minutes _____** in order to get to any appointment.
  3 … **they have just forty-eight seconds _____ to get out of the door**.

1c Explain the meaning of the expressions in **bold** in exercise **1b**.

2 Complete each gap with a phrase from the box which has the same meaning as the word(s) in brackets.

from time to time	time after time
at a time	at all times
at the time	by the time

  a I walk to school _____ (*occasionally*).
  b I wear a watch _____ (*always*).
  c _____ (*again and again*) I forget where I've put my keys.
  d I can't multi-task: I can only ever do one thing _____ (*at a particular moment*).
  e I can remember when I learnt to tell the time: I was six _____ (*at that moment*).
  f _____ (*when or before*) I get home from work I'm usually exhausted.

3a Complete each gap with an appropriate verb from the box.

| find | have | make | pass |
| set | spend | ~~take~~ | waste |

  1 It can ____*take*____ me quite **a long time to** get ready in the morning.
  2 I try to _____ **the most of my time** by planning my day carefully.
  3 I normally _____ a really **good time** on Friday night when I go out.
  4 I can never seem to _____ **the time to** read these days; I'm always busy.
  5 I try to _____ **aside time** each day for sport or other physical exercise.
  6 I _____ quite a lot of **time** every day speaking to friends on my mobile.
  7 I really don't like to _____ my **time** watching television; it's so boring.
  8 In order to help me _____ **the time** on bus or train journeys I do sudokus.

3b Discuss sentences **1–8** with your partner. How true is each one for you?

4a Rewrite **five** of the sentences in exercise **3a**.

Replace the endings in *italics* to make them true for you.
It can take me quite a long time to reply to emails.

4b Work in pairs. Compare and discuss your sentences.

Unit 9 A slave to routine

Listening Part 2
Sentence completion 2.13

1 You will hear part of a talk given by a writer called Greg Chandler, whose latest book offers alternatives to the fast pace of modern life. For questions 1–10, complete the sentences with a word or short phrase.

Greg Chandler's latest book is called
(1) '............................'.
Greg says that when we wake up, the first thing we do is to (2) ....
According to Greg, we are addicted to (3) ....
Greg says we need to slow down and (4) ....
Greg's first piece of advice to anyone who shares his beliefs is not to (5) ....
Greg recommends not eating breakfast (6) ....
Greg says it's a good idea to sit quietly before (7) ....
The Slow Food movement campaigns for good, clean and (8) .... food.
Slow Cities form part of a worldwide network of towns which share over (9) .... common aims and principles.
Slow Cities attach importance to more (10) .... ways of doing things.

2 Do you do what Greg recommends in questions 6 and 7 of the listening? Why/Why not?

Which things do you like to do quickly and which do you do more slowly? Why?

3 Which of the following would you consider doing to help you slow down? Give reasons for your answers. If you do any of them already, would you say they improve your quality of life?

- Read long novels rather than magazines
- Have a siesta after lunch
- Open your emails only once a day
- Switch off your mobile phone for two hours each day
- Walk more
- Have baths rather than showers
- Play a musical instrument
- Listen to music without doing anything else

Word formation
Nouns 2

1 Complete each gap in these extracts from the listening with the correct noun form of the word in brackets. Then check your answers in the listening script on pages 140–141.
1 … it's the clock that determines our _____ (behave) …
2 So what's my main _____ (advise) in the book?
3 … it's important to embrace the _____ (believe) that your life would indeed be better if you took things more slowly.
4 The first step to taking control of your time is to … give it less _____ (think).
5 There are around two hundred towns in the _____ (net) now …

2 For 1–6, complete sentence b so that it has a similar meaning to sentence a. You will need to complete the gap in b with the noun form of the underlined verb in a.
0 a Sue spoke for three hours.
   b Sue gave a three-hour _speech_ .
1 a Ian's selling his house.
   b Ian's house is for _____ .
2 a It's the first time we've lost this season.
   b It's our first _____ of the season.
3 a It took us six hours to fly to Rio.
   b Our _____ to Rio took six hours.
4 a We gave Eli a present.
   b We presented Eli with a _____ .
5 a Tim suddenly started laughing.
   b Tim burst into _____ .

Unit 9 A slave to routine

3a For questions **1–8**, read the text below. Use the word given in capitals at the end of some of the lines to form a noun that fits in the gap in the same line. The noun required may be formed by adding a suffix (e.g. *behave* → *behaviour*), changing the spelling (e.g. *think* → *thought*) or creating a compound noun (e.g. *net* → *network*). There is an example at the beginning (**0**).

When he finished his exams, Paolo felt a huge sense of **0** ....*RELIEF*...., as if an enormous **1** .... had been lifted from his shoulders. It was the **2** .... of summer, of course, so he'd only been able to work in the evenings, as the midday **3** .... slowed him down and made studying virtually impossible. In response to his teacher's advice, he had made himself a revision **4** ...., which he'd kept to, and he had worked hard to commit the **5** .... of the past year to memory. This course had not been his first **6** .... and he had found it difficult, **7** .... of which were the low marks he had received for much of his coursework. There could be no complaints, however, if he failed; he had done his best. Now the holidays were in **8** .... and he could look forward to a well-deserved rest.	RELIEVE WEIGH HIGH HOT TIME KNOW CHOOSE PROVE SEE

3b Do you plan your revision when studying for exams? Why/Why not?

Speaking Part 3
Collaborative task

1 Your local community centre, which offers a range of activities to those aged 16 and over, is planning to introduce a number of new activities aimed at helping people relieve stress. Some of the activities they are thinking about are shown below. Match them to the pictures.

2a Talk to your partner about what type of people these activities might appeal to.

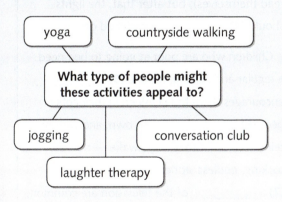

2b Now decide which two activities would be most popular.

3 Now do the Speaking Part 4 on page 99.

Help

When discussing who these activities might appeal to, you could mention:
- people's age, their work or studies, where they live, their family situation
- why they might be suffering from stress
- why a particular activity might be suitable for them.

Unit 9 A slave to routine

Listening Part 3
Multiple matching 🔊 2.14–2.18

1 💬 Discuss the following questions with your partner.
  1 How well do you sleep at night?
  2 What are some of the common reasons why some people sleep badly?
  3 What advice would you give to someone who isn't sleeping well?

2 🔊 You will hear five short extracts in which people are talking about how well or how badly they sleep. For questions **1–5**, choose from the list (**A–H**) what each speaker says. Use the letters only once. There are three extra letters which you do not need to use.

A I sleep badly because of frequent changes in my routine.
B Being active is the only thing that helps me sleep.
C I sleep better when I am not in my own bed.
D Worrying about someone gives me sleepless nights.
E I cannot sleep well unless there is total darkness.
F Eating too much before I go to bed affects my sleep.
G I have never had any problems getting to sleep.
H Lying in bed can be painful for me.

Speaker 1 [1]
Speaker 2 [2]
Speaker 3 [3]
Speaker 4 [4]
Speaker 5 [5]

3 💬 Do you share any of the same problems as the speakers you have just heard or the people they mention?

Reading and Use of English Part 2
Open cloze

1 💬 What do you think you should and should not do to help toddlers and young children get to sleep in the evening?

2 Read the text below quite quickly, ignoring the gaps. Are any of your ideas from exercise **1** mentioned?

3 Now read the text again and for questions **1–8**, think of the word which best fits each gap. Use only **one** word in each gap. There is an example at the beginning (**0**).

Bedtime routines for children

Parents should create a clear bedtime routine and clear bedtimes for their children from (0) ..*AN*.. early age. This means following a fixed pattern (1) .... evening at a similar time. Give your children dinner, allow them (2) .... play, watch television or finish homework and then put them in the bath. Afterwards, it's straight into pyjamas and bed. Parents can read a story for a (3) .... minutes (or let older children read themselves), but after that, the lights should (4) .... switched off.

Children who are poor at going to bed need a regular and calming routine (5) .... encourages them to fall asleep in their cots or beds (6) .... their own, and with no reinforcement if they stay awake — bottles, rocking, endless stories or going to sleep in (7) .... of the television are common, but ultimately unhelpful strategies. Encouraging your child to sleep (8) .... much as is needed is just as important as ensuring that they eat properly and go to school.

4 💬 Do you remember what your bedtime routine was when you were a young child? What is your bedtime routine now?

Unit 9 A slave to routine

Writing Part 2
Letter and email

1 💬 Read this Part 2 question and Helena's answer. Do you think the advice she gives Robin is good? Why/Why not?

> This is part of a letter you have received from your English-speaking friend, Robin.

> I've got my exams soon and I'm having real problems sleeping at night. You never seem to have any trouble – do you have any advice you could give me on what to do to help me sleep?
> Thanks,
> Robin

Write your **letter**.

> Letter to Robin
> I'm your friend Helena. I hope you are well. Guess what? I'm going to Scotland in August. I'm going to study English in Edinburgh. I'm realy looking forward to it. I'm sure my English will improve. Your probably looking forward to your holiday in Ireland. I'm sure it will be beautifull at this time of year. (I went last year at Easter. I went to Cork. The weather wasn't good. It rained a lot.) You will have a nice brake after your exams. I'm sure you will do very well. You say you are finding it dificult to sleep. It must be terrible for you. I would be very nervious. Here are some tips.
> 1 Never drink coffee after 5 o'clock.
> 2 Do exercise every day.
> 3 Don't eat two late.
> 4 Read a book before you go to bed.
> 5 Don't study late.
> 6 Have a warm bath.
> 7 Drink herbal infusions.
> That is all. I hope my advise is useful. If it doesn't work, you should go to the doctor's.

2 💬 Read Helena's letter again and discuss the following questions. Give examples from the letter to justify your answers.

Content	Is all the information given in the letter relevant?
Organisation	Is the letter organised into logical paragraphs?
Cohesion	Is there an appropriate range of linking words and expressions?
Range	Is there a range of grammatical structures and vocabulary?
Accuracy	Is the English reasonably accurate?
Register	Is the style of the letter appropriate and consistent?
Format	Is the answer clearly set out as a letter?
Target reader	Would Robin have enough advice to help him sleep?

3 Helena's letter contains eight spelling mistakes. Find the mistakes and correct them.

4 Helena's answer would not be given a high mark in the *First* exam. Write your own **letter** to Robin in **140–190** words.

Help

Aim to ensure that the answer to each question in exercise 2 is *Yes* for your letter.

More information in the Writing Bank page 120.

10 Getting on

Vocabulary 1
Relationships

1 Complete both gaps in **1–5** with the correct form of the same verb from the box.

| break | fall | get | keep | ~~make~~ | take |

0 It was a huge argument, but he phoned her the next day and managed to _____make_____ **up with** her. Now they're inseparable again – they were clearly _____made_____ **for each other**.

1 We used to _____ **on well with** our neighbours, but the noise from their constant arguing and loud music started to _____ **on our nerves** and we hardly talk to them now.

2 Mike and Luke were the best of friends, but they _____ **out** over an apartment they both wanted to buy. Mike _____ **for** it the first time he saw it, but it was Luke's offer which was accepted.

3 I _____ **to** my sister's boyfriend immediately; I thought he was a great laugh. My mum _____ **an instant dislike to** him though, and hardly ever speaks to him.

4 It's important to _____ **on the right side of** the boss, otherwise she can make life difficult for you. I still _____ **in touch with** two of the three people who lost their job not long after she arrived.

5 It _____ **my heart** last year when the lead singer left because of his 'difficult' relationship with the drummer. The band didn't _____ **up**, though; they got a new singer, but he's not as good.

2 💬 Discuss the following questions with a partner.
   1. Do you get on well with your neighbours? Why?/Why not?
   2. What kinds of people or things get on your nerves? Why?
   3. Are you good at keeping in touch with friends?
   4. Is there anyone you always try to keep on the right side of? Why?

Unit 10 Getting on

Reading and Use of English Part 6

Gapped text

1. 💬 You are going to read an article about a website which enables you to meet up with someone and pay them to be your friend for a few hours.

   For what type of people and in what situations do you think this website might be useful?

   What, if any, are the disadvantages of using such a site?

2. Read the base text and compare it with your ideas from exercise **1**. Do not read sentences **A–G** yet.

3. Six sentences have been removed from the article. Choose from the sentences **A–G** the one which fits each gap (**1–6**). There is one extra sentence which you do not need to use.

   A This is not a dating site.
   B Many friendships continue long after that first encounter.
   C It's about getting away from boring lives and office jobs and expanding where you go and who you meet.
   D A look through the website sets my mind at rest.
   E Until recently my options were limited.
   F In some ways, though, it's a great idea.
   G So in that way it's not so different from a dating site.

4. 💬 Discuss the following questions with your partner.
   1. Would you be interested in using this website? Why/Why not?
   2. The writer of the article says:
      Perhaps if we were a bit more friendly in the 'real world', we wouldn't need to use the virtual one to explore it.
      Do you think we rely too much nowadays on the Internet for our friendships? Why/Why not?

The cost of friendship gains new meaning when you can rent a friend

There's an open-air concert this weekend and I'd love to go. The trouble is I've got no one to go with. My friends fall into two categories: those that don't share my interest in music and those who do but don't want to pay to sit on the grass, probably in the rain. ☐ **1** Don't go or go alone and look like a man with no mates, like the man I saw once in a theatre waving to a pretend friend on the other side of the auditorium. Now I have a third possibility. I can hire someone to come with me.

American businessman Scott Rosenbaum set up Rentafriend.com, an introduction website for people like me who need a mate for a day. ☐ **2** However, you could hire a fake boyfriend if you wanted one badly enough. 'Friendships' can last an hour or longer depending on the agreement between the parties.

Scott was in online dating until 2009 when he heard about the Japanese trend for renting friends. Many people work long hours, he reasoned, and they often don't have time to make friends. Through his site you can meet up with someone and pay them to spend time with you. He sees it as 'a unique way to explore the real world. ☐ **3** '

The website has photos of the volunteer friends who you can choose on basis of height, and hair colour as well as a biography to see if you like the same things. ☐ **4** Members pay £14.50 a month to access the site. The volunteers set their own rate, but many don't charge anything if they like the activity promised.

If it's easy to become a member, it's just as easy to become a friend. You simply fill in the online form, upload a photo, hit the Finish button and you'll be approved 'usually within an hour of signing up', the website informs me. Call me suspicious but isn't that just a bit too easy? How do you know whom you are meeting? ☐ **5** The volunteers in my area look reassuringly nice and normal. Nevertheless I can't get rid of the little voice that tells me this is at best, a bit weird and at worst, convenience society gone mad.

☐ **6** Some of the friendship suggestions include hiring a tour guide if you're in a strange town or a dining companion if you don't want to eat alone. It could be good for old people or the housebound. But is hiring a pal to wait in line to purchase the latest must-have gadget or concert tickets for your favourite band in the true spirit of the enterprise? If that's the way you treat your real friends, possibly it explains why you need the website. Perhaps if we were a bit more friendly in the 'real world', we wouldn't need to use the virtual one to explore it.

87

Unit 10 Getting on

Writing Part 2
Article

1 Which of the activities in the photos do you do with your friends?

2 Read the following Part 2 writing question. Before you write your answer do exercises 3–5 below.

> You have seen this announcement in an English language magazine.
>
> **Articles wanted**
> **Friendship**
> - What qualities do you look for in a friend?
> - Why are these qualities important to you?
>
> Write us an article answering these questions.
> We'll publish the best articles in next month's magazine.

Write your **article**.

3 Complete the gaps in sentences 1–6 with the words from the box. Use the words in **bold** to help you.

| at | by | down | in | of | on (x2) | to | up | with |

1 A friend has to be understanding, **good** _____ listening, someone I can **turn** _____ if I have a problem.
2 I need a friend I can **depend** _____ – someone who won't **let me** _____.
3 They'd have to be well-informed and share my **interest** _____ current affairs.
4 I like to be **surrounded** _____ friends who don't take things too seriously and enjoy a good laugh.
5 I'm not an easy person to **get on** _____ ; friends have to **put** _____ **with** my changes of mood and take me as I am.
6 I'm not **keen** _____ selfish people; I warm to people who **think** _____ others before themselves.

4 Match these adjectives to the type of friend described in **1–6** of exercise **3**.

1 *sensitive*

knowledgeable	humorous
considerate	reliable
~~sensitive~~	tolerant

5 💬 Which, if any, of the sentences in exercise **3** express your own feelings about friends?

What other qualities do you look for in a friend? Why?

6 Now write your own answer in 140–190 words.

Remember
- Give your article a title.
- Interest your readers from the start.
- Use a lively style throughout the article.
- Include direct questions and/or statements addressed to the reader.
- If possible, end with a statement or a question which leaves the reader something to think about.

More information in the Writing Bank page 118.

Unit 10 Getting on

Speaking Part 2
Talking about photos

1 Look at these photographs. They show people arguing.

Student A: Compare the photographs, and say why you think the people are arguing.

Student B: When your partner has finished, answer the following question.

How often do you argue with other people?

> Why do you think the people are arguing?

2 Now change roles. Turn to page 100 and follow the instructions.

Useful language

Use a variety of language to speculate.
She might have been …
It looks as if he is …
I think she has probably just …
It's quite likely that they …
I'm sure that …

Listening Part 3
Multiple matching 2.19–2.23

1 Work in pairs. What do you think are the biggest sources of conflict between parents and teenagers these days?

2 You will hear five short extracts in which people are talking about their relationships with their parents when they were teenagers. For questions **1–5**, choose from the list (**A–H**) what each speaker says about their relationship. Use the letters only once. There are three extra letters which you do not need to use.

A I didn't think my parents' rules were unreasonable.
B I am still angry about a particular incident.
C I made a decision that I now think was wrong.
D My parents never took any of my opinions seriously.
E I thought my parents had little understanding of a teenager's life.
F I was allowed to go on holiday with friends when I was quite young.
G My parents each had a different approach to dealing with a particular problem.
H I think it's healthy for children to argue with their parents.

Speaker 1 [1]
Speaker 2 [2]
Speaker 3 [3]
Speaker 4 [4]
Speaker 5 [5]

3 Are you like any of the speakers in the listening?

4 Underline the correct word in *italics*. The words in **bold** are from the listening.
  1 I once **went** *through/by* **a stage** of not eating meat.
  2 I've got far too many old clothes; I need to **get rid** *off/of* some.
  3 My parents **approve** *of/for* most of my friends.
  4 I often **stay** *to/out* **late** on Saturday and sometimes don't get home until two or three in the morning.
  5 I don't always **stick** *to/for* **the rules**; rules are made to be broken.

5 Work in pairs. Discuss how true the sentences in exercise 4 are for you. Give reasons and examples.

Unit 10 Getting on

Language focus 1
Wish, if only and hope

1 We use *wish* and *if only* when we talk about things we would like to be different in the present, future or past. Read the following comments from a young adult.
   a *I wish I hadn't argued so much with my parents when I lived at home.*
   b *If only I were eighteen again! There are so many things I'd like to do.*
   c *I wish my parents would move closer to where I live, but they're happy where they are.*
   d *I wish I could go to my school reunion, but I'm going to be busy on that date.*

2 Match each comment **a–d** to a reason **1–4**. Then underline the correct alternative in **bold** to complete the rules.
   1 The speaker is expressing a wish about the present which is clearly impossible.
   wish/if only + **present tense/past tense** *b*
   2 The speaker would like to do something, but knows it is not possible.
   wish/if only + **could/would**
   3 The speaker would like someone else to do something, but knows it is unlikely to happen
   wish/if only + **will/would**
   4 The speaker expresses regret about something that happened in the past
   wish/if only + **past simple/past perfect**

3 Explain the difference in meaning between these two sentences.
   1 *I wish/If only it would stop raining.*
   2 *I hope it stops raining.*

⚙ Read more about *wish*, *if only* and *hope* in the Grammar Reference page 115.

4 Correct the mistakes in these sentences.
   1 I wish I would get higher marks for my English essays.
   2 We all wish it is warmer today because we're going to the beach later.
   3 I wish Jack would win his race tomorrow. He's trained really hard for it.
   4 If only I had ask you to help when I had that problem with my car yesterday.
   5 Clare wishes they will stop building new houses on the edge of her village.
   6 If only I hadn't got carsick every time I travel.

A   B

5 Rewrite these sentences about things you 'regret doing' or 'would like to do' using *wish*.
   0 I argued with my mum a lot when I was younger.
   I wish I hadn't argued with my mum so much when I was younger.
   1 I never listened to my parents when I was a teenager.
   2 I'm not old enough to take my driving test.
   3 I'm sorry but I can't come to your birthday party on Saturday.
   4 My parents refuse to let me go abroad with my friends this summer.
   5 I was horrible to my brother when I was younger.
   6 I have to go to school early for an exam tomorrow.

Should have/ought to have

1 We can also use *should/shouldn't have done* and *ought to have/ought not to have done* to express regret about the past. For example:
   I should have worked much harder.
   I shouldn't have thrown her coat away.
   I ought to have been more independent.
   I ought not to have followed his advice.

Find sentences in exercises **4** and **5** that show regret and rewrite them beginning with *I should(n't) have* or *I ought (not) to have …*
   0 I argued with my mum a lot when I was younger.
   I shouldn't have argued with my mum so much when I was younger.

2 💬 Work in pairs. One of you is 102 years old. The other is a reporter. The old person talks about their wishes and regrets. Then swap roles.
   I wish I had better eyesight.
   I should have travelled more when I was younger.

Unit 10 Getting on

Vocabulary 2
Age

1 Match the nouns, adjectives and phrases in the boxes to the people in the photographs A–F on these two pages. There are a number of possible answers.

Nouns: newborn   preteen   senior citizen
teenager   toddler   youngster

Adjectives: adolescent   elderly
middle-aged   retired

Phrases: in their twenties/thirties/forties, etc.
getting on in years

2 At what age can you legally do the following in your country?

leave school   vote   drive a car   get married

Do you think these age restrictions are appropriate, or should the minimum age limit be lowered or raised for any of the activities? Why?

Speaking Part 3
Collaborative task

1 Work in pairs. A television producer is planning a series of five documentaries, each dealing with a different age group.

a Talk to each other about the advantages and disadvantages of being in these different age groups.

```
preteens        people in their twenties

    What are the advantages and
    disadvantages of being in these
         different age groups?

senior citizens                teenagers

          middle-aged people
```

1b Now decide which two television documentaries would attract most viewers.

2 Now do the Speaking Part 4 on page 101.

Useful language

- Use contrast linkers when talking about the advantages and disadvantages. For example:
  *on the one hand   on the other hand
  however   although   but   whereas*
- Further useful expressions:
  *One advantage/disadvantage of being a teenager is …
  A good/bad point about being a preteen is …
  A positive thing about being middle-aged is …
  Something that's not so good about being in your twenties is …
  It can be difficult when you're retired because …*

91

Unit 10 Getting on

Listening Part 4
Multiple choice 2.24

1. Look at the photograph of the teenager teaching the elderly woman to use a tablet. Why do you think the woman wants to learn to use one? What difficulties might she have?

2. You will hear an interview with a woman called Helen James, who runs a volunteer programme called *Age Exchange*. For questions 1–7, choose the best answer (**A**, **B** or **C**).

1. Helen says that the elderly people on the *Age Exchange* programme sometimes
   - A read from their diaries to the young people.
   - B help the young people with their homework.
   - C pass on knowledge and skills to the young people.

2. Helen says that many of the elderly people want to use new technology to
   - A send photographs to other people.
   - B keep in touch with family members.
   - C find health information on the Internet.

3. What does Helen say about the images of buildings on the Internet?
   - A They help to start conversations between the young and the old.
   - B The older people use them to make a photographic record of their past.
   - C The buildings often look different to how the older people remember them.

4. According to Helen, what is an important benefit of the programme to the volunteers?
   - A They improve their communication skills.
   - B They become more valued members of the community.
   - C They learn to behave naturally with older people.

5. What does Helen say about the teenage boy who learnt to sew?
   - A His friends made fun of him.
   - B It made him popular with some people.
   - C He now repairs all his own clothes.

6. What does Helen say about the training sessions?
   - A Volunteers are given a list of objectives to achieve.
   - B Both teenagers and elderly people attend.
   - C They can be difficult to organise.

7. What does Helen say about both young and elderly participants in the *Age Exchange* programme?
   - A They often share the same interests.
   - B They sometimes do not get on with each other.
   - C Their perceptions of each other's age group can change.

3. How good do you think you would be at explaining to an elderly person how to use digital equipment? Why?

Language focus 2
have/get something done

1. Read the following sentence, then match the underlined parts, **1** and **2**, to uses **a** and **b** below.

   My gran **(1)** had her house broken into recently, so she's going **(2)** to have a burglar alarm installed.

   We use *have* + object + past participle:
   - a for actions which the subject arranges to be done by someone else.
   - b for unpleasant events which the subject did not arrange to be done.

2. *Get* can be used as an informal alternative to *have*. Rewrite the example in exercise **1**, using *get* instead of *have*.

   Read more about *have/get something done* in the Grammar Reference page 115.

3 Complete the first gap in each sentence with the correct form of *have* and the second gap with the past participle of a verb from the box.

check	steal	redecorate
restyle	service	

1 My mum goes to the local chemist's every month to _____ her blood pressure _____ .
2 We _____ the lounge _____ last week. It looks awful, so I'll do it myself next time.
3 My grandad _____ his car _____ every year, even though he hardly drives it now.
4 Lucy's just _____ her bike _____ . She should have locked it up.
5 I'm _____ my hair _____ tomorrow. I'm bored with the way it looks.

4 Work in pairs. Tell your partner about something:
- you have done regularly
  I have my teeth checked every six months.
- you would like to have done
- you would never have done
- you need to have done.

Reading and Use of English Part 1
Multiple-choice cloze

1 What factors do you think enable some people to live to more than a hundred years of age?

2 Read the text below, ignoring the gaps. Does it mention any of the ideas you discussed in exercise 1?

Eternal Youth?

What is the secret of long life? **(0)** ..*B*.. calorie intake by 30% is thought to lead to a longer lifespan, but for many, this can mean **(1)** ..... a starvation-like diet. However, scientists are now developing a drug which they believe can switch on a particular gene that has the **(2)** ..... effect without the pain.

A recent **(3)** ..... of centenarians found, though, that many in the over-100 age **(4)** ..... had led unhealthy lifestyles with some of them smoking over 40 cigarettes a day for a long **(5)** ..... of their lives. For these people a long life is the **(6)** ..... of a longevity gene and scientists have been working on a drug that can imitate this gene.

Or is it all down to the mind? Some scientists believe that if we 'think' younger our bodies will follow. Research has shown that by **(7)** ..... people imagine they are twenty years younger, many of the **(8)** ..... of ageing actually go into reverse.

3 Read the text again and decide which answer (A, B, C or D) best fits each gap. There is an example at the beginning (0).

0	A	Falling	B	Reducing	C	Holding	D	Stopping
1	A	following	B	making	C	leading	D	going
2	A	compared	B	same	C	similar	D	like
3	A	finding	B	search	C	study	D	proof
4	A	group	B	level	C	class	D	section
5	A	time	B	decade	C	period	D	stage
6	A	cause	B	reason	C	aim	D	result
7	A	allowing	B	getting	C	forcing	D	making
8	A	looks	B	notices	C	signs	D	symbols

4 Would you like to live to be over a hundred if you were still fit and healthy? Why/Why not?

Review | Units 9 and 10

Reading and Use of English Part 4
Transformations

For questions 1–6, complete the second sentence so that it has a similar meaning to the first sentence, using the word given. **Do not change the word given.** You must use between **two** and **five** words, including the word given.

1. Dave and Lina regret going abroad for their honeymoon.
   WISH
   Dave and Lina .... abroad for their honeymoon.

2. I would really like to hear from my friend Alex.
   GET
   I wish my friend Alex .... touch with me.

3. It was wrong of me to stop taking the tablets without asking the doctor.
   SHOULD
   I .... the tablets without asking the doctor.

4. It's a pity we don't have enough money for the car we looked at.
   AFFORD
   If .... buy the car we looked at.

5. The best heart surgeon will perform Russell's operation.
   PERFORMED
   Russell will .... by the best heart surgeon.

6. We missed the beginning of the film because Harry arrived late.
   TURNED
   If Harry .... time, we wouldn't have missed the beginning of the film.

Reading and Use of English Part 3
Word formation

For questions 1–8, read the text below. Use the word given in capitals at the end of some of the lines to form a word that fits in the gap in the same line. There is an example at the beginning (0).

Slow Sunday

There was a time in Britain when Sunday was a day of rest and **(0)** ...*RELAXATION*..., a chance to recover from the many tensions and **(1)** .... of everyday life. Many families would spend the whole day together, listening to the radio at home or perhaps going out for a walk or visiting relatives. The day revolved around the **(2)** .... Sunday roast, a lunchtime meal which brought all the family together at the same table.

However, with the **(3)** .... of Sunday shopping in 1994 came the gradual **(4)** .... of these customs and a change in people's **(5)** .... For many now, a typical Sunday involves a **(6)** .... trip to a shopping centre with a hurried meal in a fast-food restaurant. For others it's just a normal working day, no different from any other in the week. **(7)** .... of the *Slow Sunday* initiative call for a return to the old ways. They **(8)** .... people to engage in more restful activities, not only for the sake of their own health, but also that of the planet. Less human activity means fewer carbon emissions.

RELAX
PRESS

TRADITION

INTRODUCE
LOSE
BEHAVE
STRESS

SUPPORT
COURAGE

Remember

You must change the words in capitals in some way: you cannot leave them in the same form in which they appear.

94

Vocabulary

1 Underline the correct word in *italics*.

1 It *spends/takes/lasts* about three hours to get to the coast by bus.
2 You could make the *fast/most/last* of your time at the doctor's and do some homework while we're waiting to see her.
3 The tour guide told us to carry our passports with us at *each/every/all* times.
4 Time *to/and/after* time I've told you not to go into my bedroom without asking!
5 Don't put so much food in your mouth. Eat the biscuits one *in/at/of* a time.
6 Your watch is ten minutes *fast/quick/long* – it's twenty past three not half past.
7 Keep these old toy cars – don't *throw/get/give* rid of them. They might be worth a lot of money one day.
8 I went *through/on/along* a stage of drinking herbal tea instead of coffee, but it didn't last long.

2a Match the sentence beginnings **1–8** with the sentence endings **a–h**.

1 If I have a problem, the first person I **turn**
2 Our neighbours are awful. We have to **put**
3 We have lots of rows but we always **make**
4 Tim tried jogging but he didn't really **take**
5 The band announced its intention to **break**
6 If I ask my friends for help, they never **let**
7 Adriana has a busy life, but she tries to **set**
8 If we bought another dog, it wouldn't **get**

a **up with** each other soon afterwards.
b **up** after the current European tour.
c **on** with Rufi; they'd fight all the time.
d **to** is my dad; he's a great listener.
e **aside** some time each day for reading.
f **to** it; I think he found it quite boring.
g **up with** constant noise from parties.
h me **down**; I know I can rely on them.

2b Study the sentences in exercise **2a** for one minute. Then cover up the endings **a–h** and see how many of them you can remember.

Language focus

1 Rewrite the following sentences using third or mixed conditionals.

0 I'm only tired because I went to bed late last night.
   If I hadn't gone to bed late last night, I wouldn't be tired.
1 Rachel only got to the station on time because her dad gave her a lift.
2 I read an article about Slow Food. That's why I know so much about it.
3 Richard only played football last Saturday because the usual goalkeeper had flu.
4 I didn't realise it was Jackie's birthday, which is why I didn't buy her a present.
5 You've got wet feet because you didn't wear the right kind of shoes.

2 Complete the first gap with a verb, and the second gap with a preposition.

0 If author Ian Fleming __had__ lived to see the modern James Bond films, do you think he would have approved __of__ them?
1 I really do wish you _____ stop tapping your foot – it's getting _____ my nerves.
2 We _____ our house decorated last week by the same firm we always use, because we know we can depend _____ them to do a good job.
3 I think I should _____ ordered the fish – I'm not very keen _____ this type of meat dish.
4 You've left it too late to _____ a suit made _____ time for next week's wedding.
5 If only I _____ play tennis better – I'm just not very good _____ racket sports.

Additional Material

Unit 1

Speaking Part 1: Personal questions Exercise 3 Page 10

Student A

💬 Write one more question for each topic. Then ask your partner the questions.

FREE TIME
1. Who do you enjoy spending your free time with? What do you do?
2. What interesting things have you done recently?
3. What are you planning to do next weekend?
4. _____ ?

SHOPPING
1. Do you prefer to go shopping alone or with friends?
2. Tell us about something you've bought recently.
3. Do you do a lot of shopping online? Why/Why not?
4. _____ ?

Unit 2

Speaking Part 2: Talking about photos Exercise 2 Page 15

💬 Look at the photographs below. They show people who have succeeded in something.

Student A:
Compare the photographs and say **how difficult you think it was for the people to achieve success**.

Student B:
When your partner has finished, answer the following question.

What successes have you had recently?

> How difficult do you think it was for the people to achieve success?

Unit 4
Word formation: Prefixes Exercise 3 Page 37

In **1–6**, one of the four words in **bold** has been given the wrong prefix. Find the words and correct them.

1 Paul's teacher said she was growing **impatient** with his behaviour problems. According to her, he is extremely **impolite** and **impleasant** in the classroom, and she is finding him increasingly **impossible** to teach.

2 **Unfortunately**, Chris is still **unemployed**. He was arrested for driving while drunk last June and **unqualified** from driving for two years. So he lost his job with the delivery company and he's **unlikely** to find work as a driver again.

3 Most youngsters who start work with us at 16 are **incapable** of making decisions for themselves. Helen's **independence** and ability to work on her own is **inusual** in someone so **inexperienced**.

4 The safety measures at this funfair have been introduced to **enable** you to enjoy yourself without **endangering** your own life or that of others. Furthermore, in order to **ensure** that everyone has the best time possible, we **encourage** adults from allowing children to go on any ride they consider inappropriate.

5 Jake's **irregular** attendance at football practices annoyed his teammates, who considered him to be an **irresponsible** and **irreliable** member of the team. They felt it was **irrelevant** that he was going through a bad time with his girlfriend.

6 Chris maintained that scientists had been **dishonest** in their attempts to persuade the public of the seriousness of global warming, which he said was not as bad as they made it out to be. I **disagreed** strongly, pointing to the **disappearing** Arctic ice as proof of the problem, but was **disable** to convince him.

Unit 4
Speaking Part 2: Talking about photos Exercise 2 Page 38

What would it be like to live and work in places like these?

Unit 5

Speaking Part 2: Talking about photos Exercise 2 Page 42

💬 Look at the two photographs. They show groups of people in different places.

Student A
Compare the photographs and say **why you think one of the people is not doing the same as the others**.

Student B
When your partner has finished, answer the following question.
Do you prefer to be on your own or with a group of people?

> **Useful language**
>
> Use modal verbs to speculate about why the person is doing something different.
> He **might/could/may** find it difficult to speak to other people.
> She **might/could/may** have noticed something interesting in the newspaper.

> Why do you think one of the people in each photograph is not doing the same as the other people?

Unit 9

Language focus: Conditionals Exercise 7 Page 80

Student A

1a Look at the sentence beginnings below. Consider the work and daily routines of the speakers in **bold** and complete each sentence in an appropriate way. Include one or two clues which will help your partner guess the profession of each speaker.

1 **Footballer:** I often go to a night club on Tuesday, unless … *we have a cup match on Wednesday night.*
2 **Long-distance lorry driver:** I'd better stop for a rest soon, otherwise …
3 **Firefighter:** If I didn't use the gym at work every day, …
4 **Teacher:** I'd enjoy this job more if …
5 **Model:** It's a great life. If I hadn't chosen this as a career, …
6 **Golfer:** I might have won if …

1b 💬 Read out your completed sentences to **Student B** who will try to guess the profession of the speaker.

Unit 5

Speaking Part 4: Further discussion Exercise 2 Page 48

💬 Discuss the following questions with your partner.

1. Do you think it would be interesting to work in an isolated place? Why/Why not?
2. How important is it to be happy in your job?
3. Some people would prefer not to have to work. Why do you think that is?
4. How well do you think schools prepare young people for the world of work?
5. Some people think that all young people should work in the summer holidays to earn money. What do you think?
6. How difficult is it for young people in your area to find work?

Useful language

- When you give your opinion, use expressions such as:
  In my opinion …   Personally, I think that …   Actually, I completely disagree …
  I would certainly go along with that …   My feeling is that …

- In a discussion you should ask for the other person's opinion too. Use expressions like:
  What do you think?   How do you feel about it?   Do you agree?   How about you?

Unit 7

Speaking Part 4: Further discussion Exercise 3 Page 60

💬 Discuss the following questions with your partner.

1. Is it better to read from books or e-readers? Why?
2. How difficult would you find it to survive without a mobile phone? Why?
3. How easy is it for people of your parents' or grandparents' generation to survive in today's fast-moving world?
4. Do you think it is important to save minority languages from extinction? Why/Why not?
5. What can individuals do to help the environment?
6. Do you think life in the future will be better or worse than it is now? Why?

Unit 9

Speaking Part 4: Further discussion Exercise 3 Page 83

💬 Discuss the following questions with your partner.

1. What do you do to prevent or relieve stress?
2. How important is it to eat healthily?
3. Do you think a healthy body makes a healthy mind? Why/Why not?
4. Some people say we have become too obsessed with personal fitness. Why do you think they say this?
5. How important is it to go away on holiday each year?
6. Some people think we don't spend enough time talking to each other nowadays. What do you think?

Unit 10

Speaking Part 2: Talking about photos Exercise 2 Page 89

💬 Look at these photographs. They show families doing different things together.

Student A:
Compare the photographs, and say **why you think the families have chosen to do these things together**.

Student B:
When your partner has finished, answer the following question.
Which of these things would you prefer to do with your family?

> Why do you think the families have chosen to do these things together?

Unit 10
Speaking Part 4: Further discussion Exercise 2 Page 91

💬 Discuss the following questions with your partner.

1. Which stage of life do you think most people look forward to? Why?
2. Some people say that school days are the best time of our lives. How far do you agree?
3. Is it important to have a lot of life experience before having children of your own? Why/Why not?
4. Should elderly people live with their children? Why/Why not?
5. Teenagers often disagree with their parents. Why do you think this is?
6. What do you think is a good age for young people to leave home? Why?

Unit 1
Speaking Part 1: Personal questions Exercise 3 Page 10

Student B

💬 Write one more question for each topic. Then ask your partner the questions.

INTERESTS
1. What sport do you enjoy playing? Why do you like it?
2. Tell us about a book you've read recently.
3. Is there anything you would like to learn to do in the future? Why?
4. _____ ?

TECHNOLOGY
1. Do you watch a lot of television? Would you like to watch more or less?
2. What have you been using the Internet for recently?
3. Do you enjoy playing computer games? Why/Why not?
4. _____ ?

Unit 9
Language focus: Conditionals Exercise 7 Page 80

Student B

1a Look at the sentence beginnings below. Consider the work and daily routines of the speakers in **bold** and complete each sentence in an appropriate way. Include one or two clues which will help your partner guess the profession of each speaker.

1. **Waste collector:** I'd better have a shower now, otherwise …
   I'll smell of rotten food and other rubbish.
2. **Novelist:** I'll never finish this book unless …
3. **Farmer:** If I went on holiday, …
4. **Tourist guide:** I'd enjoy this job more if …
5. **Soldier:** It's a great life. If I hadn't chosen this as a career, …
6. **Tennis player:** I might have won if …

1b 💬 Read out your completed sentences to **Student A** who will try to guess the profession of the speaker.

Grammar Reference

UNIT 1

Present tenses

Present simple

The present simple is used to talk about:
- a situation that is permanent or long term.
  *We **live** on the edge of town.*
  *Ken **speaks** Russian.*
- facts or things that are always true.
  *Too much sun **causes** skin damage.*
- regular, habitual actions.
  *I **catch** the 8.30 bus every morning.*

We often use frequency adverbs to show how regularly an action takes place. The most common are: *always, normally, usually, frequently, often, sometimes, occasionally, seldom, rarely, hardly ever, never.*

These are usually placed before the main verb or after the verb *to be* or an auxiliary verb.
   *I **often** go swimming at the weekend.*
   *We are **always** on time for class.*
   *I don't **usually** enjoy detective stories.*

Frequently, normally, occasionally, (very/quite) often, sometimes and *usually* can also be placed at the beginning of the sentence or clause.
   ***Normally** I take sandwiches to work, but **occasionally** I go out to a restaurant for lunch.*

- scheduled or timetabled events in the future.
  *The exam **starts** at 10.30 tomorrow morning.*

See also Grammar Reference Unit 5 page 109.

Present continuous

1 **The present continuous is used:**
- to talk about an activity in progress at the time of speaking.
  *I'**m listening** to the news. Please be quiet.*
- to talk about an activity that is in progress but not necessarily happening at the time of speaking.
  *We'**re setting** up a new school website. Perhaps you can help us?*
- to talk about something that is in the process of changing.
  *Things **are getting** better; our profits **are increasing**.*
- to talk about a temporary situation.
  *Mr Dee **is teaching** us while Ms Flint is away.*
- with *always* to refer to a repeated action that annoys the speaker.
  *My brother **is always borrowing** my bicycle without asking me.*
- to describe future arrangements.
  *I'**m getting** the 9.30 train tomorrow; I've reserved a seat.*

See also Grammar Reference Unit 5 page 109.

2 We do not normally use the present continuous with stative verbs such as *be, have, know, live, think* and *understand.*
   *I **have** a new laptop. Do you want to see it?*
   ***Do** you **think** it'll rain today?*

However, sometimes these verbs can be used with an active meaning. In these cases, the continuous form can be used.
   *I'**m having** dinner now. I'll phone you back.*
   *Tim's quiet. I wonder what he'**s thinking** about.*

Present perfect simple

The present perfect simple is:
- used to talk about events that happened before the present time. The exact time is either not known or not important. It can refer to a single event:
  *I'**ve seen** the new James Bond film.*
  *I'**ve never** eaten sushi.*
  or it can refer to several events:
  *I'**ve been** to America three times.*
- used to talk about the first/second/third, etc. time an event has occurred. We are making the comment in present time.
  *This is the first time I'**ve eaten** Indian food.*
- also common after superlatives.
  *Pierre is the nicest person I'**ve** ever **met**.*
- used to talk about a recent event that has a relevance to the present.
  *The taxi'**s just arrived**. Hurry up!*
- used to talk about an event or events that occurred in a time period which has not finished yet. Time phrases such as *this year/today/this morning* are often used.
  *Helen **has eaten** six chocolate bars this morning!*
- used with the words *just/yet/already/ever/never*
  *The teacher hasn't given us the results **yet**.*
  *Have you **ever** done a bungee jump?*
- used to talk about activities and situations that began in the past and continue up to the moment of speaking. They may or may not continue in the future. This use often involves stative verbs, such as *be, have, know, live, think* and *understand.* We use *for* to introduce the time period and *since* to introduce the moment that the time period began.
  *I'**ve known** Katy for sixteen years.*
  *My brother'**s had** his laptop since his birthday.*

Present perfect continuous

The present perfect continuous is used:

- to refer to an activity that began in the past and is still continuing at the present time. It emphasises the length of time spent on the activity. We use *for* to introduce the time period and *since* to introduce the moment that the time period began.

    I**'ve been studying** for two hours. I need a break.
    She**'s been reading** since she got up this morning!

- to refer to an activity that finished recently and has a result in the present.

    I**'ve been playing** tennis and my arm aches.

- to suggest that a situation or activity is temporary.

    My mum's ill so I**'ve been looking after** her.

Note the difference between the present perfect simple and present perfect continuous.

The continuous form focuses on the activity, which may or may not be completed:

I**'ve been writing** emails all morning.

The simple form focuses on completed actions:

I**'ve written** about fifty emails this morning.

The continuous form is not used when we mention the number of things that have been completed.

- to refer to a repeated action in the recent past that has a result in the present. The focus here is not on a single, prolonged activity but a series of actions.

    I**'ve been travelling** a lot recently. I'm tired.

Past tenses

Past simple

The past simple is used to refer to:

- a completed action at a specific time in the past. The time can be stated or implied.

    The plane **landed** at 10.30.
    I **bought** this coat in Paris.

- an activity or situation that continued for a period of time in the past. The period finished in the past.

    I **lived** in New York for six months when I was a student.

- a past habit or regular action in the past.

    On our holiday we **had** dinner every evening at 10 o'clock.

- a series of consecutive actions in the past.

    I **got up, had** breakfast and **left** the house.

Past continuous

The past continuous is used to refer to:

- an activity or situation that was in progress at a particular moment in the past.

    This time yesterday I **was travelling** to Rome.

- an activity or situation that was already in progress when another event occurred. The activity in the past continuous may or may not have continued after the other event occurred.

    When Peter **phoned** me I **was watching** a film.

- activities or situations occurring at the same time.

    My brother **was doing** his homework while I **was reading**.

- the background events in a story.

    The sun **was shining** in the park. Office workers **were eating** their lunchtime sandwiches and a young girl **was playing** happily with her dog. No one noticed the black van pull up by the gates.

Past perfect simple

The past perfect simple is used:

- to refer to an activity or situation that happened before another activity or situation in the past.

    I saw Paul last month. He **had** just **started** a new job.

- with time linkers such as *when/after/before/by the time/as soon as/until* to emphasise the order of events in the past.

    I emailed Sara after **I'd downloaded** the file.

For more information on Time linkers with past tenses, see Grammar Reference Unit 5 page 108.

- to talk about an activity or situation that continued for a period of time leading up to another point of time in the past. This use often involves stative verbs, such as *be, have, know, live* and *understand*.

    I saw the doctor on Friday. **I'd had** a headache for four days.

Past perfect continuous

The past perfect continuous is used to describe and focus on the duration of an activity before and continuing up to a point of time in the past. The activity may have stopped at that point or continued after it.

It was three o'clock. **I'd been waiting** for Joe for an hour and he still wasn't there.
When Dave got here he was very tired. **He'd been driving** for twelve hours.

Used to and *would*

1   *Used to* + infinitive is used to talk about regular actions or situations in the past that have now changed.

    I **used to take** the train to work but now I go by car.
    My sister **used to hate** eating vegetables but now she loves them.

2   Note how we make negatives and questions using *used to*.

    We **didn't use to** go on holidays abroad very often. Now I go every year.
    Did you use to go to Middleton School? I think I recognise you.

3 *Used to* can only be used for talking about the past, not the present. To talk about regular actions or situations in the present, we can use an adverb such as *usually* or *normally* with the present simple.

   *I don't **usually** watch the news on television.*

4 *Would* + infinitive without *to* is also used to talk about regular actions in the past. However, it is NOT used with stative verbs to talk about permanent states in the past. It often describes typical behaviour and can be used with *always/usually/never/often*.

   *My gran **would always give** me a piece of cherry cake and a cup of hot chocolate after school.*
   *Our teacher **would never let** us use a dictionary during tests!*

5 It is possible to use *would* in the negative and question form but it is not common.

UNIT 2

Comparisons

Form

One-syllable adjectives

Add *-er* to make the comparative form, and *-est* to make the superlative form.

   short – short**er** – short**est**

If the adjective ends in *-e* (e.g. *safe, late, large*), add *-r* and *-st*.

   strang**e** – strang**er** – strang**est**

If the adjective ends in a single vowel and a consonant (e.g. *thin, hot, wet*), double the consonant and add *-er* and *-est*.

   big – big**ger** – big**gest**

Adjectives with more than one syllable

Use *more* and *most* in front of the adjective to form the comparative and superlative.

   modern – **more** modern – **most** modern comfortable – **more** comfortable – **most** comfortable

If the adjective ends in *-y* (e.g. *funny, noisy, unhappy*), change *-y* to *-i* and add *-er* and *-est*.

   dirt**y** – dirt**ier** – dirt**iest**

With some two-syllable adjectives both types of comparative and superlative forms can be used. These include the following: *clever, common, friendly, gentle, narrow, pleasant, polite, quiet, simple, stupid*.

   narrow – narrow**er**/ **more** narrow – narrow**est**/ **most** narrow

Adverbs

Use *more* and *the most* in front of most adverbs.

   quickly – **more** quickly – **the most** quickly

Adverbs with the same form as an adjective, such as *early, fast, hard, late, long*, have comparative and superlative forms which end in *-er* (or *-r*) and *-est* (or *-st*). The adverb *soon* is another example.

   soon – soon**er** – soon**est**

Irregular adjectives and adverbs

Some adjectives and adverbs have irregular comparative and superlative forms.

   good and *well* – better – the best
   bad and *badly* – worse – the worst
   far – farther/further – the farthest/furthest

Use

Comparative and superlative adjectives and adverbs

1 To make a comparison between two people or things we can use comparative forms of adjectives and adverbs with *than*.

   *Alison is **more confident than** her brother. My order arrived **earlier than** expected.*

To describe small differences, use *a bit, a little, slightly*.

   *I'm feeling **a little better than** I was this morning.*

To describe big differences, use *(quite) a lot, much, far*.

   *This house is **much more spacious than** our old flat, and the neighbourhood's **a lot quieter**, too.*

2 To make a comparison between more than two people or things we can use superlative forms of adjectives and adverbs. The definite article *the* is used before superlative adjectives. To specify the group we use *in* before the noun.

   *Amy's **the most intelligent** student **in the class**.*
   *The Burj Khalifa in Dubai is **the tallest** building **in the world**.*

It is possible to use single-word superlative adverbs with or without *the*.

   *Let's see who can sing (the) **loudest**.*

To emphasise the difference between one person or thing and all the others, use *by far, easily*.

   *This is **easily the worst** holiday I've ever had!*

3 **less and least**

Less and *least* are the opposites of *more* and *most*; they can be used with all adjectives and adverbs, regardless of the number of syllables.

   *I bought **the least expensive** coat I could find.*

Like *more* and *most*, they can be used as adverbs; in this case, *the* is optional before *most* and *least*.

   *Most women here **work more than** the men and **get paid less**.*
   *Which school subjects do you **like (the) most** and **(the) least**?*

4 Use *more* or *less* with uncountable nouns, and *more* or *fewer* with plural countable nouns.

   *You may have **less money than** him, but he's got **fewer friends**.*

Similarly, use *most* or *least* with uncountable nouns, and *most* and *fewest* with plural countable nouns. In this case, these words are preceded by *the*.

*We aim to sell your house for **the most money** in **the least amount** of time with **the fewest problems**.*

(just) as + adjective/adverb + as

1 This structure can be used to talk about people or things that are the same in some way.

*Don't ask me – I'm **just as confused as** you are!*

Use *almost, nearly* to qualify the comparisons.

*She sings **almost as well as** her mum.*

2 In negative sentences *so* can replace the first *as*.

*Alan **isn't so optimistic** about the future **as** I am.*

Use *not quite* with this structure to describe small differences.

*It **isn't quite so cold** today **as** it was yesterday.*
(= it's a little warmer)

Use *not nearly* for big differences.

*The exam **wasn't nearly as hard as** I thought it would be.* (= it was much easier)

3 Use *as much* with uncountable nouns, and *as many* with plural countable nouns.

*I've got **just as much work** to do today as yesterday.*
*There weren't **as many people** at the party **as** I expected.*

This structure can also be used without nouns.

*I didn't eat **as much as** you but I still feel full.*

4 Use *not/never … such* before adjective + uncountable or plural countable noun.

*We did**n't** have **such good weather** on our holiday this year.*
*I've **never** seen **such ugly buildings as** these.*

Use *not/never … such a* before adjective + singular countable noun.

*Mr Phillips **isn't such a good teacher as** Mrs Reid.*

Other structures

1 *the* + comparative, *the* + comparative
Use this structure to show that two changes happen together; the second is often the result of the first.

***The easier** I find a subject, **the less interesting** it is for me.*
***The harder** you work, **the more** you can earn.*

2 *like* + noun, pronoun or gerund

*You children behave **like animals**!*

3 *(not) a lot of/a great deal of/much/little/no difference between*

*There is**n't a lot of difference between** the film and the book.* (= the film is very similar to the book)

4 *the same* + noun + *as* can be used as an alternative to *as* + adjective + *as* to talk about people or things that are the same in some way.

*I'm **the same height as** my mum.*
*I'm **as tall as** my mum.*

UNIT 3

Modals of speculation and deduction

Speculating and making deductions about the present

1 When we are certain something is true we use *must* + simple infinitive/continuous infinitive without *to*.

*You **must know** Lucy. She goes to the same yoga class as you.*
*Dan **must be working** hard. He's been in his office all day.*

2 When we are certain something is not true we use *can't/couldn't* + simple infinitive/continuous infinitive without *to*. We do not normally use *mustn't* to express this idea.

*We **can't be** out of petrol. I filled up two days ago.*
*He **couldn't be having** a shower. There's no hot water.*

3 When we think something is possibly true we use *may (not)/might (not)/could* + infinitive/continuous infinitive without *to*. We do not use *could not* to express this idea.

*Jack **could be** in his room, but I'm not sure.*
*I have no idea of the answer. Alan **might know**. Kathy looks sad. She **may not be feeling** well.*

Speculating and making deductions about the past

1 We use *must/can't/couldn't* + perfect infinitive (= *have* + past participle) to express certainty about past situations. We can also use the continuous form of the perfect infinitive.

*Their holiday **must have cost** a fortune – they went to Japan.*
*Emma **can't have been listening** to the lecture; she was sending messages on her phone the whole time.*

2 We use *may (not)/might (not)/could* + perfect infintive to express uncertainty about the past. The continuous form is also possible.

*I can't find my book. I think I **may have left** it on the train.*
*Police think the art thief **might not have been working** alone.*

Relative clauses

Relative clauses give information about someone or something in the main clause. They usually begin with a relative pronoun (*who, which, that, whose, what*) or a relative adverb (*where, when, why*).

Defining relative clauses

1. Defining relative clauses identify, or define, who or what we are talking or writing about and are essential for our understanding of the whole sentence.
Commas are not required at the beginning or end of the relative clause. The relative pronoun *that* can be used instead of *who* and *which*.

   *I've got a friend **who/that** can speak four languages.*
   *A widower is a man **whose** wife has died.*
   *There are few places **where** you can enjoy complete silence.*

2. The relative pronouns *who*, *which* and *that* can be omitted, but only if they are the object of the verb in the defining relative clause.

   *Who was in that film (**which/that**) you saw last night?*
   (The relative pronoun is the object of *saw* and can be omitted.)
   *People **who/that** say they never cry are liars.*
   (The relative pronoun is the subject of *say* and cannot be omitted.)

3. The relative adverbs *when* and *why* can also be omitted in defining relative clauses.

   *I'll never forget the time (**when**) you fell in that lake.*
   *The reason (**why**) he resigned remains a mystery.*

4. The relative pronoun *what* can be used in defining relative clauses and means 'the thing which'.

   *He showed me **what** he'd bought.*

Non-defining relative clauses

1. Non-defining relative clauses contain information which is not essential to our understanding of who or what we are writing or talking about. The main clause would make sense, even without this information.

2. Commas are used to separate the relative clause from the main clause. *That* cannot be used instead of *who* or *which*, and the relative pronoun cannot be omitted.

   *JK Rowling, **who** is now a multi-millionaire, once taught English in Portugal.*
   *The Most Valuable Player award went to Sánchez, **whose** eight goals helped his team to victory in the tournament.*
   *We went to Gouda, **where** the cheese comes from.*

3. The relative pronoun *which* can be used in non-defining relative clauses to refer to the whole of the main clause.

   *Alex arrived on time, **which** surprised everyone.*

Whom

In both defining and non-defining relative clauses *whom* can be used instead of *who* when it is the object of the verb in the relative clause.

*Tim's art teacher was Mr Jay, **whom** he had always disliked.*
*There is someone **whom** I would like you to meet.*

However, many speakers consider *whom* to be too formal and avoid using it.

*There is someone (**who**) I'd like you to meet.*

Relative clauses and prepositions

1. Prepositions can be placed at the end of both defining and non-defining relative clauses. In defining relative clauses the relative pronoun can be omitted.

   *It was directed by Ken Loach, **who** I have a lot of respect **for**.*
   *This is not a subject (**which/that**) I want to comment **on**.*

2. In more formal English, the preposition often appears immediately before the relative pronoun: *whom* for people and *which* for things. *That* cannot be used and the relative pronoun cannot be omitted.

   *It was directed by Ken Loach, **for whom** I have a great deal of respect.*
   *The Finance Minister said it was not a subject **on which** he wished to comment.*

UNIT 4

Gerunds and infinitives

Gerunds

The gerund is used:

- as the subject, object or complement of a sentence or clause.

  ***Walking** makes me hungry.*
  *Rob's given up **smoking**.*
  *Joe's favourite pastime is **doing** nothing.*

- after prepositions.

  *Are you interested **in going** to the cinema tonight?*

- after *look forward to* and *be/get used to*, where *to* is a preposition.

  *I've **got used to being** on holiday, and I'm not **looking forward to going** back home on Saturday.*

- after certain verbs, e.g. *admit, adore, advise, appreciate, avoid, can't help, can't stand, consider, delay, deny, detest, dislike, enjoy, feel like, finish, imagine, involve, keep, mind, miss, postpone, practise, prevent somebody, resist, risk, suggest*.

  *I like the countryside but I **miss living** in the city.*
  *We planted that tree to **prevent people looking** into our house from the street.*

not is placed before the gerund to make it negative:

*It's hard to **imagine not having** a mobile phone.*

- after these expressions.

have difficulty/problems/trouble   it's/there's no use   it's (not) worth   there's no point (in)

*It's **worth buying** a good guidebook before you go to Rome.*
*She **had difficulty understanding** his accent.*

If the subjects of the main verb and the gerund are different, an object (pronoun) is added or, in formal English, a possessive determiner.

*I can't **imagine him** (or **his**) **playing** football.*

Infinitives

1   **The infinitive with *to* is used:**
- to say why you do something.

    *We gave the children some sweets **to keep** them quiet.*

- after certain adjectives, e.g. (It is/was, etc.) *difficult, easy, essential, important, lovely, (un)necessary, (im)possible, (un)usual, wonderful,* (I am/She will be, etc.) *delighted, disappointed, (un)happy, (un)lucky, sad, surprised.*

    *We're **sad to hear** you can't come; it would have been **wonderful to see** you again.*

- after certain nouns, e.g. *ability, chance, decision, failure, idea, opportunity, plan, refusal, right, way.*

    *What's the best **way to get** to the station?*

- after certain verbs, e.g. *afford, agree, appear, arrange, attempt, choose, decide, demand, deserve, hesitate, hope, learn, manage, offer, prepare, promise, pretend, refuse, seem, threaten.*

    *Patty's **arranged to meet** Mike on Saturday.*

not is placed before the infinitive to make it negative:

*Jodie called to her son but he **pretended not to hear** her.*

2   With some verbs a direct object is needed, e.g. *advise, allow, enable, encourage, force, invite, order, persuade, recommend, remind, teach, tell, warn.*

    *Patty's **persuaded him to go** to the opera with her!*

3   Some verbs can be used either with or without a direct object, e.g. *ask, expect, help*, need, want, would like, would love, would hate, would prefer.*

    *Julie **wants to buy** a new coat and she **wants me to go** with her.*
    * Help can also be used with an infinitive without to: see below.

4   **The infinitive without *to* is used:**
- after modal verbs.

    *You **can go** to the party, but you **must be** home by midnight.*

- after *help, let, make, would rather, had better.*

    *I'**d better go** – it's very late. I'**d rather stay** here, though.*

Make and *let* are followed by a direct object; *help* can be used with or without a direct object.

*Can you **help (me) clean** the kitchen?*

Verbs followed by either a gerund or an infinitive with *to*

1   *Begin, start* and *continue* can be followed by either a gerund or infinitive with *to*, without any difference in meaning. The gerund is not usually used after a progressive form of these verbs.

    *He continued **writing/to write** until his hand began **aching/to ache**.*
    *It's **starting to rain**.*
    It's starting raining. ✗

2   Either form can also be used after *hate, like, love* and *prefer* with no difference in meaning.

    *I **like singing/to sing** in the shower.*

3   With *remember, forget, stop* and *go on* the gerund refers to actions or states occurring before these verbs; the infinitive with *to* refers to things occurring afterwards.

remember doing something = to recall a previous action
    *I **remember reading** an article on tea recently.*

4   *forget doing* something is not often used to talk about an action you do not recall. Instead, *not remember* is used.

    *I d**on't remember lending** any money to you.*

remember/forget to do something = (not) to do something you have to do or intend to do

    *I **remembered to buy** your stamps – here you are. But I **forgot to post** your letter – I'm really sorry.*

5   *stop doing* something = no longer do something
    *Put your umbrella down – it's **stopped raining**.*

stop to do something = interrupt one activity to do another
    *On his way home, Ian **stopped to buy** a pen.*

6   *go on doing* something = continue doing something
    *If you **go on eating** like that, you'll feel sick.*

go on to do something = do something after doing something else

    *After losing their first two matches, the Italians **went on to win** the tournament.*

7   *mean doing* something = involve
    *If you come fishing with me, it'll **mean getting up** early.*

8   *mean to do* something = intend
    *I didn't **mean to break** the window – it was an accident.*

9. *try doing* something = do something to see what will happen

> If your laptop is running slowly, **try restarting** it.

try to do something = attempt/make an effort to do something

> I **tried to tell** her I was sorry, but she didn't want to listen.

10. *need* + gerund has a passive meaning.

> This kitchen **needs cleaning**. (= needs to be cleaned)

11. *need* + infinitive with *to* has an active meaning.

> We **need to clean** this kitchen.

UNIT 5

Time linkers with past tenses

1. *After, as soon as, before, once, until, when, whenever* can be used with the past simple. The gerund is also common with *after* and *before*.

> I recognised him **as soon as** I saw him.
> **Before** she **went/Before going** to bed, Sue had a glass of milk.

Two past simple tenses often indicate that the second action resulted from the first, and that it happened soon afterwards.

> I **cried when** I **heard** the news.

Whenever means 'every time that'.

> **Whenever we went** camping, it used to rain most of the week.

After, before, as soon as can be qualified in the following way:

> soon after, (not) long after, shortly after; (not) long before, shortly before; almost as soon as.

Just can be used with all three.

> **Just/Shortly/Soon/Not long** after he got married, Tim lost his job.

The past perfect can be used, especially if we want to emphasise that the first action finished before the second one started.

> My mum wouldn't let me go out **until I'd tidied** my room.
> **Once I'd eaten** something, I felt a lot better.

2. *As, when, while* and *whilst* can be used with the past continuous to introduce an action or situation which was in progress when another, shorter action occurred. *Whilst* is usually only used in formal English.

> **When/As/While** we **were having** our picnic, we **saw** a deer.

They can also be used with two clauses in the past continuous to talk about two actions or situations occurring at the same time. *While* is more common in this use.

> **While** you **were having** fun and making lots of noise, I **was trying** to do my homework!

3. *During* and *for* are prepositions and followed by a noun.

During tells us <u>when</u> something happened.

> I stayed at my sister's house **during the summer**.

For tells us <u>how long</u> something took or lasted.

> My brother was on the phone **for two hours**!

4. **At first, at last, finally, eventually, at the end, in the end, by the end**

At first is used to talk about the beginning of a situation and to contrast it with what happens later. It is often followed by *but*.

> **At first** it was cold and grey, **but** then the sun came out.

At last indicates very strongly that you have been waiting for something to happen for a long time. *Finally* has a similar meaning.

> After ten years in prison he was free **at last**!
> Mike **finally** passed his driving test on the sixth attempt.

In the end and *eventually* suggest that something happens after some problems, changes or uncertainty.

> Lucy wasn't sure about the job, but she accepted it **in the end/eventually**.

At the end refers to the point at which something finishes. It can be followed by *of* + noun.

> I spoke to the teacher **at the end of the class**.

By the end can also be followed by *of* + noun and means 'at some time during the period before something finishes'.

> I started reading the book at lunchtime and **by the end of the day** I'd finished it.

5. **By the time, at the time**

By the time is used for saying what had already happened before something else occurred. It can be followed by the past simple or the past perfect.

> **By the time we (had) arrived** at the station, our train had left.
> (= The train left before we arrived at the station.)

At the time means 'at the particular point when something occurred'. It may suggest a contrast with what happens later.

> It seemed like a good idea **at the time** (but I know now that it wasn't).

The future

Will

Will + infinitive without *to* can be used to:

- talk about hopes, expectations and predictions. It is often used after these verbs: *hope*, *expect* and *think*. A present tense can also be used after *hope*.

    *I **expect** Tom **will arrive** late – he usually does.*
    *We **hope** you **come/will come** back and visit us.*

Adverbs such as *probably* and *definitely* are normally placed after *will* and before *won't*.

*I **think** she**'ll definitely pass** but she **probably won't get** an 'A'.*

- make factual statements about the future.

    *Spring **will be** here soon.*
    *Alex **will be** twenty in April.*

- talk about decisions made at the moment of speaking, including offers.

    *You're cold, aren't you? I**'ll close** the window.*

Going to

Be going + infinitive with *to* can be used to talk about:

- intentions and plans formulated before the moment of speaking.

    *Owen says he**'s going to leave** school at 16.*

The infinitive *to go* can be omitted.

*I**'m not going (to go)** to Sarah's party tomorrow.*

- predictions, as an alternative to *will*.

    *I don't think Taylor **is going to/will win** the election.*

If there is evidence now that something is certain to happen, we usually use *going to*.

*That car is out of control – it**'s going to crash**!*

Modal verbs

Modal verbs express degrees of certainty when talking about:

- intentions.

    *We **may/might have** a barbecue on Sunday.* (Possibility)

- predictions.

    *It **may/might/could well rain** tomorrow.* (Probability)
    *You **should find** a parking space quite easily.* (Probability)

Present simple

The present simple can be used:

- to talk about timetabled or scheduled events.

    *Our train **leaves** at 6.30 tomorrow morning.*

- to refer to the future after time linkers such as *after*, *as soon as*, *before*, *until*, *when*. The present perfect and present continuous can also be used.

    *I'll call you just **before we get on** the plane.*
    ***After we've had** our lunch we're going shopping.*
    ***While I'm driving** to work, you'll still be in bed.*

Present continuous

The present continuous can be used to describe future arrangements we have made, usually with other people or organisations.

*I**'m picking** Gavin **up** at 1.30 and we**'re having** lunch at 'Le Bistro'. I've booked a table for two o'clock.*

Future continuous

The future continuous, *will + be + present participle*, is used to talk about:

- actions that will be in progress at a particular moment in the future.

    *I can't go to the parents' meeting; I**'ll be working** then.*

- plans and decisions we have made for the future.

    *My son's ill, so he **won't be going** to school tomorrow.*

Future perfect simple

The future perfect, *will + have + past participle*, is used to talk about actions which will be completed before a certain time in the future.

*I think I**'ll have finished** this book by the end of the week.*

Future perfect continuous

The future perfect continuous, *will + have + been + present participle*, is used to talk about actions which continue up to, and possibly beyond, a certain time in the future.

*I**'ll have been working** here for six months on Friday.*

Other ways of talking about the future

1 *Be (just) about + infinitive with to* is used to talk about the immediate future.

    *I'm sorry, I can't talk – I**'m just about to go** out.*

2 *Be (un)likely + infinitive with to* is used to express probability.

    *It**'s likely to snow** later on so take a hat.*

3 *Shall I* and *shall we* are used to ask for suggestions, advice and instructions.

    *What time **shall we meet** this evening? Where **shall we go**? **Shall I phone** Peter?*

4 The infinitive with *to* is used after some verbs to talk about future hopes, plans, intentions and expectations.

    *We **expect/hope to get** home before 9 o'clock. I **plan/intend to go** to bed early tonight.*

5 The verbs *plan* and *think* can be followed by a preposition and a gerund.

    *Mick and Irene **are planning on getting** married next year. They**'re thinking of going** to Tahiti for the honeymoon.*

UNIT 6

Reported speech

Reported statements

1. When we are reporting what someone has said we can use either direct speech or reported speech.

   Direct speech: *'I've bought a new car,'* said Dan.
   Reported speech: Dan said that he had bought a new car.

2. When we report statements, we may have to make changes to the actual words that the person used. We can use *that* after the reporting verb but it is optional.

   He said (**that**) he wanted to live in Poland.

3. We usually have to make changes to the verb tenses. This is sometimes called 'backshift' as most tenses move back one tense.

Direct speech	Reported speech
Present simple	
'We **live** in the city.'	She said they **lived** in the city.
Present continuous	
'I**'m waiting** for Tina.'	He said he **was waiting** for Tina.
Present perfect	
'I**'ve worked** here for ten years.'	She said she **had worked** there for ten years.
Present perfect continuous	
'Jack**'s been looking** for you.'	She said Jack **had been looking** for me.
Past simple	
'We **spoke** to Tim after school.'	He said they **had spoken** to Tim after school.
Past continuous	
'I **was lying**.'	He said he **had been lying**.
Future	
'I**'ll meet** you at 6.30.'	She said she **would meet** me at 6.30.

The modal verbs *must/may/can* are reported in these ways:

I **can** sing well.	She said she **could** sing well.
I **may** be late.	He said he **might** be late.
You **must** work harder.	He said we **had to** work harder.

4. We do not need to change the tense:
   - for verbs in the past perfect.
     'I**'d** never **thought** about it.'
     He said he'd never **thought** about it.
   - for the modal verbs *might/could/would/should/ought to*.
     'You **should** buy a car.'
     He said I **should** buy a car.
   - if the statement is still true.
     I **want** to talk to Mia.
     Bill said he **wants** to talk to Mia.
   - if we are reporting a statement using a present reporting verb.
     The answer **is** 264.
     Paula says the answer **is** 264.

5. Other changes we may have to make are:
   - to pronouns and possessive adjectives.
     'I've forgotten **your** phone number.'
     He said **he** had forgotten **my** phone number.'
     'If **you** haven't got a ruler **you** can borrow **mine**.'
     She said if **I** hadn't got a ruler **I** could borrow **hers**.
   - to *this/that/these/those*. We sometimes replace them with *the*.
     '**This** article is very interesting.'
     He said that **the** article was very interesting.
   - to words and phrases indicating time and place.

Direct speech	Reported speech
now	then
today	that day
tomorrow	the next/following day
yesterday	the previous day/the day before
the day after tomorrow	in two days' time
three days ago	three days before/earlier
next week	the next/following week
last month	the previous month/the month before
this morning	that morning
here	there
come	go

6. The reporting verbs *say*, *explain* and *complain* can be used with or without an indirect object.

   I **said/explained/complained (to the receptionist)** that the heating in my room wasn't working.

   The verb *tell* must be followed by a direct object.

   I **told him/the receptionist** the heating wasn't working.

Reported questions

When we report questions we have to make the same changes as for reporting statements regarding tenses, pronouns and words and phrases indicating time and place. We also need to remember the following:

- the word order in a reported question is the same as for a statement.
- we do not use auxiliary verbs *do*, *does* or *did*.
- we do not use question marks.
  'Where does Sam live?'
  I asked her **where Sam lived**.
  'Who is your English teacher?'
  He asked her **who her English teacher was**.

- when we are reporting a *yes/no* question (a question without a word such as *when, who, how*, etc.) we use *if/whether*.

  '*Do you speak Spanish?*'
  He asked me **if/whether** I spoke Spanish.

- when we report a request we use the pattern *ask* + object pronoun/noun + infinitive with *to*

  '*Could you shut the window please?*'
  She asked **me to shut** the window.

Reporting verbs

See Reported statements above for information on using *complain, explain, say* and *tell*.

Verb patterns for other reporting verbs are:

- verb + infinitive with *to*
  ask, offer, promise, refuse, threaten

  '*I won't take the test.*'
  He **refused to take** the test.

- verb + object pronoun/noun + infinitive with *to*
  advise, ask, beg, encourage, invite, order, persuade, recommend, remind, tell, urge, warn

  '*You really should go to university.*'
  My parents **encouraged me to go** to university.

- *Suggest* cannot be followed by an infinitive.
  She **recommended me to do** more exercise. ✔
  ~~She suggested me to do more exercise.~~ ✗

- verb + gerund
  admit, deny, recommend, suggest

  '*Let's go to the new Thai restaurant.*'
  He **suggested going** to the new Thai restaurant.

- verb + preposition + gerund
  apologise for, insist on

  '*Sorry I'm late.*'
  He **apologised for being** late.

- verb + object pronoun/noun + preposition + gerund
  accuse of, advise against, blame for, congratulate on, praise for, thank for, warn against

  '*You stole my pen!*'
  She **accused me of stealing** her pen.

- verb + *that* clause with *should*
  insist, recommend, suggest

The words *that* and *should* are optional.

  '*I'd order the fish if I were you.*'
  She **suggested (that) I (should) order** the fish.

UNIT 7

Countable and uncountable nouns

Countable nouns have a singular and a plural form. In the singular they are always preceded by a word such as an article, a number or a determiner.
a garden, four students, each day, some animals

Uncountable nouns have no plural form. They can appear alone or be preceded by a word such as *the* or a determiner, but not *a/an* or a number. They are used with a singular verb form.

Knowledge is strength. **The news** was good. We've made **little progress**.

These nouns are usually uncountable:

accommodation	advice	behaviour	damage
equipment	food	furniture	graffiti
health	help	homework	housework
information	knowledge	luggage	money
news	pollution	progress	research
smoke	spaghetti	traffic	transport
travel	water	weather	work

Languages (e.g. *English, Polish, Swiss*) are also uncountable.

Nouns which can be used both countably and uncountably

1. Some words for food and drink can be used both countably [C] and uncountably [U], but with a slight change in meaning.

   *Would you like a **coffee**?*
   ([C] = a cup of coffee)
   *No, thanks. I don't drink **coffee**.*
   ([U] = coffee in general)
   *I've made a **cake**.*
   ([C] = a whole cake)
   *Can I have some **cake**?*
   ([U] = a piece of cake)

2. Other words, such as *paper, room, time* and *work* change their meaning completely.

   *The story's in all the Sunday **papers**.*
   ([C] = a newspaper)
   *Can I have some **paper**, please?*
   ([U] = paper to write/draw on)
   *Three of Taylor's **works** are on display.*
   ([C] = a work of art)
   *Jo's having trouble finding **work**.* ([U] = a job)

Making uncountable nouns countable

1. Some uncountable nouns have countable equivalents with a similar meaning.

Uncountable	Countable
accommodation	a room/hotel/guesthouse
advice	a tip/suggestion
luggage	a bag/suitcase
travel	a trip/journey/holiday
work	a job/an occupation/a profession

2. Some other nouns can be made countable by using *piece(s)* or *item(s)*.

   a piece of advice/chewing gum/equipment/ food/furniture/homework/information/luggage/news/ research
   an item of clothing/equipment/jewellery/luggage/news

*What a lovely **piece of news**! When's the wedding?*
*Passengers are limited to **one item of luggage**.*

Words and phrases used with countable and uncountable nouns

Before countable nouns	Before uncountable nouns	Before countable and uncountable nouns
(very) few	(very) little	some
(quite) a few	a little	any
many	much	no
too many	too much	(quite) a lot of
several	a great deal of	plenty of
a couple of	a large/small amount of	most
a large/small number of		all
each		enough
every		more

1. *(Very) little* and *(very) few* mean *not much/many* or *not as much/many as you would like* or *expect*.
   I've got **very little money** left. Can you lend me some?
   Very few people attended the meeting.

2. *A little* and *a few* mean *some* or *a small number of*.
   A little knowledge is a dangerous thing.
   I've got **a few sweets** left. Would you like one?

3. *Quite a few* and *quite a lot of* mean *a fairly large number/amount of*.
   Quite a few people came to our concert – we were very pleased.

4. *Plenty of* means *a lot of* or *more than enough*.
   Paul's got **plenty of toys** – don't buy him any more.

5. *Each* is used to talk about two or more people or things; *every* is only used to talk about more than two. They both precede a singular countable noun and a singular verb.
   Each side of the bridge **has** a customs checkpoint.
   Nearly **every player** in the team **is** a foreigner.

Obligation, prohibition, advice and necessity

Obligation

1. *Must* + infinitive without *to* can be used:
   - to express strong obligation.
     Teacher to student: You **must finish** your essay by tomorrow.
   - in signs and notices indicating rules and laws.
     Notice on building site: Hard hats **must be worn** at all times.
   - to give strong advice.
     You really **must go** to that new Indian restaurant.
   - to make polite invitations.
     You **must come** and have dinner with us sometime.
   - to tell ourselves what we personally feel is necessary.
     I **must remember** to buy some more bread.

2. *Have to* can also be used to express obligation, particularly when this is imposed by someone else or by external circumstances.
   The teacher says I **have to finish** my essay by tomorrow.
   My eyesight's getting worse so I **have to wear** glasses for reading.

3. *Must* only has a present form; *have to* is used for all other forms.
   You**'ll have to hurry** if you want to get there on time.
   I **had to buy** some more bread.

   Mustn't + infinitive without *to* is used to express prohibition (see below).

4. *Don't have to* expresses a lack of obligation. Compare:
   You **mustn't eat** those chips – you're on a diet!
   You **don't have to eat** all those chips if you don't want to, but you must finish the fish.

5. *Make* + noun/pronoun + infinitive without *to* is used to express obligation.
   I hate fish but my parents **make me eat** it.

6. In the passive, *make* is followed by the infinitive with *to*.
   Liam **was made to apologise** to the teacher for his behaviour.

Prohibition

1. The modal verbs *cannot/can't* and *must not/mustn't* can be used to express prohibition.
   You **cannot/must not talk** during the exam.

2. Negative forms of *let* + infinitive without *to*, and *allow* + infinitive with *to* can be used with a direct object.
   My parents **won't let me have** a tattoo.
   The hotel **does not allow guests to have** pets in their rooms.

3. The passive *am/are/is not allowed* + infinitive with *to* can also be used.
   The dog**'s not allowed to come** into the kitchen.

4. To talk about past prohibition, use *couldn't*, *didn't/wouldn't let*, *didn't/wouldn't allow* or *was/were not allowed to*. There is no past form of *mustn't* and no passive of *let*.
   When I was your age, we **couldn't wear** trainers to school.
   Mark **wasn't allowed to go** fishing; his parents wouldn't let him stay out all night.

Advice

1. *Should/shouldn't* and *ought (not) to* are used to give advice.

   *You **should see/ought to see** a doctor about your headaches.*

   They can also be used to say what we think is the right thing to do.

   *Supermarkets **ought not to give** customers free plastic bags; they **should charge** for them.*

   In the negative, *I don't think you should …* is more usual than *I think you shouldn't*.

   ***I don't think you should** eat any more sweets.*

2. *Had/'d better (not)* + infinitive without *to* is used to give advice and warnings. It suggests that the speaker thinks there will be negative consequences if the advice is not followed.

   *We**'d better get** the tickets soon – they'll sell out very quickly.*
   *You**'d better not be** late – I'll be furious if you are!*

Necessity

1. *Need to* + infinitive is used to express necessity.
   *Have you got a minute, Sven? **I need to talk** to you.*

   Needn't and *don't need to* both express a lack of necessity.

   *The doors open at seven thirty but we **needn't get/ don't need to get** there until eight.*

2. *Needn't have* + past participle is used to indicate a past action that was completed but that was not necessary.

   *I **needn't have taken** a coat: it was very warm.*

3. *Didn't need to* + infinitive is used to indicate a past action that was not necessary. The context usually makes it clear whether the action was performed or not.

   *We **didn't need to wear** a suit to the party, but I wanted to look smart so I did.*

4. *There is/was no need (for someone)* + infinitive with *to* can also be used to express a lack of necessity in the past or present.

   ***There's no need (for you) to shout!** I can hear perfectly well.*

UNIT 8

The passive

Form

To form the passive we use the appropriate tense of the verb *to be* and the past participle of the main verb.

Present simple:	*My salary **is paid** directly into my bank.*
Present continuous:	*My car **is being repaired** at the moment.*
Present perfect:	*I**'ve been asked** to give a speech.*
Past simple:	*Luke **was given** his results on Friday.*
Past continuous:	*I didn't know I **was being filmed**.*
Past perfect:	*The food **had been eaten** before we got there.*
Future simple:	*You **will be met** at the airport.*
Gerund:	*Do you like **being photographed**?*
Infinitive with *to*:	*I'd like **to be invited** to the party.*
Infinitive without *to*:	*All phones **must be switched off**.*

Use

1. We use the passive to focus attention on the person or thing affected by the action, rather than on the agent (the person or thing that does the action).

   *My husband **was made** redundant last month.*

2. If we want to indicate the agent in a passive construction, we use the preposition *by*.

   *This book was written **by P.J. Stone**.*

   If we want to indicate the instrument used by the agent to do the action, we use *with*.

   *The graffiti was painted **with a spray can**.*

3. The passive cannot be used with intransitive verbs.

   ~~The glass was fallen off the shelf.~~ ✗

4. When there are two objects in a sentence, the person usually becomes the subject of the passive sentence.

   The teacher gave Trudy a prize.
   *Trudy **was given** a prize by the teacher.*
   (These are more usual than: *A prize was given to Trudy by the teacher.*)

Non-use of agent

The agent is not usually included in passive constructions:

- when we do not know the agent or the agent is unimportant.

  *Jemma's bike **has been stolen**.*
  *These houses **were built** fifty years ago.*

- when the agent is obvious from the context.

  *Our rubbish **is collected** every Monday.*

- when the agent is people in general.

  *Sri Lanka used **to be called** Ceylon.*

- in official notices or advice to avoid using *you*.

  *One pill **should be taken** before each meal.*

- when we want to avoid mentioning the agent.

  ***It has been decided** not to increase salaries this year.*

Passive of reporting verbs

Reporting verbs can be used with passive constructions when we want to introduce a widely held opinion or fact. There are two ways of doing this:

- It + passive + *that* clause.

  It is said that fish is good for our brains.
  It is believed that the economy is getting worse.
  It is thought that global warming caused the floods.

- Subject + passive + *to* + infinitive/continuous infinitive/perfect infinitive without *to*.

  Fish is said to be good for our brains.
  The economy is believed to be getting worse.
  Global warming is thought to have caused the floods.

Verbs commonly used with these constructions are *believe, consider, expect, feel, know, say* and *think*.

UNIT 9

Conditionals

Conditional sentences contain:

a a subordinate clause expressing a **condition** and introduced by words such as *if, unless, as long as*.

b a main clause describing the likely **result** of the condition becoming reality.

   If I miss the last bus, I'll phone you.
   (condition)   (result)

When the result clause appears first in the sentence, there is usually no comma.

   I'd learn to sail if I had more time.
   (result)   (condition)

Zero conditional

The zero conditional is used to talk about situations which are always or generally true. We use the present simple in both the conditional clause and the main clause. *If* has the same meaning as *when, whenever* or *every time* in these sentences.

   Everyday situations: I usually **feel** sick **if I read** in the car.
   Scientific facts: **If you add** salt to water, it **dissolves**.

First conditional

The first conditional is used to talk about possible future situations and their likely results. We use the present simple in the conditional clause and a future tense in the main clause.

   We**'ll** probably **go** swimming **if** the weather**'s fine** tomorrow.
   If you **don't let** me play, **I'm going to tell** my mum.

Modal verbs such as *can, may, might* and *could* can also be used in the main clause.

   If the pain **gets** worse, **I might go** to the doctor's.

Second conditional

1 The second conditional is used to talk about imaginary, impossible or unlikely situations in the present or future. We use the past simple or, less frequently, the past continuous in the conditional clause and *would/might/could* + infinitive without *to* in the main clause.

   If I **lived/was living** in Spain, **I'd eat** paella every Sunday. (imaginary)
   I **could do** this job a lot faster **if** I **had** six pairs of hands. (impossible)

2 When the second conditional refers to the future, the implication is that the condition is less likely to become reality than if it were expressed with a first conditional. Compare:

   If Ian phones tonight (possible), what will you say to him?
   If Ian phoned tonight (unlikely), what would you say to him?

3 *Were* instead of *was* is often used after *if* in second conditional sentences.

   If I **were/was** you, I wouldn't worry about it.

Third conditional

The third conditional is used to talk about imaginary situations in the past and to speculate about how things might have been different. We use the past perfect simple or continuous in the conditional clause and *would/could/might* + perfect infinitive without *to* in the main clause.

   If I**'d lost** my job, we **would have sold** the house.
   (I didn't lose my job so we didn't sell the house.)
   If my wife **hadn't been working** last night, we **could have gone** to the concert. (My wife was working last night so we couldn't go to the concert.)

Mixed conditional

A mixed conditional is a combination of a second and a third conditional. The time reference in the conditional clause is different from that in the main clause.

   My parents **would be** happier **if** I **hadn't bought** a motorbike.
   If the car **wasn't** so unreliable, we **would have** driven to Wales.

Alternatives to *if* clauses

1 *As long as* and *provided/providing (that)* can be used in place of *if* to emphasise the condition.

   I'll let you borrow my bike **as long as** you promise to look after it.
   You can go out **provided** you finish your homework first.

2. *Otherwise* can be used to introduce the result clause. We use it to talk about the negative consequences of something not happening.

   *I hope it stays sunny, **otherwise** we won't be able to have a barbecue.* (= If it doesn't stay sunny, we won't be able to have a barbecue.)
   *It's a good job we took our umbrellas, **otherwise** we would have got soaking wet.* (= If we hadn't taken our umbrellas, we would have got soaking wet.)

3. *Or* can be used in a similar way, especially in warnings, threats and advice.

   *You'd better go now, **or** you'll be late for school.* (= If you don't go now, you'll be late for school.)
   *Stop being silly, **or** I'll send you to bed early.* (= If you don't stop being silly, I'll send you to bed early.)

UNIT 10

Wish, if only and hope

We use the verb *wish* when we would like things to be different. We can also use *if only* to express the same ideas as *wish*. We use *if only* when we want to make the wish stronger. It is often considered more dramatic.

   *I **wish/If only** I had enough money to buy a bike.*

Wish/If only + past simple

1. We use *wish* or *if only* + past simple when we are unhappy with a present situation and would like it to be different, even though this may not be possible. The verbs used with *wish* for present situations are normally stative verbs such as *be*, *have*, *know*, *live* and *understand*.

   *I **wish we lived** in the town centre.*
   *If only I **knew** how to dance.*

2. Verbs other than stative verbs can be used if we are referring to regular or habitual actions.

   *I wish **it didn't rain** so much in this country.*

Wish/If only + would/could

1. When we want someone to do something or something to happen now or in the future but it is unlikely, we can use *wish* + subject pronoun/noun + *would*

   *I wish it **would rain** – it's so dry everywhere.*

2. We often use this form when something irritates us and we want it to stop/change.

   *I wish the neighbours **would stop** arguing – they're so noisy.*

3. We do not normally use *I wish I would*. Instead, we use *I wish I could* to talk about something that we would like to do in the future but cannot.

   *I wish I **could go** on holiday with you but I've got to work.*

4. We use *hope* + present when a future event is possible.

   *I **hope I do** well in the exam tomorrow.*

Wish/If only + past perfect

When we want to express regret about the past we use *wish/if only* + past perfect.

   *I **wish I had gone** to Tony's party. Sue says it was really good.*
   *If only **I hadn't eaten** that extra cake. I feel a bit sick now.*

Should have/ought to have done

1. We can also use *should/shouldn't* + *have* + past participle and *ought/ought not* + *to have* + past participle to express regret about the past.

   *I **should have revised** more for the test. I got a very low mark.*
   *We **ought to have left** home earlier. We're going to be late.*

2. These structures can also be used to express criticism.

   *You **shouldn't have stayed out** so late last night. No wonder you're tired!*

3. *Ought not to have* + past participle is formal and rarely used in spoken English.

   *The judge **ought not to have accepted** his appeal.*

Have/get something done

1. When we refer to actions that we do not do ourselves but pay for or ask others to do, we use this structure: subject + correct form of *have* + object + past participle.

   *I **had my laptop repaired** last week.*
   *Our friends **are having their house extended**.*

   Get can be used as an informal alternative to *have*.

   *I**'m going to get my hair cut** tomorrow.*

2. We can use the same structure to talk about unpleasant events that we have not asked to be done.

   *This is the third time our shop **has had its windows smashed**.*
   *He put the fire out but **got his hand burnt** quite **badly**.*

Writing Bank

Part 1: Essay

In your English class you have been talking about the world of work. Now, your English teacher has asked you to write an essay.

Write an essay using **all** the notes and giving reasons for your point of view.

Model answer 1

In the following model answer, the writer gives their opinion in the first paragraph and then provides arguments to support this opinion.

> Is it better to be self-employed or work for another person, organisation or company?
> **Notes**
> Write about:
> 1 job security
> 2 income
> 3 .... (*your own idea*)

> *Is it better to be self-employed or work for another person, organisation or company?*
>
> A country's economic situation or our own abilities may decide which job we do, and we might have no choice about whether we work for ourselves or for someone else. If we could choose, however, I personally feel there are more advantages in being self-employed.
>
> Firstly, as a self-employed person you have much more independence. You are your own boss and you can decide how to do things in your business, who works for you and what hours you work. In addition, if your business is successful, it may be possible to decide how much you pay yourself. Consequently, you have the chance to earn a much bigger income than if you work in a company or organisation.
>
> Some people argue that there are bigger risks and less job security if you are self-employed and you have no protection if things go wrong. However, in the current economic crisis, working for a company is not much safer: businesses are closing all the time, and employees can lose their jobs without warning.
>
> In conclusion, whilst there may be some risks in being self-employed, it seems better than working for someone else.

Annotations:
- If possible, avoid repetition of language used in the title.
- use of formal linking devices
- appropriately formal style throughout essay
- introduction, stating opinion
- first and second reasons (points 2 & 3 of Notes)
- third reason (point 1 of Notes)
- conclusion, summarising opinion

Useful language for essays

Saying what people think
Some/Many people feel that …
Others argue that …
One/Another point of view is that …
It is sometimes said/claimed that …
It is widely believed that …
It is generally agreed that …

Expressing your opinion
I personally feel that …
I firmly believe that …
I partly/fully agree that …
In my opinion …
My personal view is that …

Expressing contrast
On the one/other hand …
However, …
… whereas …
Having said that, …

For further linking words and phrases, see the relevant writing sections in Units 1 and 6.

Model answer 2

In this model answer, the writer considers both sides of the argument before giving their opinion in the final paragraph.

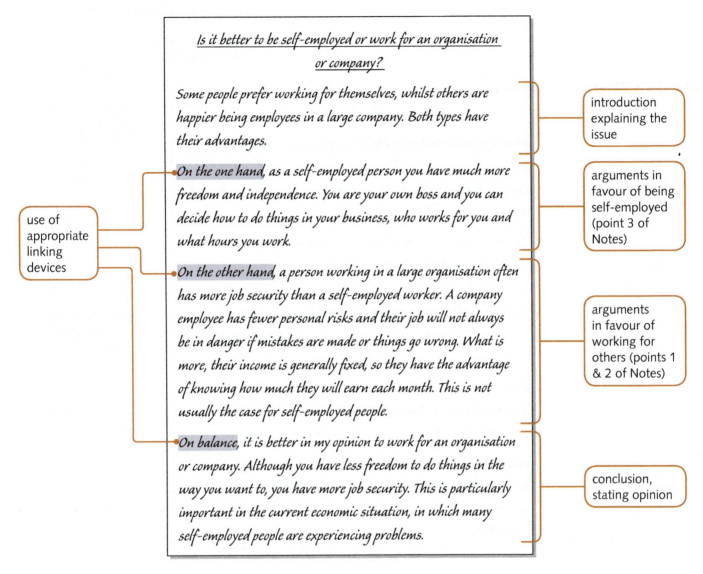

Is it better to be self-employed or work for an organisation or company?

Some people prefer working for themselves, whilst others are happier being employees in a large company. Both types have their advantages. — introduction explaining the issue

On the one hand, as a self-employed person you have much more freedom and independence. You are your own boss and you can decide how to do things in your business, who works for you and what hours you work. — arguments in favour of being self-employed (point 3 of Notes)

On the other hand, a person working in a large organisation often has more job security than a self-employed worker. A company employee has fewer personal risks and their job will not always be in danger if mistakes are made or things go wrong. What is more, their income is generally fixed, so they have the advantage of knowing how much they will earn each month. This is not usually the case for self-employed people. — arguments in favour of working for others (points 1 & 2 of Notes)

On balance, it is better in my opinion to work for an organisation or company. Although you have less freedom to do things in the way you want to, you have more job security. This is particularly important in the current economic situation, in which many self-employed people are experiencing problems. — conclusion, stating opinion

(use of appropriate linking devices)

Task

In your English class you have been talking about life in cities compared with life in the countryside. Now, your English teacher has asked you to write an essay.

Write an essay using **all** the notes and giving reasons for your point of view. Write your **essay** in **140–190** words.

Is it better to live in a city or in the countryside?
Notes
Write about:
1 noise
2 health
3 .... (your own idea)

Making additional points
In addition (to this), …
Furthermore, …
Moreover, …
What is more, …

Concluding
To conclude, …
To sum up, …
In conclusion, …
On balance, …

Part 2: Article

You see this announcement in *Technology Today* magazine.

Write your **article**.

LIFE WITHOUT A COMPUTER?

How different would your life be if you did not have a computer at home?

Write and tell us and we will publish the best articles.

Model answer

> *A computer-free home? Yes, please!*
>
> What a pleasure that would be! For one thing, it would be much easier to move in our house if we got rid of our three PCs and two laptops. And with no printers, speakers, keyboards or wires, there'd be less dust everywhere.
>
> Can you imagine, too, how family relations would improve? My brother might come out of his bedroom more often, and my dad could look at me rather than the computer screen when we're having one of our rare conversations. We would have more time to play games together, cook real food or even talk to each other.
>
> Naturally, homework might be more difficult — I'd have to use books to find information, and write everything with a pen instead of typing it. But at least I'd be able to concentrate more without interruptions from emails and online chat messages.
>
> Last but not least, just think of the benefits to my health. My eyesight might improve and my back wouldn't ache from sitting down all the time. It makes you wonder why we all have computers.

Annotations:
- opening sentence relevant to title
- direct question addressed to the reader
- a closing comment
- interesting title to attract reader's attention
- informal linking devices
- For this particular question type use comparatives and *would*, *might* and *could*.
- a lively informal style throughout the article

Task

Either write your own answer to the task above *or* write an answer to the following question in 140–190 words.

You see this announcement in *Music plus* magazine.

Life without MUSIC?

How different would your life be if you could not listen to music?

Write and tell us and we will publish the best articles.

Write your **article**.

Useful language for articles

Involving the reader
Can you imagine …?
Just think …
Have you ever …?
How would you feel if …?
Did you know that …?

Introducing points
Firstly … Secondly …
Finally …
For one thing …
For another thing …
First of all …
What's more …
Last but not least …

Attitude adverbs
Naturally, …
(Not) surprisingly, …
Interestingly, …
Worryingly, …
Personally, …
(Un)fortunately, …

Part 2: Review

You have seen this notice in your school library.

Write your **review**.

REVIEWS NEEDED

We want to buy some new books for the library. Have you read a good book in English recently?

Write us a review of a book you enjoyed, explaining why you liked it and why you think it would be a good choice for the school library.

We will use your reviews to help us decide which books to buy.

Model answer

The Thieves of Ostia

'The Thieves of Ostia' by Caroline Lawrence is the first in a series of books entitled 'The Roman Mysteries' and I think it's an absolute must for the school library. — *introducing the book*

The book is set in the Roman port of Ostia nearly two thousand years ago. It tells the story of Flavia and her three friends, and their attempts to discover who has been killing the dogs of Ostia and why. It's full of mystery and excitement, and the plot has many twists and turns, which make you want to keep reading. — *information about plot and characters, and reasons why you liked the book*

The book is aimed at ten- to twelve-year-old native English speakers, but it is very popular with older children and would be ideal for teenagers studying English. What's more, it gives a fascinating insight into life in Roman times, so readers learn about history as well as improving their language skills. — *reasons why the book would be a good choice for the library*

After finishing 'The Thieves of Ostia', students will want to borrow further books from the series. By buying it, then, the library would be doing a lot to encourage students to read more in English. — *concluding comments*

use of linking words and phrases (What's more, After finishing, By buying it, then)

Task

Either write your own answer to the task above or write an answer to the following question in 140–190 words.

You have seen this notice in your school's English-language magazine:

ANIMATION FILMS
REVIEWS NEEDED

Have you seen an animation film recently?

If so, send us a review of the film, saying what you did and did not like about it. Include information on the characters and the story, and say whether you would recommend the film to other people.

We will publish the best reviews.

Write your **review**.

Useful language for reviews

Giving information about a film, book, musical or play
- It is set in (France) in (the nineteenth century).
- It tells the story of (Gemma) …
- It is based on a novel/a true story.
- The film stars (Angelina Jolie) as (Maleficent).
- The main character is (Flavia Gemina).

Expressing an opinion
- It is full of mystery/suspense/humour/action/twists and turns.
- It gives a fascinating insight into (life in the last century).
- The plot is straightforward/predictable/complicated/gripping.
- The acting/soundtrack/direction is impressive/disappointing.
- I particularly enjoyed … / I didn't particularly like …

Giving a recommendation
- This (book) would be ideal for (teenagers).
- It is a must/an absolute must for (the film club).
- I'd recommend this (hotel) to (families with young children).
- It is certainly/not worth reading/watching/going to see/buying.

Part 2: Email and letter

This is part of a letter from an English pen friend, Lee.

Write your **letter**.

> My sister Amy will be seven next month. I was thinking of getting her a pet for her birthday. You know a lot about animals – what would you recommend for a child of her age? If you could give me some information on how to look after it, that would be great too.
>
> Thanks,
>
> Lee

Model answer

Dear Lee

It was great to hear from you. I can't believe Amy's nearly seven! It'll be a lovely surprise for her to have a pet on her birthday.

If I were you, I'd go for a hamster, as it's a very small animal and won't take up much room in your flat. There are several different varieties to choose from, but the best type to get for somebody like Amy is a Syrian hamster, because they're really affectionate and don't mind being picked up by young children.

The other good thing about hamsters is that they're easy to take care of. You need to feed them and change their water every day, though sometimes once every two days is enough. Supermarkets usually sell hamster food, and you should give them fresh fruit and vegetables as well. Hamsters can get quite smelly, so you have to clean their cage out once a week – I expect Amy will ask you to do that!

I hope that's helpful. Let me know what you buy her.

All the best

Pedro

Annotations: use of phrasal verbs; use of linking words; brief, relevant opening paragraph; language for giving advice; information on how to look after the pet; appropriate ending

Task

Either write your own answer to the task above **or** write an answer to the following question in 140–190 words.

This is part of a letter from an English pen friend, Chris.

> My grandmother lives on her own and she's thinking of getting a pet to keep her company. You know a lot about animals – what would you recommend for someone like her? If you could give me some information on how to look after it, I'd appreciate that too.
>
> Thanks,
>
> Chris

Useful language for emails and letters

Beginning the letter
It was great/lovely to hear from you.
Thanks for your letter.
I'm pleased/delighted to hear that …
Sorry to hear about your …

Giving advice
It's (not) a good idea to …
It's best (not) to …
You should/shouldn't …
If I were you, I would/wouldn't …
Whatever you do, make sure you (don't) …
Try to ensure you (don't) …
One thing that works for me is to …

Ending the letter
I hope that's useful/helpful.
Write back soon and let me know …
Give my love/regards/best wishes to …
Looking forward to hearing from you.
Hope to see you soon.

Closing phrase
All the best
Best wishes
Bye for now
(Lots of) love

Write your **letter**.

Part 2: Report

You are now reaching the end of your studies for the *Cambridge English: First (FCE)* examination. Your teacher has asked you to write a report for new students at your school, explaining what resources are available in the school to help students prepare for the exam. You should include information on the resources in your school and advice on how to use them.

Write your **report**.

Model answer

(a suitable heading for each section of the report)
(a range of language for giving advice)
(Summarise the aim of the report without copying the wording of the question.)
(a variety of words and phrases to describe amounts and quantities)
(a consistent style throughout, in this case formal)
(Conclude with summarising comment and/or final recommendation.)

Introduction
The purpose of this report is to describe the resources on offer in the school for students preparing for the Cambridge English: First examination and consider ways to make the best use of them.

Books
The library contains a wide selection of readers and novels suitable for students at this level. It is a good idea to read at least one book a month in order to become familiar with a range of vocabulary and structures. There are also a number of relevant grammar practice books, which should be consulted if you are having problems with a specific feature of the language.

Computers
Students are also advised to spend thirty minutes or so a day doing computer-based practice tests. The multimedia room has sixteen computers for study use, with several First practice exams installed on each. Internet access also enables students to listen to podcasts and read online newspapers – an excellent way to improve listening and reading skills.

Conclusion
A daily visit to the school's library and multimedia room is recommended to help ensure success in the First examination.

Task

Write an answer to the following question in 140–190 words.

A group of teenage students is going to be staying in your town for a week. You have been asked to write a report for the group leader about shopping in your town. Give information on the shopping facilities available in your town and make recommendations on where the students should go.

Write your **report**.

Useful language for reports

Giving advice and making suggestions
I would recommend/advise (them to go to a seafood restaurant).
I suggest you/they (shop for clothes at 'Brown's').
The best place for (DVDs) is 'The Film Shop'.
You/They should/really must/are advised to (try a salad bar).
(A visit to the cathedral) is an option worth considering.
(A boat trip) is a must/to be recommended.
It is advisable/a good idea to (wear a raincoat).

Talking about facilities
The shopping/sports/cultural/leisure/restaurant, etc. facilities are …
… excellent/outstanding/second to none.
… adequate/quite good.
… poor/inadequate/basic.

Part 2: Letter of application

You see this advertisement in an English-language newspaper.

> **VOLUNTEERS REQUIRED FOR SUMMER WORK**
>
> We are looking for people to spend afternoons and Saturdays with groups of young children who have learning or physical disabilities and want to have fun. As well as accompanying the children to the swimming pool and on trips to the countryside, volunteers will be asked to organise further activities of their choice.
>
> Write to Mr Brent and explain why you would be suitable.

Write your **letter of application**.

Model answer

Dear Mr Brent

I saw your advertisement in yesterday's edition of the 'Evening News' and I would like to volunteer to work with the disabled children. — *reason for writing*

I am a nineteen-year-old Italian studying English here this summer. My classes are in the morning, and I am keen to do something useful in my free time. I have some experience of looking after a disabled child. My seven-year-old cousin has Down's Syndrome and I often take her to the park *in order to* give her parents a rest. I *also* teach her ballet, *which* she thoroughly enjoys. — *relevant experience* / *use of linking words*

There are a number of activities I could organise for the children. *In addition to* my ballet dancing, I can play the guitar and know several songs for children, both English and Italian ones. I am interested in birdwatching, too, so I could bring that knowledge to the countryside excursions. — *possible further activities*

I have an outgoing and friendly nature, and feel I have the necessary patience and energy to make a positive contribution to your programme. — *personal qualities and suitability* / *appropriately formal style*

I look forward to hearing from you

Yours sincerely

Angela Balducci — *appropriate ending*

Task

Write an answer to the following question in 140–190 words.

You see this advertisement in an international magazine.

VOLUNTEERS REQUIRED

If you want to work with elderly people, why not spend this summer at the **Wildflowers Nursing Home**? Food and accommodation are provided. Duties include:

- playing cards and board games and going for walks with residents
- teaching basic computer skills
- organising further activities of your choice

Write to **Mrs Redman** and explain why you would be suitable.

Write your **letter of application**.

Useful language for letters of application

Beginnings and endings
Dear Sir or Madam and Yours faithfully
Dear Ms Bentley and Yours sincerely

Reason for writing
I saw/have seen your advertisement in …
I am writing to apply for the job as (a waiter) …
I would like to apply for a grant to study/for …
I would like to volunteer to work with (disabled children) …

Describing skills and experience
I have experience of (looking after children).
I spent (three months) working as (an au pair).
I have excellent communication/computer/organisational skills.
I have a good knowledge of (history/English/computers).

Personal qualities and suitability
I have a/an friendly/sensitive/easy-going/enthusiastic nature.
I feel I have the necessary (patience) and (energy) for the job.
I am confident I would be well suited to the job.
I believe I am an ideal candidate for a grant/the job.

Closing remarks
I enclose my curriculum vitae.
I hope you will consider my application.
I look forward to your reply/hearing from you.

Wordlist

This wordlist contains key vocabulary that is highlighted in Units 1–10. The wordlist is also available on the Student's Resource Centre, where the phonetic script, definitions and sample sentences are provided.

adj = adjective   n = noun   v = verb   sbdy = somebody   sthg = something

Unit 1 Influence
Influences

copy sbdy's every move
encourage sbdy to do sthg v
have an influence on
idolise sbdy v
role model n
set a good example
shape sbdy's opinion

The weather

blazing sun
cold spell
dropping temperatures
fine and sunny
gale-force winds
hard winter
heavy snow
intense heat
light breeze
pour with rain
torrential rainfall

Unit 2 Success!
Sport

beat v
court n
draw v
field event n
(football) boots n
(football) match n
(football) pitch n
goggles n
(golf) club n
(golf) course n
helmet n
hole n
knee pads n
lane n
meeting n
opponent n
penalty n
pole n
practise v
racket n
referee n
rink n
Rollerblades™ n
runner-up n
running n
(silver) medallist n
slalom n
slope n
spectator n
starting blocks n
(swimming) pool n
(tennis) net n
time out n
tournament n
track n
trunks n
umpire n
vest n
viewer n
win v

Unit 3 Image and images
Describing appearance

almond-shaped (eyes) adj
bright and sparkling (eyes) adj
broad (nose) adj
clear (complexion) adj
crooked (teeth) adj
dark (complexion) adj
dull (eyes) adj
freckled (complexion) adj
full (lips) adj
hazel (eyes) adj
healthy (teeth) adj
hooked (nose) adj
narrow (nose) adj
pale (complexion) adj
perfect (teeth) adj
piercing (eyes) adj
rotten (teeth) adj
sharp (nose) adj
shoulder-length (hair) adj

slim *adj*
smooth (face/skin) *adj*
spotty (complexion) *adj*
straight (hair) *adj*
straight (teeth) *adj*
thick (hair) *adj*
thin (lips) *adj*
thinning (hair) *adj*
tubby *adj*
untidy (hair) *adj*
upturned (nose) *adj*
wrinkled (face/skin) *adj*

Types of film/TV series
adventure *n*
animation *n*
comedy *n*
horror *n*
musical *n*
period drama *n*
romance *n*
science fiction *n*
thriller *n*

People and elements of a film/TV series
actor *n*
cameraman/woman *n*
cast *n*
director *n*
episode *n*
location *n*
make-up artist *n*
plot *n*
role *n*
scene *n*
scriptwriter *n*
sequel *n*
setting *n*
special effects *n*
stuntman/woman *n*

Describing a film/TV series
convincing *adj*
dramatic *adj*
gripping *adj*
stunning *adj*

Phrases
appeal mainly to
based on
on location

Unit 4 Going away
Holidays and travel
adventure holiday *n*
board *v*
camping holiday *n*
coach holiday *n*
delay *v*
drive *v*
enjoy yourself *v*
give sbdy a lift *v*
navigate *v*
package holiday *n*
public holiday *n*
rest *n*
sailing holiday *n*
seaside holiday resort *n*
skiing holiday *n*
stay at sbdy's house *v*
taxi along (the runway) *v*
tour *n*
trip *n*
working holiday *n*

Describing places
appealing *adj*
bleak *adj*
bustling *adj*
depressing *adj*
dreary *adj*
dull *adj*
exciting *adj*
inhospitable *adj*
monotonous *adj*
overcrowded *adj*
pleasant *adj*
relaxed *adj*
stressful *adj*
tough *adj*
unhurried *adj*
vibrant *adj*

Unit 5 Fitting in
Describing people's feelings
be in a bad mood
fed up *adj*
feel down
feel sorry for yourself
miserable *adj*
sad *adj*
upset *adj*

Describing personality

adventurous adj
bad-mannered adj
bad-tempered adj
brave adj
caring adj
confident adj
decisive adj
easy-going adj
enthusiastic adj
even-tempered adj
friendly adj
fussy adj
grumpy adj
impolite adj
irritable adj
kind adj
lazy adj
moody adj
nervous adj
outgoing adj
patient adj
practical adj
relaxed adj
reliable adj
reserved adj
responsible adj
rude adj
self-assured adj
sensible adj
sensitive adj
sociable adj
thoughtful adj
tolerant adj
tough adj

Unit 6 News and views
Describing decisions

complicated adj
decisive adj
easy adj
hard adj
simple adj
straightforward adj
tough adj
tricky adj

Phrases

bear in mind
change your mind
come to a decision
leave it up to sbdy else to decide
let your heart rule your head
make up your mind
no easy matter
rush into a decision
take into account
weigh up the pros and cons

Unit 7 Survival
Surviving

be in danger of (disappearing)
be under threat from
(find it hard) to make ends meet
may not survive much longer
put the survival of something at risk
stay alive
the biggest threat to

Prepositions with verbs

agree on sthg
apologise for sthg
apply for sthg
believe in sthg
belong to sthg/sbdy
complain about sthg/sbdy
concentrate on sthg
depend on sthg
dream about sthg/sbdy
forget about sthg/sbdy
go by yourself
go on your own
insist on sthg
invest in sthg
listen to sthg/sbdy
look at sbdy
object to sthg/sbdy
participate in sthg
pay for sthg
respond to sthg/sbdy
result in sthg
save up for sthg
shout at sbdy
smile at sbdy
stare at sbdy
stay in touch
worry about sthg/sbdy

Prepositions with nouns

at fault
at home
at risk
at work
by accident
by bus
by chance
by heart
in charge
in danger

in theory
in practice
in the end
on average
on fire
on offer
on purpose
out of breath
out of date
out of order
out of sight

Unit 8 Brain games
Memory

forgetful *adj*
from memory
have a good memory for facts and figures
keep forgetting
learn by heart
memorable *adj*
memorise *v*
remember names and faces
remind you of sbdy
unforgettable *adj*

Describing people's feelings

bored *adj*
depressed *adj*
emotional *adj*
pleased *adj*
worried *adj*

Describing personality

aggressive *adj*
attention-seeking *adj*
modest *adj*
moody *adj*
placid *adj*
polite *adj*
rebellious *adj*
respectful *adj*
timid *adj*
vain *adj*

Arts and culture

abstract *adj*
ballerina *n*
ballet *n*
best-seller *n*
biography *n*
cartoon *n*
choir *n*
choreographer *n*
classical *adj*
comic *n*
composer *n*
concert hall *n*
exhibition *n*
exhibits *n*
gallery *n*
graffiti *n*
graphics *n*
graphic novel *n*
hip hop *n*
instrument *n*
jazz *n*
lead singer *n*
lyrics *n*
musician *n*
novel *n*
novelist *n*
opera *n*
orchestra *n*
painting *n*
paperback *n*
performance *n*
play *n*
playwright *n*
poem *n*
poet *n*
portrait *n*
sculpture *n*
self-portrait *n*
soap opera *n*
solo *n*
stage *n*
storyline *n*
studio *n*
venue *n*

Unit 9 A slave to routine
Phrases with *time*

at a time
at all times
at the time
by the time
find the time to do sthg
have a good time
just in time
from time to time
on time
pass the time
set aside time
spend time

take a long time

time after time

time to (do sthg)

waste your time

Other phrases

just (seconds/minutes/hours) left to do sthg

keep your watch (five minutes) fast

make the most of sthg

not stand another moment of it

Unit 10 Getting on
Relationships

break sbdy's heart

get on sbdy's nerves

made for each other

keep in touch with sbdy

keep on the right side of sbdy

take an instant dislike to sbdy

Qualities you look for in a friend

considerate *adj*

humorous *adj*

interest *n*

knowledgeable *adj*

reliable *adj*

sensitive *adj*

tolerant *adj*

Other phrases

be surrounded by (friends)

good at listening

be keen on

sbdy you can turn to

sbdy you can depend on

think about others

Age

adolescent *n*

elderly *adj*

getting on in years

in one's twenties/thirties/forties

middle-aged *adj*

newborn *n*

preteen *n*

retired *adj*

senior citizen *n*

teenager *n*

toddler *n*

youngster *n*

Phrasal Verb list

The numbers in brackets refer to the Student's Book unit in which the phrasal verb first appears. All definitions are taken from *Macmillan Phrasal Verbs Plus*.

Phrasal Verb	Meaning
break down (7)	if a machine or vehicle breaks down, it stops working
break up (10)	if a band breaks up, the members stop playing together
bring sthg **back** (8)	cause ideas, feelings, or memories to be in your mind again
carry on with/doing sthg (2)	continue doing something
catch on (5)	become popular or fashionable
clear up (7)	if the weather clears up, the clouds or rain go away
clear sthg **up** (7)	make a place tidy by removing things that you have finished using or no longer want
cloud over (1)	become darker because grey clouds are forming in the sky
come up with sthg (2)	think of an idea or a plan
cover sthg **up** (1)	hide the truth about something
cram sthg **into** (+ period of time) (9)	do a lot of activities in a short time
draw up (9)	if a vehicle draws up, it arrives at a place and stops
drop sbdy **off** (4)	take someone to a place in a car, usually without getting out of the car yourself
end up (1)	be in a particular place or state after doing something or because of doing something
fall for sthg (10)	like something immediately and decide that you want to have it
fall out (**with** sbdy) (10)	stop being friendly with someone because you have had a disagreement with them
find sthg **out** (5)	discover a fact or piece of information
fish sthg **out** (9)	pull something out of a bag or other container
get by (**on**/**with** sthg) (7)	have just enough of something, such as money or knowledge, to be able to do what you need to do
get in with sbdy (5)	begin to be involved with a particular person or group
get on with sbdy (3)	have a friendly relationship with someone
get through sthg (7)	manage to deal with a difficult situation
give sthg **up** (1)	stop doing something that you do regularly
go away (4)	leave your home for a period of time, especially for a holiday
go back on sthg (6)	fail to do something that you have promised or agreed to do
go on to do sthg (2)	do something after you have finished doing something else
grow up (2)	change from being a child to being an adult
hang around together (5)	spend time with each other
lash out at sbdy (9)	try to hit someone suddenly
leave sbdy/sthg **out** (5)	not include someone or something

Phrasal Verb list

let sbdy **down** (1)	make someone disappointed by not doing something that they are expecting you to do
live on sthg (7)	have a particular amount of money to buy the things that you need to live
look back on sthg (1)	think about a time or event in the past
look forward to (doing) sthg (5)	feel happy and excited about something that is going to happen
look up to sbdy (1)	admire and respect someone
make up (**with** sbdy) (10)	become friendly with someone again after having had a disagreement
pick sbdy **up** (4)	go and meet someone, usually in a vehicle
pick sbdy/sthg **up** (Writing Bank)	lift someone or something up from a surface
put sbdy **down** (7)	criticise someone, especially when other people are there, in a way that makes them feel stupid
put sthg **off** (6)	delay doing something, especially because you do not want to do it
put sbdy **up** (4)	let someone stay in your house
put up with sbdy/sthg (5)	accept an annoying situation without complaining, even though you do not like it
rub off on sbdy (1)	if a quality that someone has rubs off, it begins to affect another person so that they begin to have that quality too
see sbdy **off** (4)	go somewhere such as a station or airport with someone in order to say goodbye to them
set time **aside** (9)	reserve time
set off (1)	start a journey or start going somewhere
set sthg **up** (2)	start a business or an organisation
settle in (5)	become familiar with a new way of life, place, or job
show sthg **off to** sbdy (5)	show people something you are very proud of so they will admire it
sign up for sthg (2)	join a course or organisation
stand out (5)	be easy to see or notice because of being different
stay out (10)	not return to your home, especially when it is late
stick to (10)	obey rules or instructions
stick with sthg (5)	continue to do something
sum up (1)	give a summary of something
take off (4)	if an aircraft takes off, it leaves the ground and starts flying
take sbdy **on** (2)	start to employ someone
take sthg **up** (2)	start doing something new as a habit, job or interest
take up (time/space) (Writing Bank)	fill a particular amount of space or time
take to sbdy/sthg (5)	begin to like someone or something
touch down (4)	if an aircraft touches down, it lands
turn away from sthg (6)	refuse to accept or use something any longer
turn up (9)	come somewhere unexpectedly
weigh sthg **up** (6)	consider the good and bad aspects of something in order to reach a decision about it
work sthg **out** (2)	calculate

Listening scripts

Unit 1 Influence

Listening Part 2: Sentence completion

🔊 1.01

Tim Lee

Hello, I'm Tim Lee, and in today's programme in our series on advertising, I'd like to talk about 'product placement'. That's where products are included, or to use the correct term, 'placed' in television programmes or films for commercial reasons. For example, when a company pays a programme-maker to show an actor drinking a particular brand of bottled water, or eating a **chocolate bar.** It's a rather more subtle way of influencing people's buying choices than the typical advertisement.

Of course, something like this often occurs quite by chance. You might see a **company logo** for example, that just happens to be on the clothes of someone being interviewed. This is not product placement – just a bit of good luck for the company concerned.

Product placement, of course, is nothing new – it has existed on UK television for many years. It used to be allowed only in films or **international** programmes, like the American drama series we see so many of. Then the law changed and since February 2011, we've been able to see it in a number of other programme types, including UK-produced TV series, entertainment shows and sports programmes. But not news or **children's** programmes – at least, not yet. We all know how the very young are influenced by adverts and how they in turn influence their parents and what they buy. So I'm sure advertisers will be working very hard to try to get the law changed again in the future.

Now, even if it's OK for a programme to include this form of advertising, there are, thankfully, a number of conditions which apply. Firstly, the product has to be **relevant**. You cannot create the action or dialogue around the product; the product has to fit in with whatever's happening at a particular moment. So for example, a particular brand of washing powder might be OK on a table in a kitchen scene, but it would *probably* be out of place, and therefore not permitted, on a table in a **restaurant**. That all, of course, depends on the script – and very possibly somebody can think of a programme where this might occur quite naturally – but I think you understand the point I'm trying to make.

Secondly, a placed product shouldn't benefit from any obvious **promotion** in a programme. Actors are not allowed to go on about how good it is or mention its name so many times that viewers feel they're clearly being encouraged to buy it. And finally, for obvious reasons, a number of products that might negatively affect people's **health** or lead to addiction are banned from product placement – that of course includes cigarettes and alcohol, which are also banned from normal television advertising.

Now, viewers have to be told when a programme includes a placed product. To do that, the TV channel will show a symbol with the letter 'P' on the screen. And they have to do this on a minimum of **two** occasions – once at the beginning of the programme and once at the end. It also comes on after any advertising breaks, so it could appear as many as three times during a programme, and maybe even more.

Understandably, perhaps, there are a few concerns associated with product placement. Some people worry that it might affect the quality of programmes. Personally, with all these rules in place, I think that's unlikely. Certainly, it might be **distracting** for viewers, and take their mind off what's happening on screen. But that's hardly a cause for concern. No, what I think we should be most worried about is the …

Unit 2 Success!

Listening Part 3: Multiple matching

🔊 1.02–1.06

Speaker 1

My career on the pitch lasted twenty years, and during that time I was lucky enough to play for three of the biggest clubs in the country, so I had plenty of valuable experience. But of course, working with some of the players nowadays requires an additional kind of skill. They earn a lot of money and some of them have a very high opinion of themselves and their abilities. Dealing with *that* can be difficult, so when I started out, <u>I'd often pick up the phone and talk to my old bosses … ask them for a few tips.</u> They were my teachers when I was a player, but <u>they were also a great help to me in my early years as a manager</u>. I owe a lot of my success to them.

Speaker 2

Experience has taught me not to listen too closely to what other people say. Theatre critics have written some rather nasty things about me over the years. As I'll be explaining in my autobiography – when I eventually find the time, and the patience, to write it. But, no, you just have to ignore everyone else and get on with it. The key to success is to believe in yourself, to convince yourself you can do it every time you go on stage. I usually spend five minutes before a performance, looking in my dressing room mirror, telling myself how good I am. Terribly vain, I know, but it works.

Speaker 3

Young people nowadays think that success is all about being on the telly and having loads of money. For me, success is just deciding what you want from life, what your aims are, and then achieving what you set out to do … doesn't matter how much you earn or how famous or important you become. Not everyone can make it to the top, can they? As a matter of fact, when I left school I started training to be a chef – could have worked in some of the best restaurants if I'd qualified. But I decided early on that I'd be much happier running my own store and selling kitchen equipment. I've actually got two now – so I'm doubly successful!

Speaker 4
Success didn't come overnight for me. Indeed, it was several years before I actually had anything published. During the day I taught English in a private language school – for not very much money, I have to say – and by night I would scribble away in my flat until the early hours of the morning. Essays, short stories, novels – you name it, I had it rejected by publishers. But I was quietly determined and prepared to wait. I knew that it was just a question of time. Then, sure enough, one bright young editor read some of my work, liked what I was doing and gave me an opportunity. And I gave up the day job.

Speaker 5
It's never just one thing, is it? I mean, to begin with, luck often comes into it – like bringing out your product at the right time, just when people need it, or think they do, anyway. You can't always plan for that. And then there's skill, of course – knowing how to manage people, for example, or understanding how the market works. But in my book, success mostly comes down to hard work. You have to be prepared to spend seven days a week at the office and work maybe fourteen or fifteen hours a day. That's always my advice to budding entrepreneurs.

Listening Part 4: Multiple choice

🔊 1.07

(I = Interviewer; M = Mark Grant)
I: With me today is local man, Mark Grant, who spent the last eight months travelling round the world. Nothing particularly unusual about that, you may say, except that Mark successfully completed the 18,000 miles … on his bike. Mark, why did you do that? Were you hoping to break a record?
M: If I was, I failed miserably. The record stands at 175 days and it took me quite a lot longer than that. No, my aim was to raise funds through sponsorship for the Alzheimer Care Trust. My grandfather received a lot of support from them, and as he was the one who encouraged me to take up cycling when I was a teenager, I thought this would be a good way to repay them for all their help. I hope to give the charity a cheque very soon for four hundred thousand pounds.
I: Very impressive. And how do you feel now that you've achieved your goal?
M: Exhausted! No, naturally I'm delighted to have completed the journey and to be in a position to make such a large donation to the Trust. And I have to say I got very emotional last Sunday when I saw all the people who turned out to meet me at the finishing line. I had to get my handkerchief out to dry the tears. It was actually quite funny, though, to see the look of shock on a lot of people's faces when they saw my beard. Shaving wasn't part of my daily routine while I was cycling, so I wasn't quite as handsome as when I started out!
I: You mention daily routine. Tell us about that Mark. What was a typical day like for you?
M: Well, I tried to spend about twelve hours a day in the saddle, so I'd usually get up fairly early, somewhere between five and half past, maybe a bit later, do a few stretching exercises and listen to some relaxing music on my phone, just to ease myself into the day. Then it was breakfast. I don't normally eat very much in the morning but that had to change for this trip. I always made sure every night that I had plenty of food for when I got up. And then, after I'd eaten, I'd clear away and start cycling.
I: And didn't you ever get *bored* of it all? I mean twelve hours a day is a lot, isn't it, especially on your own.
M: I went through 23 different countries, most of which I'd never been to before, so I couldn't very well get bored. And I met so many friendly people on the way that I was hardly ever conscious of the fact I was doing it alone. I also had my music to entertain me, of course – *and* keep me awake. It was often a struggle at the end of the day to keep my eyes open and concentrate on the road.
I: Hm, dangerous. Did you ever have any accidents?
M: I didn't, fortunately. I nearly got blown off my bike, once or twice though. In fact the wind was by far the most difficult thing I had to deal with during the whole trip – particularly in south-east Asia where strong headwinds tore at my face and were really quite painful. It seemed as if the harder I pedalled, the stronger the wind decided to blow, which wasn't the case of course. But I did lose a bit of time and I got to Australia a little later than I'd intended.
I: Right, now, a lot of listeners were able to follow your progress via your blog. Did you have to take a lot of technological gadgets with you for this kind of thing?
M: Well, I wrote the blog on my phone, which I also used to send texts and listen to music. And phone people as well, of course. Then, on the handlebars I had a GPS, to show my position. And to power them I had a solar panel fixed to the top of the pannier rack at the back. But none of it weighed very much and it didn't take up too much space, so apart from worrying about getting it stolen, it wasn't really a problem.
I: And did anyone ever steal anything?
M: On the contrary. Everyone kept trying to give me things! I was amazed. In some places, people would come up to me and offer me small gifts. Or they'd invite me into their homes, and refuse to accept any money for the food they gave me. It was very heartwarming.
I: Mark, we're going to take a break for news. Don't go away just yet, though. After the news summary, we'll be opening up the phone lines for listeners' questions. So if you want to ask Mark …

Unit 3 Image and images

Listening Part 3: Multiple matching
🔊 1.08–1.12

Speaker 1
It's part of our lives today, isn't it? No one's really hiding anything – people know it's happening. When I buy a magazine and look at the photos of celebs and models, I know full well that they've been digitally altered. People can't look *that* perfect, can they! And surely, it's not just me. Everyone knows that retouching goes on, so there's nothing dishonest about it. As far as I'm concerned, it's fine. People should moan about something else!

Speaker 2
If I were one of those people on the cover of a magazine, I'm sure I'd want a bit of retouching to look fit and healthy – particularly when you're getting on a bit! Quite honestly, I think it's only fair. Famous people have their photos everywhere and we're looking at them all the time. I know people say that if they want the publicity then they have to accept everything that goes with it. But we've all got a job to do. If theirs is to look good in magazines, then the more help they get the better!

Speaker 3
I know we're seen as the bad guys here, but really, we're only doing what our readers want. We're producing the best-looking pictures that we can because that's what people expect to see. So, if anyone, they're the ones to blame. Our readers don't want to see models with black bags under their eyes because they had a late night! Or a spotty face! And if we make an actor's face a little slimmer – that's not going to hurt anyone is it? People have always liked to look at good-looking people – think of all the film stars in the past. And quite honestly, if we're talking about making people look good – maybe we should be talking about banning make-up!

Speaker 4
Sometimes you just have to laugh! I look at some of these photos and think – you must be joking! No one has a neck that long or legs that skinny! It gets a bit ridiculous at times. Personally, I don't object to a bit of retouching here and there, but frankly some of the pictures are so unrealistic. I mean, they have to be believable, don't they? Magazine artists need to limit themselves and accept that they can't go over the top and change people's appearance to the point that they no longer look human.

Speaker 5
For me, it's all about the fact that most people today are obsessed with appearance and how we all look. There's something in the newspapers nearly every day about all the eating disorders that young kids are suffering from, and why is that? Because many of them want to look like the people they see in the magazines. Photo manipulation simply makes it all worse and puts young people at risk. I'm well aware that the magazines want to sell more copies – it's a business for them. But I think they should behave more responsibly.

Listening Part 1: Multiple choice
🔊 1.13–1.20

1
You hear a man talking on a radio phone-in about a quiz programme he saw during the week.

Man: I felt I had to phone in because I was really surprised at some of the answers given on the 'Challenge Quiz' on Thursday evening. I'm no car enthusiast but even I know that the correct answers given to the contestants weren't always right. On at least three occasions the car makes weren't what was shown in the pictures. I'm usually impressed by the standard of this particular quiz, so it was a bit of a shock. The programme researchers really need to check their facts when planning to ask questions like these because I'm sure I'm not the only person who noticed this.

2
You overhear two friends talking about a film they've just seen.

Girl: Did you enjoy it? I loved the film. Robert Downey Junior is definitely one of my all-time favourites.

Boy: It's odd – I'm so used to seeing him in adventure movies. They suit his style of acting. You know, the fast-moving stories with lots of clever stunts and the love interest too.

Girl: I think it was good to see him trying something else. I mean, I've seen him in funny films before but not quite like this. I thought it was hilarious!

Boy: He's so talented, I reckon he could do nearly anything and do it well. How about Robert Downey Junior as a vampire – that would be worth seeing!

3
You hear someone leaving a voicemail message.

Man: I'm just phoning to say I won't be able to come round this afternoon because I've got an audition at 3.30! I couldn't believe it – it's ages since I last went for a part but this could be big. You said I should keep trying and you were right! I'm going for a part in 'Together', you know, the soap opera on Channel 6. I think I'm up against some stiff competition and I didn't sleep at all last night. We couldn't meet up somewhere this morning, could we? You always manage to calm me down! I'll buy you the biggest cappuccino and if I get the part you can come along and watch the filming? OK? Give me a ring soon.

4
You hear two mothers talking about their children's birthday parties.

Mother A: How was the party yesterday? Did Mia have a good time, and more importantly – did everything go smoothly?

Mother B: It was fantastic. And thanks for giving me the name of that magician. He was terrific. Mia was thrilled when he pulled an egg from behind her ear!

Mother A: That's a new one! Tommy's friends loved him when we had him last year. I still don't understand how he does those card tricks. Did the kids like those?

Mother B: I think he ran out of time. Maybe we'll get those next year. The high spot of the afternoon was when the rabbit came out of the hat!

Mother A: At our party it was a pigeon! The kids just love that sort of thing, don't they?

5

You hear part of a TV review programme.

Man: On paper, the new detective series on Channel 4 last week should have been a huge success. It had everything it needed to succeed – a lot of big names always help a new show. Also they had one of the best scriptwriters in the business who's written over a dozen successful crime series in his career. Somehow, though, it didn't work and a lot of people – myself included – felt let down by the first episode. The story line wasn't that strong and some of the acting could have been better. However, it was only the first episode and maybe next week's instalment will be an improvement. Let's hope so.

6

You hear a man phoning his friend.

Man: Hi! Are you going to see 'Coldplay' in London next Friday? I know you're a big fan.

Woman: Yeah. I'm so looking forward to it. I've never seen them on stage before. I was really lucky and got tickets at the last moment. How about you?

Man: You must have got the last ticket then. When I managed to get through they were sold out. I was hoping you might be able to take me into London, because I'm going to the première of the new James Bond film and I know the train will be packed.

Woman: I really wanted to see that too. But you can't do everything! Sure, no problem.

7

You hear a newscaster talking about an art exhibition at a local gallery.

Man: If you're going to the Walker exhibition at the Main Gallery this week, don't expect to see his painting of London Bridge. It won't be there. Visitors yesterday afternoon were shocked to see a space where the great canvas should be and there were worries that the painting had been stolen. There have been a lot of thefts from art exhibitions in the recent past, as we all know. In fact, the painting has been withdrawn because art experts are concerned that this may not be the original painting. They believe the colours lack the warmth of a genuine Walker. The American owners of 'London Bridge' had been reluctant to allow the painting to come to England and it's now been suggested they were aware it might not be the genuine article.

8

You hear a writer talking about her work.

Woman: When inspiration refuses to come I can't just sit there on my own and wait for something to happen. I have to get on with other things, talk to other people. That's often when I get my best ideas – when I'm concentrating on something else entirely. And once the ideas are flowing, my characters quickly take on a life of their own. Very often I have no idea what they're going to do or say next. In fact, when I start writing, I never know how my books are going to end. And I love that aspect of my work – it keeps me on my toes and stops me turning out the same, tired old stories.

Unit 4 Going away

Listening Part 2: Sentence completion

🔊 1.21

Mark Mitchell

Thanks mainly to concerns about climate change, the term 'food miles' has entered our vocabulary. Food miles tell us how far food travels between the place where it is grown or produced and the place where it is eaten – in other words, the distance from 'field to **fork**'. Go into any British supermarket nowadays and you might find pears from Argentina, grapes from Chile, strawberries from Spain or tomatoes from Saudi Arabia. In fact, around forty-five per cent of the vegetables and **ninety** per cent of the fruit eaten in the UK comes from abroad. These figures are a cause for concern to those consumers who want to reduce the negative effect of their everyday lives on the environment. Why? Well, because much of our imported produce arrives by plane and air travel is responsible for giving off large quantities of gases such as carbon dioxide, which, as we know, is a major cause of rising **global temperatures**. Indeed, at one point, in response to consumer demand, and in order to warn shoppers of the possible environmental impact of what they were buying, some supermarkets began putting a **sticker** of an aeroplane on produce flown in from abroad. Many people would refuse to put any food with one of these aeroplanes into their shopping basket, particularly so-called 'locavores', who avoid, if possible, any produce which has been imported, preferring instead to buy **locally grown** fruit and vegetables, and meat from nearby farms. As well as doing their bit for the environment, locavores will tell you that locally grown food is much healthier than imported food, which can lose important vitamins on long journeys.

But do we really need to be quite so worried about the distance our food travels? Some experts now say that the whole idea of food miles is too **simplistic** and therefore unhelpful to environmentally conscious consumers. Take apples for example. British apples are picked from

September to October. Some are sold fresh and the rest are kept in cold storage for use throughout the year. This is fine, initially, but keeping apples cold uses a lot of energy, and this of course creates those carbon emissions which are so bad for our planet. From **June** onwards, then, it becomes kinder to the environment to start shipping apples from New Zealand. Similarly, in summer, you can eat British lettuces with a clear conscience. But in winter, the energy needed to grow lettuces in heated greenhouses in Britain is greater than the environmental cost of importing them from Spain.

So it's not only a question of how far food travels but when it travels. And also, of course, how it travels, because the **form of transport** used makes a big difference. For example, food transported by sea is considered by some experts to be better than that which is flown in, because sea transport produces fewer carbon dioxide emissions.

Quite apart from environmental considerations, though, there's also the fact that **one** million people living in Africa are employed in the trade supplying fresh fruit and vegetables to the UK, a business which is worth several million pounds. If that business came to an end, many people in a number of African countries would be affected. This includes Kenya, which exports green beans to the UK at times when these are no longer in season here. 'Environmentally unfriendly,' say some. 'Not at all,' say others, because Kenyan farmers do not use **tractors**, and they use natural rather than chemical fertilisers, so their growing methods are far less polluting than in Britain.

The concept of food miles, then, is not wrong, it is simply incomplete as it does not consider the total energy used during the growing, transportation, production, storage and distribution of what we eat.

Unit 5 Fitting in

Listening Part 3: Multiple matching

🔊 1.22–1.26

Speaker 1
I often laugh about it now, but at the time it was quite hurtful. I felt I was being **left out**. I was the new girl in the department and they'd all been working together for years. Whenever someone had a birthday, they would all go out for a drink after work, but they'd never ask me if I wanted to go. They were the best of friends and I was an unwelcome outsider – that's what it felt like, anyway. And this went on for ages. I never thought about leaving, though – which is just as well because things are really good now. But it wasn't until I'd been in the job for about nine months that I began to feel like I was one of the crowd.

Speaker 2
When my dad got his promotion, we had to move to a different part of the country. And of course that meant me having to change schools, which I got a bit stressed out about. I thought everyone would make fun of my accent and I'd have trouble making new friends and everything. It wasn't long before I'd **settled in**, though. By the end of the first week I'd **got in with** a group of lads from my class who all played football at break time. We always had a good laugh, and we used to **hang around together** outside of school as well. I'm still in touch with some of them, even after all this time.

Speaker 3
When we first moved over here I had a pretty strong accent, which some of the other kids seemed to think was quite humorous. They had a bit of a joke about it, trying to imitate me and everything. It was all good-natured, but at first it used to get me down, and made me wish I was back in Australia. My parents **found out** fairly early on what was happening, and they told me just to ignore them all. So I did. And actually, the accent thing probably made it easier for me to get accepted. I was a novelty, almost like some kind of exotic creature from a faraway land that they could **show off** to their mates.

Speaker 4
Many moons ago, when I was about eleven, my parents wanted me to join the scouts. My dad had been in a group when he was younger and he kept telling me what a great time he'd had, camping and tying knots and all that sort of stuff. He even managed to convince me I might enjoy it. But I never really **took to** it like he had – mainly because there was no one there I particularly liked or **got on with**. I was very shy and I didn't mix well with other kids. I **stuck with** it for a while, but I left eventually – not long after my mum and dad had bought the uniform. They were fed up about that.

Speaker 5
I couldn't wait to move out to the countryside. I hated my job and I couldn't **put up with** the noise and the stress any longer. Some of my friends advised me against it – they said I'd miss the people, the energy and the hustle and bustle of the city. But they were wrong. I loved the peace and quiet, and the pace of life. And almost as soon as I'd moved in, I made a really good group of friends. But not long ago, while I was sleeping upstairs, someone broke into my cottage and stole a few things. It's been great living here, but I don't feel safe now on my own and I probably won't stay much longer.

Listening Part 1: Multiple choice

🔊 1.27–1.34

1
You hear a teenager talking to a friend about becoming a firefighter.

Boy: So how come you're still working in the supermarket? I thought you were going to apply to be a firefighter. Aren't you tall enough or something?

Girl: Cheeky thing! I'm not *that* short. And anyway, it doesn't matter how tall or short you are, as long as you pass the fitness tests. No, I've still got to wait another six months – till my eighteenth. I'll be old enough to start training then.

Boy: And what about your glasses? You never see firefighters wearing specs, do you?

Girl: Yeah, I was a bit worried about that. But I checked it out on their webpage, and I don't think it'll be a problem. You can be a firefighter with worse vision than I have.

2
You hear a wildlife cameraman talking on the radio about his work.

Man: Obviously, there's an element of risk involved. I often spend long periods on my own in some very isolated places, and if I'm attacked by a bear or bitten by a snake there's no one there to help me. But I value my personal safety and take precautions to prevent that kind of thing happening. Actually, to be honest, it's a rather dull and monotonous existence much of the time. Last year I spent six weeks alone in a Himalayan hut for just five minutes' footage of snow leopards. Next month I'll be trying to film pumas in the Andes. Of course, I may not succeed, but that's the attraction for me. Never knowing if you'll get what you want. Because when you do, it's priceless.

3
You hear a woman talking about a walking holiday she is going on soon with some friends.

Woman: We're spending another week in the Lake District next month. Just a small group of us. I have to say I'm looking forward to not having someone telling me what to do every day. We had a guide the last two times we went. Steve his name was. Nice chap – very competent. Not like these guides you hear about that get lost or make you walk further than you really want to. In fact, he phoned Julie up to see if we'd be needing him again. But we're going to do it without him this year. We'll be able to get up when *we* decide and we can plan our own walks. It should be fun.

4
You hear a commercial fisherman being interviewed on the radio.

Interviewer: Is it hard being away from home for so long?
Fisherman: It would be really tough if I was married and had kids, like some of the other guys. But in my case I guess you could say the crew is my family. We live, work, eat and breathe together for weeks on end.
Interviewer: Do you ever get fed up with each other?
Fisherman: Sure, we have arguments from time to time, just like families do. But we talk together and sort things out. You have to. The thing is that living conditions are cramped, even on the larger boats, and it's difficult to get away from each other. Sometimes I'd do anything for a bit of space to myself.

5
You hear a British woman talking about travelling to Mongolia.

Woman: The whole reason for going to a place like Mongolia is to experience a different way of life. And to do that you need to be prepared to put up with conditions you might complain about on a holiday at home. Let's face it, you aren't likely to get much of a feel for the country if you stay in a five-star hotel. Spending a week with the nomads on the other hand gives you a wonderful insight into life in Mongolia. OK, so you might not sleep so well in a tent, and maybe some of the food isn't what you would normally choose to eat. But it's a real privilege to spend time in the presence of these warm and fascinating people.

6
You hear an elderly man talking about retirement.

Man: I'm still very active, so I can't complain. Not like some people I know who've retired. You see it with some of my neighbours – they're grumpy, irritable and they spend half their time moaning. Probably because they never do anything. The couple who live next door to me just sit in front of the telly all day – you never see them. You can't cut yourself off like that – you've got to get out and do things. If I'm not up in the hills walking, I'm in the local library or playing bowls. I never stop. I just get a bit worried now and then that one day I won't have my health and I won't be able to do all the things I do now. I wouldn't like that.

7
You overhear a woman talking about her husband.

Woman: Jim likes what he does. He seems to get on well with everyone, especially the young lads who are in there for long sentences. Some of the officers act as if they're in the army – they're good at giving orders but they don't talk much to the prisoners. Jim's different, though – he's just naturally friendly. You know, some of the inmates don't get a lot of visits, so they tell him all their problems. He's a really good listener. Actually, next month he'll have been working there for ten years. He's never stayed in a job for as long as that before. He used to be in the police force, of course, but he never really took to it. It was too stressful, so he left after a couple of years.

8
You hear an extract from a radio play.

Man: Here's a good job for you – in the hotel business.
Girl: Yeah, I saw that one. I'm not going to apply for it, though.
Man: Why not? You got some decent qualifications at school, and you've had a bit of experience here. I think you've got a good chance.
Girl: There's no point. It says you need *two years'* experience – like every other job that's going. I don't know how people like me are supposed to find work. Age discrimination, my dad calls it.
Man: Bah, don't worry about that. They say that so they don't get millions of applications. I'll write you a good reference. You've been a real help to me working here. I'm just sorry I've got to sell the café.

Unit 6 News and views

Listening Part 4: Multiple choice

🔊 2.01

(I = Interviewer; E = Emma Baines)

I: Today in the studio we have 18-year-old Emma Baines, who last year went to Barcelona to take part in an International Session of the EYP, the European Youth Parliament. Emma, I believe there was quite a tough selection process?

E: Yes, that's right. First of all, our school team got chosen at the regional meeting of EYP UK to represent the South-East at the National Session. And then at the National Session we were selected to represent the UK in Barcelona. I remember when I told my family – my little sister's face lit up with joy, and my dad could hardly speak, he was so emotional. And my mum – well, she said she'd known all along I'd be going and couldn't understand what all the fuss was about. I know she was proud of me, too, though.

I: How did you become involved in the European Youth Parliament in the first place, Emma?

E: Well, my mum's in local politics and she's always encouraged me to take an interest in what's going on in the world. Plus, I've always had strong views on everything. So, anyway, last year, the teacher in charge of the school debating society decided to take a team to the regional meeting, or Forum, as it's called, and she was particularly keen for me to go. I think she appreciated the fact that I have such a strong belief in my own opinions and abilities. The other teachers were always irritated by that, but she saw it as a strength.

I: So what was it like when you got to Barcelona?

E: Well, the first thing at any EYP event is the team-building. That's where you go off in groups and do loads of activities together to get you pulling together as a team and respecting each other's views. All the people in my group were from different countries, but because everyone's English was so good, I hardly noticed that, to be honest – at least not at that stage, anyway. The games and tasks we did were great fun – we had such a good laugh, and for that reason it was one of the highlights of the week.

I: And did you stay with the same group for the rest of your time in Barcelona?

E: Yes, that's right, we did. On the second day, all the team-building groups became working groups, or committees, and that's when we got down to the more *serious* work. Each committee had a different problem to deal with … um … ours was the effect of overfishing and pollution on Europe's seas – and we had to come up with solutions. I found this quite tough at first – I had very clear views as to what should be done, but of course, so did everybody else in the group. So we had to take every single suggestion into account, and weigh up the pros and cons before coming to any decisions. And that took time.

I: And then did you and your group share your solutions with the other committees?

E: Yes, we did. Each committee produced a written resolution, which we had to present to all the other participants on the last day, at the General Assembly. Then it was debated and put to the vote. This was what we'd been working towards over the previous few days and I was immensely pleased with what we'd produced and proud of how we defended it. One or two in my group were nervous at having to speak in front of so many people, and they were quite glad when it was all over. But I didn't want the moment to end.

I: What do you think you gained from going to Barcelona?

E: Oh, I came away with a greater understanding of Europe and what it means to be European. And I made a lot of friends – I just wish I'd been able to speak to some of them in their own language, instead of English all the time. Great people with great ideas – they're the next generation of politicians and I'm confident they'll take Europe forward – and improve it.

I: So, Emma, what are *your* plans for the future?

E: Well, I'm not going to rush into any decisions – there's no hurry. I'll probably go abroad next year to do voluntary work, and after that I want to go to university. Then *maybe* a career in politics – we'll see. But not local politics like my mum. The EYP has opened my eyes to bigger issues, problems which affect several different countries at once. That's where my interest lies.

I: Well, good luck with that, Emma – and thanks for coming to talk to us.

Language focus: Reported speech: Reported statements: Exercise 1b

🔊 2.02

1. My mum's in local politics and she's always encouraged me to take an interest in what's going on in the world.
2. Last year, the teacher in charge of the school debating society decided to take a team to the regional meeting.
3. I'll probably go abroad next year to do voluntary work and after that, I want to go to university.

Unit 7 Survival

Listening Part 1: Multiple choice

🔊 2.03–2.10

1

You hear a man talking about a documentary he saw on television.

Man: So this guy, right, he was taken up to this really remote part of Canada and just left there for three months to survive on his own. It was summer, so it wasn't too cold, and he camped in this really picturesque area, next to a lake, surrounded by snow-covered mountains and these spectacular pine forests – you know, the kind of thing Canada's famous for – but he was completely alone. Well, apart from all the animals that live there. In fact, I couldn't believe just how many different types of creatures he came across in such a small area – moose, beavers, eagles, porcupines, and these enormous grizzly bears! Incredible.

2

You hear a shop owner being interviewed on the radio.

Interviewer: In the face of the present financial crisis, many small businesses are having to close. How are you coping, Mrs Strong?

Mrs Strong: Well, to be honest, we've survived worse recessions than this one. We've managed to build up a reputation for selling only good quality items produced in this country. We find that people are prepared to pay a little bit extra for something they can rely on, rather than risk buying something made abroad which is low-priced but not guaranteed to last. We're more worried about the fact that a large number of hypermarkets seem to be popping up everywhere. Their prices are no better than ours, but people prefer to do all their shopping in one place.

3

You hear a teacher being interviewed on the radio.

Interviewer: Tiger Day is the last Sunday in September. Paul, your school is marking the occasion this coming Friday. What's the purpose of the event?

Paul: We want to draw our pupils' attention to the dangers facing tigers, and the different factors which threaten their survival. Children are used to seeing them in zoos, which is no bad thing, but most of them simply don't realise that there are very few tigers left in the wild. We want to put that right. I know that several schools in the area are hoping to raise a large amount of money to help with various international projects, but our children are rather young for that and we want to focus on the educational aspects.

4

You hear a woman talking about books and e-readers.

Woman: My son got me an e-reader for my birthday and downloaded some eBooks onto it for me. It's very smart and almost certainly doesn't attract as much dust as my book collection. But I've managed to get by all these years without an e-reader, and I'm pretty sure I can survive without one for many years to come, thank you very much. I don't want to sit in my armchair and look at a computer. I like to feel the weight of a book in my hands and the texture of the pages as I turn them. Call me old-fashioned, but I find it comforting.

5

You overhear a man speaking on his mobile phone.

Man: Did you survive the storm last night? ... No, nor did we. Actually, there wasn't much damage at all in our street ... no. A lot of trees were blown down and I think the house next door lost a couple of roof tiles, but that's about all ... yeah, we *were* lucky. Anyway, John, I've been trying to phone my dad, but he's not answering. He's probably alright, but I'd like to go round and check everything's OK. Would you mind if I came into the office a bit later this morning? ... Great, thanks. I've nearly finished those figures you wanted, so if my dad's alright, they should be on your desk by lunchtime.

6

You overhear a student speaking about her financial situation.

Woman: You know, I wouldn't be able to survive if I didn't work part-time. Some of my friends who aren't working are finding it really hard to make ends meet. OK, so we get a student loan, and the interest is low, and we don't pay it back till we start working, and all the rest of it, but it's not enough to live on. And anyway, I think the government should give us the money, not just lend it to us. We're the future; they should be helping us out more, like they did for my mum and dad's generation. They went to university and they both got a student grant, not a miserable loan.

7

You hear a man speaking on the radio.

Man: The main character in the story is an academic, a lecturer in Welsh at the University of Wales. Clearly I had to have some knowledge of the subject and I did a great deal of research into the history of the language while I was planning the novel. A friend of mine who's a journalist on a Welsh language newspaper gave me a lot of help and advice and I became something of an expert by the time I started putting pen to paper. I think it's wonderful that Welsh has managed to survive and prosper in the face of the growth of English, and I've tried to convey my enthusiasm through the protagonist.

8

You hear a woman talking to a friend about her first week as a teacher.

A: How was your first week? Did you get through it alright?

B: Yeah, I survived. Very tired but still alive.

A: Why's that then? Have the kids been giving you a hard time?

B: Not really. I did think I might have a few problems with bad behaviour, being so new to the job and everything, but the kids have been fine. And I can't really complain about the number of hours I have to teach – because it's my first year, I have a reduced timetable. No, what wears me out is the amount of preparation I have to do. Everything's new to me so I have to spend about three or four hours a night getting things ready for the next day. It's exhausting.

Listening Part 2: Sentence completion

🔊 2.11

John Taylor

Hello. My name's John Taylor and my passion is museums. **Surprisingly**, perhaps, given that I'm not a sailing enthusiast, one of my favourites is the National Maritime Museum in Cornwall. I've been to it every year since 2005, when I saw the **enormously popular** *Surf's Up* exhibition, about the history of surfing in the UK. The best exhibition I've been to there, though – and the one I want to tell you about today – was called *Endurance and Survival*, which I saw with my son, Paul, who was 13 at the time. We had a fantastic day and Paul, who *is* a keen sailor, always says that that was when his interest in boats and the sea **really began**.

The centrepiece of the exhibition was the *James Caird*, the small lifeboat in which Antarctic explorer Ernest Shackleton and five of his 27-man crew sailed an incredible 800 miles to South Georgia across some of the most dangerous waters in the world. They had **had to** leave the rest of the crew behind on a small island in order to go and look for help. That was in April 1916. Shackleton's ship, *Endurance*, had got stuck in the Antarctic ice almost a year and a half before that in January 1915, and their long battle for survival is surely one of the most epic adventures of all time. And did everyone **get back safely**? Well, yes, they did. **Incredibly**, Shackleton and all those who'd sailed on the *Endurance* lived to tell the tale.

Another amazing survival story which formed part of the exhibition was that of the Robertson family, whose yacht was attacked and sunk by whales in the Pacific Ocean. The disaster occurred in the summer of 1972, about 200 miles from the Galápagos islands. The five members of the family and their friend spent the next five weeks fighting for their lives, first in a life raft, and when that deflated, a small open dinghy. The only food they had was a tin of biscuits, half a pound of sweets, ten oranges, six lemons and a bag of onions! And there was enough water for just ten days.

And they still managed to survive! They had to collect rainwater and catch fish to supplement their provisions. And they also caught turtles which bumped into their dinghy. They were **eventually picked up** 300 miles west of Costa Rica by a Japanese fishing boat. And from there they were taken to Panama. There was a display of some of the objects that the Robertsons sailed with, but the thing Paul and I most remember was the dinghy. We still talk about it now and how incredibly small it was.

The exhibition also featured a fascinating look at the skills and personal qualities you need to have if you want to sail round the world. Paul's probably got what it takes, but I was left in no doubt that I would be **extremely foolish** even to think of doing it!

Now, the great thing about the National Maritime Museum is that there are always plenty of sections which **specifically cater** for children. This is not one of those museums where you **mustn't** touch anything. There are loads of interactive exhibits, with buttons to push and things to do. And when I took Paul, he was able to climb into the different boats on display and get a feel for what conditions must have been like for those who sailed in them. What really captured his attention, though, was the display of navigation equipment. He was interested by how it's developed over the centuries, and the exhibition gave him a real sense of how important it is for survival at sea.

As I said before, I'm no sailing enthusiast, but I'm always fascinated by the exhibitions at this museum. So anyone with even the slightest interest in the sea really **ought** to pay a visit.

And how much do you **have to** pay to get in? Well, the current prices are twelve pounds for adults, ten pounds for senior citizens, and eight pounds fifty for students and children aged five and over. Children under five **don't have to** pay. Students **need** to show their student card, of course, and senior citizens **should** take some proof of their age, just in case they're asked to provide it.

Now, if you get the chance, you really **must** go along and see the latest exhibition there. It's all about the … .

Unit 8 Brain games

Listening Part 4: Multiple choice

🔊 2.12

(S = Simon; R = Roberta)

S: So, how's your memory these days? Are you one of those people who can get through life without a diary – committing everything to memory and not having to write down a single thing? Or are you more like me – surrounded by lists for everything from meetings to shopping to birthdays to – well, you name it, I have to write it down or it goes straight out of my mind. And somehow I seem to have to remind myself of things more and more often these days! Well, today in the studio we have memory expert Roberta Tanner. So, Roberta – am I on the downward slope as far as my memory is concerned?

R: Not at all Simon! You just have a lot on your mind. You're also under a certain amount of pressure and when that happens we tend to forget things.

S: Mm, and what about you? Tell me – did you remember the time and date of this interview or did you have to write it down? If I looked in your bag would I find a load of lists?!

R: I admit – it was in my diary! But of course, I probably would have remembered something as interesting as this interview without that, anyway! And that's quite an important thing about memory – we tend to remember the interesting and exciting things that are coming up in our lives much more than the boring and mundane!
S: Human nature really.
R: It's also true that the harder we work at remembering something the longer we remember it for. For example, if you have to remember some things you need to buy – like chicken, potatoes and milk for example – it helps to make a funny picture with all the items. You could imagine a chicken drinking some milk with a potato on its head! Put that picture into your memory and even though it's not the most important part of your day, you'll remember to buy those things!
S: OK! Nice image! I've heard that repetition is another good way to remember things.
R: In the short term, yes it can be. Like when you need to keep information in your head before you write it down, like a phone number or an address, so you say it to yourself again and again. And it's one thing actors do to learn their lines for a part. They say them over and over again to themselves and in rehearsals until eventually they're word perfect!
S: Then after the play – when the actor has to learn a new part he forgets the last one?
R: Exactly – because he doesn't need it any more. Our brains are very good at prioritising memories.
S: I read something recently about chimpanzees and how it seems that they might have better memories than humans. What can you tell us about that?
R: Yes, it's interesting. Scientists in Japan have carried out a number of tests with chimps in recent years. And they think they have evidence that young chimps, in particular, may have a photographic memory.
S: That's where you can look at a page of text or a picture and remember everything that was on it. There was someone in my class at school who could do that. He got top marks in every test going, it was so annoying!
R: Yes. Well, it can certainly be very useful! Your classmate was very fortunate. Anyway, in one particular experiment, scientists tested chimpanzees against university students. They showed the chimps and the students a selection of different numbers, arranged in no particular order around a computer touch screen. The participants in the test had to memorise where each number was before all the numbers were quickly replaced with blank squares. They then had to touch the blanked-out numbers on the screen, one by one in the correct numerical order. The chimps performed brilliantly. They were able to do the test successfully even when the numbers were shown for very short times.
S: That's amazing. And the chimps did the test faster than the students, I believe.
R: That's right. And another interesting fact is that the chimps who did best in the test were all young. This might be relevant to human memory. It's quite possible that the photographic element of our memory is better when we're younger and we lose it with age.
S: Yes, I'm living proof that memory gets worse as you get older.
R: Well, you know what they say – 'Use it or lose it' …
S: Mm, yes, I think I ought to start doing more crossword puzzles …

Unit 9 A slave to routine

Listening Part 2: Sentence completion

🔊 2.13

Greg Chandler
Hello, I'm Greg Chandler and I'm here to tell you a little bit about my latest book and its main themes. Until now, as you may know, all my books have been novels, the last of which was called 'Fast and furious'. In contrast, the title of this new one is '**Take it slowly**' and it's my first work of non-fiction. The book came out of a realisation that we never seem to take pleasure in the moment. We spend all our time nowadays running around, always in a hurry, thinking about what we've got to do next, and not what we're doing now.

As soon as we wake up, we **check the time**: it's the first thing we do every day. And then throughout the rest of the day it's the clock that determines our behaviour, that dictates what we do and when we do it. And we seem to rush around, in this mad, non-stop race against time, doing everything as quickly as we possibly can. We have this unhealthy addiction to **speed**. We need to have the fastest possible internet connection, we want to know the quickest route from A to B, we eat fast food, we speed-read and we even look for a partner through speed-dating. What we really need to do is slow down and **enjoy life**. It's as simple as that. But we seem to have forgotten how to do it. And that's what this book is about – helping people learn to do something which should really be second nature.

So what's my main advice in the book? Well, before you do anything else, it's important to embrace the belief that your life would indeed be better if you took things more slowly. That's the key. And once you've accepted that, then my number one tip is always 'Don't **wear a watch**'. The first step to taking control of your time is to pay less attention to it, give it less thought. I don't wear a watch, and I still get to meetings on time, I'm still aware of time, but it doesn't dominate my life, and I'm not glancing at my wrist every five minutes worrying about what time it is.

Then there's the whole area of eating; taking time over your food, not rushing it. For example, always eat your breakfast sitting down, not **standing up**. It's an important meal, perhaps the most important one of the day, so set aside enough time in the morning to sit down and enjoy it. Also, chew your food. Don't swallow it before you've had time to take in the flavour. And it's worth sitting quietly for a few moments before **eating a meal** – it'll slow you right down and help you appreciate your food.

Now this leads me on to the Slow Food movement, about which there's a whole chapter in my book. The Slow Food movement is a non-profit organisation that promotes food which is good, clean and **fair**; that is, food which tastes good, which uses clean production methods that respect the environment, and whose producers are paid a **fair** wage. It's a reaction to food produced on an industrial scale which is often none of these things – fast food, ready-made meals, that kind of thing.

But Slow Food is not the only organisation in the 'slow' movement. You may also have heard about the Cittàslow, or Slow Cities. Well, towns mainly, because they all have under fifty thousand inhabitants. There are around two hundred towns in the network now, and that's in thirty different countries. To become members they all have to agree to a set of over **fifty** goals and principles, which aim to improve the quality of life there, to enable people to live at a slower, healthier, more relaxed pace.

Now, to achieve this, they do anything from planting flowers in the high street to promoting healthy eating or improving the traffic system. They value local traditions and more **traditional** ways of doing things, they prefer bikes to cars, peace and quiet to noise. It's about celebrating diversity and rejecting the fast-lane, homogenised world you see in so many cities across the globe. Have you ever thought about this town and how it could …?

Listening Part 3: Multiple matching

🔊 2.14–2.18

Speaker 1
I do everything you're supposed to do. I go to bed early, I'm careful not to eat too much in the evening, I do lots of exercise … But it usually takes me ages to get to sleep, and then I toss and turn all night, and keep waking up every half hour. The funny thing is, I never have any problems when I'm away on business. Most of my colleagues sleep really badly in hotels – there's too much noise, the bed's too small, the air conditioning keeps them awake … but *I* always go out like a light and sleep right through until the alarm goes off. It's the same when I'm on holiday.

Speaker 2
A lot of my friends at school aren't sleeping too well at the moment – we've got exams coming up and we're all a bit nervous. But *I* have to get up really early every morning to get the train to school, so it's a really long day for me. And when I eventually get to bed, I fall asleep immediately – almost as soon as my head hits the pillow. Mind you, I've always been like that, even when I was a baby. My mum or dad would put me in the cot and I'd be asleep before they'd even left the room. They got a bit worried about me, apparently – seemed to think it was strange that I didn't cry more.

Speaker 3
I can't remember the last time I had a good night's sleep. Age has a lot to do with it, but to be honest, I've always been a light sleeper. The slightest noise and I'm wide awake. There's no point just lying there, so I get up, perhaps make myself a hot drink, and then I usually get on with the housework – do some ironing, clean the bookshelves, that sort of thing. I've even been known to do a bit of gardening at 3 o'clock when it's still completely dark outside! But as long as I'm moving about, doing things, that's the main thing – it's the only chance I have of getting back to sleep.

Speaker 4
I usually wait up for my daughter when she goes out at the weekend. I like to be there for her when she comes home. It's not that I'm worried about her – we did enough of that when she was a teenager. No, I just like to hear how she got on, whether she met anyone nice … The thing is, I don't sleep that well, anyway – my back keeps me awake. It starts to hurt if I'm in the same position for too long. So I'm much happier being up and about, doing things, moving around or even just sitting in the kitchen, listening to the radio. And of course, when my daughter comes home in the early hours of the morning, I do so enjoy our chats.

Speaker 5
I do shift work – two weeks on days, then two weeks on nights. I'm working nights at the moment. It's not too bad really. I treat myself to a big breakfast when I get home – eggs, mushrooms, toast, that kind of thing – do a few household chores, watch a bit of daytime telly maybe, then go to bed around 11 o'clock. After that, I'm dead to the world for about seven hours – nothing can wake me up once I've drifted off. Well, almost nothing. I have these really thick curtains in my room to shut the light out. And I wear one of those face mask things over my eyes. Otherwise I'd have real problems sleeping.

Unit 10 Getting on

Listening Part 3: Multiple matching

🔊 2.19–2.23

Speaker 1
Like nearly every teenager I went through a rebellious stage when nothing my parents did was right. Looking back, I think I often did things just because it was the opposite of what my parents wanted. Instead of going to university I went travelling for two years and I know they disapproved. Eventually I settled down to studying and now I really wish I'd gone earlier. I had a good time in those two years but if I'd gone straight to university I think I'd have got a much better degree. Well, you can't go back. It just goes to show that parents do sometimes know what they're talking about.

Speaker 2
I actually got on really well with my parents when I was in my teens. That's not to say we didn't have our differences. There were a lot of rows, I remember, over food in particular. Once, I was on some crash diet or other and Mum got very cross and worried about me not eating enough. Dad, on the other hand, told her to let me get on with it – he recognised that it was just a phase and sure enough I soon started eating properly again. I really appreciate my dad's understanding and we still get on well today.

Speaker 3
Oh yes – I argued with my parents about everything under the sun! Our biggest conflict was about what I wore. I was very much into black at the time and my mum couldn't stand it. To be honest, neither could my dad. Once I remember, she threw out a long, black coat I'd saved up for for months. I loved that coat and wore it everywhere. When I found out that she'd got rid of it we had an enormous row. I don't think I've ever forgiven her for that. Our relationship has never been that good and I don't see them very much these days.

Speaker 4
On reflection, I think I must have been the perfect teenage daughter. I was happy to do everything my parents wanted and never thought they were being too strict. I didn't stay out late, always completed my homework on time and socialised with youngsters my parents approved of. They gave me good careers advice and I took notice of it. I guess I respected them – both of them, although my dad was a bit in the background a lot of the time. They gave me a certain amount of freedom and I never pushed the limits. Now though, I sometimes feel that I missed out in a strange way! My friends have great tales of going to forbidden concerts and breaking rules. Sometimes I wish I were young again and then I would rebel – just a bit!

Speaker 5
Dealing with my own children makes me realise what a terror I must have been to my parents. You name it, I did it. They never knew where I was or what I was doing. I stayed out till all hours some weekends. Life was just so exciting then and in my opinion my parents had no idea of the fun I'd be missing if I stuck to their rules. They were adults and didn't know how young people felt. It never occurred to me that they'd ever been teenagers themselves! My kids, on the other hand, are calm and not at all rebellious. Not that we have too many rules – and we do talk them over as a family. I hope they stay that way.

Listening Part 4: Multiple choice
🔊 2.24

(I = Interviewer; H = Helen James)

I: With us today we have Helen James, who runs a volunteer programme called *Age Exchange*. What's the aim of the programme, Helen?

H: Well, basically, it's to bring the young and the old in our community together. The young people – aged between 16 and 18 – go into care homes for two hours a week over a ten-week period, to teach residents how to use new technology – computers, smartphones, tablets and so on. And in return, their elderly students might tell the teenagers stories about their past, talk to them about the local area, or teach them something – crafts, games, songs, or any other talents they may have. The volunteers sometimes learn more than they do at school!

I: What do the older people want to use the technology for?

H: Well, often the first thing they want to do is learn how to make video calls, and send emails to sons and daughters who maybe live in another part of the country, or even abroad. And then what to do if they get an email with a photo of a grandchild as an attachment – how to open it, what to do with it. It may be obvious to you and me, but it can cause headaches, and even stress to older people coming to the Internet for the first time.

I: It's a whole new world for many of them, isn't it?

H: Yes, but they quickly see the attractions. The volunteers all say that the older people love using the Internet to look at images of buildings from their past – the house they grew up in, the school they went to, the church they got married in. This sparks off lots of different memories and gets them talking to the teenagers about their younger lives. The teenagers talk about their own lives too, and the two age groups share and compare experiences. It's of enormous value to everyone involved.

I: Yes, it must be. And you were talking to me before we came on the air about the many other benefits of the programme to the young volunteers.

H: That's right. They learn to express themselves more clearly, to explain things carefully and patiently to elderly people, who have little or no idea about something which comes so naturally to young people. They become good listeners, too – they ask questions, show interest, smile … and this, plus the feeling that they are doing something useful, gives them much greater confidence in themselves.

I: And what sort of things do the elderly participants teach them?

H: Things like card games, recipes and songs, mainly. There was one eighty-year-old lady, though, who taught a young lad to sew. He got a hole in his favourite t-shirt when he was at the care home, so she showed him how to mend it. He didn't tell his mates because he knew they'd laugh at him, but his younger sisters found out and they kept getting him to sew things for them! They were very grateful, though.

I: I should think so, too! Now, Helen, do you give the volunteers any help before they start on the programme?

H: We do, yes. We run a series of four training sessions. It's not always easy to fit them in around everything else that goes on in the volunteers' lives – exams, sports activities, part-time jobs – but we manage somehow. During the sessions, we give them a profile of the older person they're partnered with, which includes hobbies, interests and technology needs. Then we get them to make a plan of what they intend to do in their ten weeks.

I: And do they have to keep to this plan – achieve all their objectives?

H: Not at all. In fact, we encourage them to make 'just chatting' the most important activity. They learn so much from that – including the fact that old people are not boring to be with, after all. They find getting to know them just as interesting as getting to know people of their own age. And the elderly participants, for their part, realise that teenagers today are not all rude or lazy – they're often surprised to discover they can be very pleasant, caring people!

I: Well, that's reassuring! Helen, thank you so much for coming on the programme today. We're going to continue now with …

Answer key

Unit 1 Influence

Vocabulary 1: Influences page 6

2a
1 have   2 encourage, setting
3 looked   4 shape   5 copy

2b
1 A   2 C   3 E   4 D   5 B

Reading and Use of English Part 7: Multiple matching page 7

2
1 D   2 B   3 C   4 D   5 A
6 C   7 B   8 A   9 B   10 D

Listening Part 2: Sentence completion page 8

3
1 chocolate bar   2 company logo
3 international   4 children's
5 relevant   6 restaurant
7 promotion   8 (people's) health
9 two   10 distracting

Language focus 1: Present tenses: Present simple and continuous page 9

1
I'm trying describes an action in progress at the time of speaking. The same is true of *I think* and *you understand*, but these are both stative verbs, which are not normally used in the present continuous.

2
1 (*present simple*) occurs **c**
2 (*present continuous*) *'m using* **a**
3 (*present continuous*) *'re (always) advertising* **d**
4 (*present simple*) *influence* **e**
5 (*present continuous*) *is becoming* **b**

Present perfect simple and continuous page 9

1
1 These are both situations which started in the past and still continue in the present. The simple, and not the continuous, is used because the verbs *exist* and *be* are both stative verbs.
2 *For* is used with a period of time (*many years*) to show how long something has lasted.

Since is used with a point in time (*February 2011*) to show when something started.

2
1 c   2 a   3 b

3
1 In **a** the simple form is used to emphasise the fact that the activity has been completed. The continuous form is used in **b** to talk about a recent activity which may or may not have been completed; in this case, though, it clearly has not.
2 In **b** the continuous form is used to suggest that the situation is temporary; the speaker uses the simple form in **a** to indicate that the situation is permanent.
3 The continuous form in **a** conveys the idea of repetition, that the sister has been to the class on a number of occasions. The simple form in **b** indicates that this is one occasion and the sister is at her Pilates class now.
4 Both activities have recently finished and both statements could have been made by the same speaker for the same situation. In **a**, however, the focus is on the duration of the activity and this is conveyed by the continuous form; in **b** the focus is on the number of completed emails. The continuous form is not used when mention is made of the number of things that have been completed.

4
1 have/'ve been staying   2 have/'ve just started
3 do not/don't have or have not/haven't got   4 own   5 live   6 is helping/has been helping   7 have/'ve seen   8 am/'m thinking   9 costs

Vocabulary 2: The weather page 10

2
1 fine, cloud, pour
2 hard, dropping
3 light, blazing, intense
4 winds, rainfall
5 spell, heavy

Reading and Use of English Part 1: Multiple-choice cloze page 11

2
1 C   2 B   3 A   4 B   5 A
6 B   7 D   8 C

Language focus 2: Past tenses page 12

1 and 2a
1 *was walking* past continuous, *blew* past simple
2 *had finished* past perfect simple, *started* past simple
3 *had been snowing* past perfect continuous

2b *Possible answers*
1 The past continuous (*was walking*) is used to talk about an activity that was in progress when another, shorter action was completed; the past simple (*blew*) is used for the shorter action.
2 The past perfect simple (*had finished*) is used to talk about an action which was completed before another action (*started*) occurred.
3 The past perfect continuous (*had been snowing*) is used to describe and focus on the duration of an activity occurring before and up to a point of time in the past (*that morning*).

3
1 was shining   2 (had) said
3 packed   4 set
5 had been driving   6 noticed
7 got   8 had clouded   9 had dropped   10 decided   11 had promised/had been promising
12 were changing   13 (were) getting   14 opened   15 began

Writing Part 1: Essay page 12

1
1 reference sites on the Internet discourage [pupils] from thinking for themselves.
2 makes shopping very impersonal

2a
Expressing your own opinion
In my opinion
I personally feel
Saying what others think
many people believe that
many consider these to be
it is widely felt that

2b
however, for example, Whilst, as, Furthermore, (Travel) is another area, For one thing, In addition, Finally, because, To sum up, although

2c

influence (noun): *effect, impact, consequences*
cause (verb): *leads to, mean, is responsible for, have resulted in*

3

Sample answer

New technology is an important part of everyday life for large numbers of people. In my opinion, it has had a very positive influence on the way we live.

For one thing, it has improved relationships between people. We can communicate with each other at any time of the day using emails, messages or video calls, all at a low cost. This is particularly useful for people who live a long way from their friends and families.

Technology has also had a positive impact on our leisure time. The use of computers and other devices means we can do our work faster and more efficiently than before, so we have more time for ourselves. In addition, we can shop or play games on our computers or phones during this free time.

Finally, technology has led to improvements in sport. Football referees can use microphones to communicate with their linesmen in order to make better decisions. Similarly, in tennis, umpires can consult virtual 3D images when they are not sure if a ball is in or out.

In conclusion, technology is clearly a positive influence in many areas of our lives.

Unit 2 Success!

Listening Part 3: Multiple matching
page 14

1

1 C   2 H   3 E   4 A   5 F
(B, D and G are not used)

2

Speaker 1 C   I listened to the advice of other experts.
… so when I started out, I'd often pick up the phone and talk to my old bosses, ask them for a few tips.
… they were also a great help to me in my early years as a manager.

Speaker 2 H   You need to have confidence in your own ability.
The key to success is to believe in yourself, to convince yourself you can do it every time you go on stage.
I usually spend five minutes before a performance, looking in my dressing room mirror, telling myself how good I am.

Speaker 3 E   A successful person is someone who accomplishes their goals.
For me, success is just deciding what you want from life, what your aims are, and then achieving what you set out to do …
But I decided early on that I'd be much happier running my own store and selling kitchen equipment. I've actually got two now – so I'm doubly successful!

Speaker 4 A   I had to be patient for success to come.
Success didn't come overnight for me. Indeed, it was several years before I actually had anything published. But I was quietly determined and prepared to wait. I knew that it was just a question of time.

Speaker 5 F   A combination of factors is required to become successful.
It's never just one thing, is it?
… to begin with, luck often comes into it
And then there's skill, of course …
But in my book, success mostly comes down to hard work.

Word formation: Adjectives
page 15

1

lucky; (in)valuable; additional

2

1 pleasant   2 uncomfortable
3 worrying   4 exhausted
5 harmful   6 careless
7 ambitious 8 unattractive

Reading and Use of English Part 6: Gapped text page 16

3

The article mentions the following general points:
- His career before he set up his online sweet business
- How and when he came up with his idea
- How he started the business
- The early days
- A problem which was solved
- How the business has grown
- His criteria for choosing the sweets he sells
- Advice to would-be entrepreneurs

4

1 F   2 A   3 E   4 G   5 C
6 B   (D not used)

Help page 16

Possible underlinings

A   It … boxes of traditional sweets
B   success … strong vision … sweet shop from his childhood.
C   These … so much interest … 9 December.
D   continue production … traditional sweets
E   To begin with … it … small operation
F   After graduating … a company that made automatic doors
G   However, after the first half-year … as orders grew.

5

1 c   2 f   3 e   4 a   5 d
6 b

Listening Part 4: Multiple choice
page 18

2

1 C He wanted to collect money for an organisation.
… my aim was to raise funds through sponsorship for the Alzheimer Care Trust.
I hope to give the charity a cheque very soon for four hundred thousand pounds.

3

A His grandfather encouraged him to do it.
Not stated.
My grandfather … encouraged me to take up cycling when I was a teenager.
B He was trying to break the world record.
He implies he was not.
Interviewer: *Were you hoping to break a record?*
Mark: *If I was, I failed miserably. The record stands at 175 days and it took me quite a lot longer than that.*

Help page 18

Possible underlinings
3 It was <u>important</u> for Mark <u>each morning</u> to
4 While he was cycling, Mark <u>frequently felt</u>
5 Mark says that <u>high winds caused him</u> to

145

6 What does Mark say about the technological equipment he took?
7 In some countries he visited, Mark was impressed with

4 and 5
2 B   3 B   4 C   5 A   6 A
7 B

2 What does Mark say about the people who came to welcome him home?
A Some of them were crying.
It was Mark who was crying: *I got very emotional … I had to get my handkerchief out to dry the tears.*
B Many were surprised by his appearance.
Correct answer *It was actually quite funny, though, to see the look of shock on a lot of people's faces when they saw my beard.*
C There were not as many as he had expected.
Not stated (there were probably more than he expected) *I got very emotional last Sunday when I saw all the people who turned out to meet me at the finishing line.*

3 It was important for Mark each morning to
A get up at exactly the same time.
He got up early but not always at exactly the same time: *I'd usually get up fairly early, somewhere between five and half past, maybe a bit later*
B have a large breakfast.
Correct answer *I don't normally eat very much in the morning but that had to change for this trip. I always made sure every night that I had plenty of food for when I got up.*
C phone home.
Not stated *… and listen to some relaxing music on my phone.*

4 While he was cycling, Mark frequently felt
A fed up.
Not stated *I went through 23 different countries, most of which I'd never been to before, so I couldn't very well get bored.*
B lonely.
Not stated *I met so many friendly people on the way that I was hardly ever conscious of the fact I was doing it alone.*
C tired.
Correct answer *I also had my music to … keep me awake. It was often a struggle at the end of the day to keep my eyes open and concentrate on the road.*

5 Mark says that high winds caused him to
A progress more slowly than planned.
Correct answer *But I did lose a bit of time and I got to Australia a little later than I'd intended.*
B lose confidence in his cycling ability.
Not stated (he lost time, not confidence) *I did lose a bit of time …*
C fall off his bicycle and injure himself.
He says he nearly did:
Interviewer: Hm, dangerous. Did you ever have any accidents?
Mark: *I didn't, fortunately. I nearly got blown off my bike, once or twice though.*

6 What does Mark say about the technological equipment he took?
A It wasn't very heavy.
Correct answer *But none of it weighed very much …*
B There was too much.
Not stated (he simply lists the equipment and its functions)
C Some of it was stolen.
He had to be careful, but none was stolen:
Mark: *… apart from worrying about getting it stolen, it wasn't really a problem.*
Interviewer: And did anyone ever steal anything?
Mark: *On the contrary. Everyone kept trying to give me things!*

7 In some countries he visited, Mark was impressed with
A the quality of the food.
Not stated (he mentions food but not the quality) *… they'd invite me into their homes, and refuse to accept any money for the food they gave me.*
B the generosity of the people.
Correct answer this is explained in the whole of Mark's last turn. He says *I was amazed* and *It was very heartwarming.*
C the size of the houses.
Not stated (he mentions homes but not the size) *they'd invite me into their homes …*

Language focus: Comparisons page 19

1
The words given are those that appeared in the recording. The bracketed words are also grammatically possible.

1 than   2 as (so)   3 most
4 the, the   5 little (bit, lot)

2

Adjective/Adverb	Comparative	Superlative
fast	faster	the fastest
wet	wetter	the wettest
white	whiter	the whitest
early	earlier	the earliest
slowly	slower/more slowly	the slowest/most slowly
gentle	gentler/more gentle	the gentlest/most gentle
reliable	more reliable	the most reliable
good	better	the best
bad	worse	the worst
far	farther/further	the farthest/furthest

3a
1 d   2 c   3 e   4 b   5 a

3b
1 c   2 d   3 e   4 a   5 d

4a
1 Books are <u>much</u> more interesting than films.
2 It's better to try and fail <u>than</u> never try at all.
3 The people in my country are among the friendliest <u>in</u> the world.
4 The more qualifications you have, the <u>more easily</u> you will find a job.
5 The *Hunger Games* films are by far the most entertaining films that have <u>ever</u> been made.
6 Cats are not <u>quite</u> as sociable as dogs.
7 English is probably the <u>most</u> difficult language of all to learn.
8 Many of the mistakes in this exercise are the same <u>as</u> the ones that I often make.

Vocabulary: Sport page 20

1a

Underlined word	Normally associated with
a track	athletics
b pitch	football
c goggles	swimming
d court	tennis, basketball
e vest	basketball, athletics
f helmet	skiing, skating
g hole	golf
h trunks	swimming

1b

Sport	Place	Clothes & equipment	Other words
football	pitch	boots	referee, match
tennis	court	racket, net	umpire, match
basketball	court	vest	referee, time out
athletics	track	vest, starting blocks	meeting, field event
golf	course	clubs	hole, tournament
swimming	pool	costume, goggles, trunks	lane
skiing	slope	poles, helmet	slalom
skating	rink	knee pads, Rollerblades®, helmet	tournament

2

a taken up, take part, takes place
b silver, second, runner-up
c viewers, spectators, crowd
d beat, drew, won
e gone, playing, practise

Writing Part 2: Article page 21

3

Contractions: *I've (x 2), I'd (x 2), wasn't, I'm (x 2), don't, it's*
Phrasal verbs: *took up, gave up, carry on with, sign up for*
Conjunctions at the beginning of sentences: *Because, So*

4

Can you think of **a better way** of keeping in shape **than** taking part in a team sport?
as well as being **the fittest I've ever been**, I'm also **a lot happier**
… it was**n't nearly as enjoyable as** doing something together with other people.
I'm **much more able** to sit at my desk and carry on with my revision.
What could be **better**?

6

Sample answer
<u>Maximum participation; minimum disagreement</u>
Which sport should we choose if we want to include as many people in the school as possible? Swimming, of course. Most teachers and students can swim, and we could even persuade the staff in reception to take part.
 Our local swimming pool has eight lanes, so each race could involve at least eight people, and there could be many different types of races. Participating is more important than winning, of course, but think how thrilling it will be to watch four young, fit students race against four much older, slightly less fit teachers! Excitement is guaranteed and it could all take place on one evening.
 That wouldn't be the case with a tennis tournament, which would have to be played on many different days and also, wouldn't involve many people. Not everyone can play basketball or football, either, and team sports like these often lead to disagreements and disputes, which would not be good for student-teacher relations.
 Clearly, then, the swimming competition is the best choice. And anyone that doesn't participate can scream and shout from their seats. It'll be fun for everyone.

Review Units 1 and 2

Reading and Use of English Part 4: Transformations page 22

1 have/'ve been **feeling**
2 not/'nt **come** up with
3 have/'ve **known** Gary since
4 dirtiest beach I have/I've **ever**
5 are not/aren't **as** many students
6 is not/isn't **quite** as/so old

Reading and Use of English Part 3: Word formation page 22

1 different   2 easily
3 employment   4 length(s)
5 original   6 unchanged
7 successful   8 production

Vocabulary page 23

1
1 up   2 down   3 on   4 up, on   5 back   6 out

2
1 b rainfall   2 e snow
3 f winds   4 c breeze
5 d heat   6 a sun

Language focus page 23

1
1 don't believe   2 happened
3 walk   4 have just had
5 I'm going   6 was coming
7 noticed   8 picked   9 realised
10 belonged   11 has been living
12 had written   13 phoned
14 had found   15 was walking
16 went   17 had been worrying
18 contains   19 had dropped
20 had chosen

2
1 least, in, a, by
2 not, as, as, bit/little
3 many, as, such, less
4 many, worse, fewer
5 more, the, ever, quite

Unit 3 Image and images

Vocabulary: Appearance page 24

1
1 clear   2 wrinkled   3 slim
4 straight   5 full   6 thick
7 narrow   8 dull

2
1 b   2 d   3 a   4 e   5 c

Listening Part 3 Multiple matching page 24

2
1 D   2 F   3 B   4 H   5 A
(C, E, G not used)

3

Speaker 1: *people know it's happening … Everyone knows that retouching goes on, so there's nothing dishonest about it.*

Speaker 2: *I think it's only fair … But we've all got a job to do. If theirs is to look good in magazines, then the more help [famous people] get the better.*

Speaker 3: *that's what people expect to see. … Our readers don't want to see models with black bags under their eyes because they had a late night! Or a spotty face! … People have always liked to look at good-looking people*

Speaker 4: *I don't object to a bit of retouching here and there, but frankly some of the pictures are so unrealistic … Magazine artists need to limit themselves and accept that they can't go over the top and change people's appearance to the point that they no longer look human.*

Speaker 5: *all the eating disorders that young kids are suffering from … Photo manipulation simply makes it all worse and puts young people at risk.*

Language focus 1: Modals of speculation and deduction page 25

1
must be, can't have grown
could be
must have had
must be wearing

2a
a *could*   b *must*   c *can't*
may and *might* can be used in place of *could*

2b
1 perfect infinitive   2 continuous infinitive   3 simple infinitive

3
1 Jack **can't** have gone
2 This can't **be** Bath already
3 he **might/may/could** be there.
4 I must have been **doing** something else
5 it **might/may** not be – it's difficult to tell.

4 *Possible answers*
1
She must have passed because she's got a really big smile on her face.
She can't have passed because she's crying so much.
She might have passed – she seemed fairly confident this morning.
2
He must have gone shopping because the fridge is full.
He can't have gone shopping because there's no milk.
He could have gone shopping because he's been out all morning.
3
He must live near the college because he always walks here.
He can't live near the college because he spends a lot on buses.
He might live near the college because I often see him at the local café in the evening.

Reading and Use of English Part 5: Multiple choice page 26

4
It is mainly about Pixar.

5
1 D   2 A   3 C   4 B   5 A
6 C

Language focus 2: Relative clauses page 28

1

1 Yes. Both sentences are **defining relative clauses**: these clauses identify, or define, the thing (*cartoons* in **a**, *the film* in **b**) being talked about and are essential for our understanding of the sentence. Commas are not used in defining relative clauses and the relative pronoun *that* can be used in place of *which* or *who*.
2 The relative pronoun can be omitted in defining relative clauses only if it refers to the **object** of the verb in the relative clause. In **a**, *which* refers to *cartoons*, the object of the verb *adore*. In **b**, *which* refers to *the film*, the **subject** of the verb *won*.
3 In **c**, *which* refers to the whole of the preceding clause ('*Up*' was also nominated for Best Picture). In **d**, *which* refers to '*Up*'.
4 Both sentences are **non-defining relative clauses**. The information in non-defining relative clauses is not essential to our understanding of who or what is being written or spoken about in the main clause, so commas are used to separate the two clauses. The relative pronoun *that* cannot be used in place of *which* or *who* in non-defining relative clauses.
5 No, *which* after a preposition, and *whose* can never be omitted or replaced by *that*, whether the relative clause is defining or non-defining.

2
1 Last Saturday, *when* she stayed at my house, Sally slept in the attic, *which* my parents have converted into a guestroom.
2 I got exactly *what* I wanted for my birthday – a new wallet. It was the only thing *which* I really needed.
3 I don't see any reason *why* my parents won't let me have a sleepover party for my birthday.
4 Our headteacher, *who* is retiring at the end of the year, has been at this school for over twenty years.
5 An equinox is one of two days during the year on *which* night and day are of equal length.
6 There's a prize for anyone *who* can tell me the name of the actor *who* was born in Los Angeles in 1974 and *whose* films include *Titanic*, *The Aviator* and *The Wolf of Wall Street*.
7 I slept until half past nine this morning, *which* is very unusual for me.
8 The only person *who* I really get on with at work is leaving next week. She's got a job at The Grand Hotel, *where* her dad works as a doorman.

3
a) *The relative pronoun can be omitted in:*
2 It was the only thing I really needed.
3 I don't see any reason my parents won't let …
8 The only person I really get on with at work …

b) *The relative pronoun can be replaced by 'that' in:*
2 It was the only thing that I really needed.
6 There's a prize for anyone that can tell me the name of the actor that was born …
8 The only person that I really get on with at work …

Listening Part 1: Multiple choice page 30

1 C   2 C   3 A   4 B   5 B
6 B   7 A   8 B

Writing Part 2: Review page 30

3
1 **Plot:** the story of Merlin the wizard and King Arthur when they were both young. Each week they have a new adventure, often fighting magical monsters; brings in characters from the old legends
2 **Actors:** Bradley James and Colin Morgan, whose acting is superb
3 **Setting:** the time of King Arthur; location in a spectacular French castle and the Welsh forests,
4 **Special effects:** excellent use of special effects to create the monsters.
5 **Writer's opinion:** It's well acted, cleverly written and directed, and totally addictive.

4
1 appeal   2 episode   3 tells
4 cast   5 based   6 set

5 *Possible answers*
Paragraph 2: We learn some details about the main characters and the plot.
Paragraph 3: We learn about some aspects of the series that the writer particularly liked.
Paragraph 4: The writer sums up his opinion and says whether he thinks other people will enjoy it.

6
Sample answer
Are you a fan of science fiction? Even if you're not, you should try watching one or two episodes of one of the most successful TV series ever shown on British television – 'Doctor Who'.

The main character is the Doctor, a humanoid alien who travels backwards and forwards through time in a blue police box known as the Tardis. Police boxes were a common sight in Britain in 1963, when the series first appeared on television. The fact that 'Doctor Who' has lasted for over 50 years is proof of its popularity, and a good reason why you should give it a try.

So why is it so successful? Because it doesn't take itself too seriously. There's plenty of humour, particularly in the relationship between the Doctor and his human assistant, who face all types of aliens trying to harm or take over our planet. And the series stays fresh as the setting changes every week, so you never get bored. Every few years, the Doctor changes his appearance and you get a new set of actors, too.

Whichever version of 'Doctor Who' you see, you're sure to enjoy it.

Unit 4 Going away

Vocabulary and Speaking: Holidays and travel page 32

3
1 C taxied, B took off
2 D give you a lift, C pick you up
3 D rest, B enjoy
4 A delayed, C boarded
5 B put, D stayed
6 D trip, C tour

Reading and Use of English Part 2: Open cloze page 33

1
1 up   2 on   3 it
4 who/that   5 because/as
6 have/'ve   7 not   8 the
9 little   10 all

2
1 Samantha Lazzaris went to Puerto Rico instead of Costa Rica.
2 The travel agent had used the wrong booking code.
3 She had to spend £800 on three extra flights.

3
1 up   2 had   3 As   4 to
5 It   6 instead   7 other
8 would/will

4
1 phrasal verb   2 auxiliary verb
3 fixed phrase/preposition
4 preposition   5 pronoun
6 *instead of* is a preposition
7 pronoun   8 auxiliary verb

Reading and Use of English Part 7: Multiple matching page 34

2
1 B   2 C   3 D   4 C   5 A
6 B   7 D   8 C   9 B   10 A

Language focus: Gerunds and infinitives page 36

1a
1 letting, watch
2 to calm
3 afford, to have

2
1 a, f   2 c   3 e, d

3
- they kept <u>asking</u> us <u>to let</u> them <u>take</u>

asking: gerund after the verb *keep*
to let: infinitive with *to* after the verb *ask* (followed by the direct object, *us*)
take: infinitive without *to* after the verb *let*

- <u>to prevent</u> costly accidents (we now buy them each a disposable camera)

to prevent: infinitive with *to* to say why you do something

- They're cheap <u>to buy</u>

to buy: infinitive with *to* after the adjective *cheap*

- we don't have <u>to worry</u> about them <u>being dropped</u>

to worry: infinitive after the verb *have (to)*
being dropped: gerund after the preposition *about*

- the girls have stopped <u>asking</u> <u>to use</u> our cameras

asking: gerund after the verb *stop* meaning 'no longer do something'
to use: infinitive with *to* after the verb *ask*

- they keep <u>wanting</u> us <u>to stop</u> <u>to take</u> photos

wanting: gerund after the verb *keep*
to stop: infinitive with *to* after the verb *want*
to take: infinitive with *to* after the verb *stop* meaning 'interrupt one activity to do another' (also, infinitive with *to* to say why you do something)

- we always enjoy <u>looking</u> at their photos

looking: gerund after the verb *enjoy*
Note: in *Having said that* in Section C, the word *having* is a present participle (= although I/we have said that).

4
1 **to** protect
2 before **going**
3 need **to** put
4 Avoid **going** out
5 do not let your skin ~~to~~ burn.
6 don't forget **to drink**
7 Correct
8 get used to **wearing**
9 Correct
10 **Spending** time

Listening Part 2: Sentence completion page 37

1
food mile noun [C] a measure of the distance travelled by foods between the place where they are produced and the place where they are eaten.
Source: Macmillan English Dictionary

2
1 fork   2 ninety/90
3 global temperatures   4 sticker
5 locally grown   6 simplistic
7 June   8 (form of) transport
9 one/1   10 tractors

Word formation: Prefixes page 37

1
a unfriendly   b incomplete

2
1 dishonest   2 unlucky   3 illegal
4 impractical   5 incorrect
6 irrational

149

3
1 unpleasant   2 disqualified
3 unusual   4 discourage
5 unreliable   6 unable

Writing Part 2: Email and letter page 38

2
Sam has not said anything about the nightlife. You will lose marks in the exam if you do not address all the points in the question.

3
Paragraph 1: general reference to Paul's email
Paragraph 2: location and description of beaches
Paragraph 3: things to see and do in the local area
Paragraph 4: closing comments

4
a *If … then, and, As well as, as, also, where, when, Or else*
b *I'd recommend, One idea is to, Make sure you, you could*
c *top quality, lovely soft sand, extremely clean, so clear, colourful fish, warm sea, surrounding area, nearby mountains, pretty medieval villages, a craft market, local pottery is fantastic, a boat trip, seals and seabirds*

5b
Sample answer
Hi Susi,
Your friends are so lucky to be able to come to Spain on holiday in May. The weather is very pleasant in spring, and there aren't as many tourists as in summer.
  One place I'd recommend them to go to is Salamanca. It's full of historical buildings that they could visit, such as the twelfth-century university – the oldest in Spain – and two cathedrals. The countryside near the city is beautiful, too, especially the mountains to the south west – the Sierra de la Peña de Francia – where they could go for some lovely, long walks.
  Another area they should visit is Galicia, in the north-west of Spain. It has a stunning coastline, with sandy beaches in the west and rocky cliffs in the north. Tell your friends that it rains quite a lot there, but of course, the countryside wouldn't be so lovely and green if it didn't. The capital of Galicia, Santiago, has an amazing cathedral, and I'm sure they'll be impressed by the romanesque portico at the front.
  Let me know where they decide to go – maybe I could meet them somewhere.
All the best,
Javier

Review Units 3 and 4

Reading and Use of English Part 4: Transformations page 40
1 might have/might've thrown
2 must have/must've been tired because/as
3 had/'d better go
4 feel like doing anything
5 did not/didn't mean to
6 is somebody whose

Reading and Use of English Part 1: Multiple-choice cloze page 40
1 B   2 C   3 B   4 A   5 B
6 C   7 D   8 C

Vocabulary page 40
1 crooked   2 clear   3 thinning
4 wrinkled
5 trip   6 put   7 all

Language focus page 41
1
1 can't be, must/may/might/could be
2 can't have spent
3 might/could/may have phoned
4 must speak

2
1 which seems quite early
2 who was going camping
3 which/that had been prescribed
4 whose working day
5 for which they're not qualified
6 the reason why he decided
7 the café which/that is next to
8 when it snowed all day

3
1 visiting   2 to go   3 to do
4 looking/to look   5 go
6 seeing   7 to miss   8 having
9 to buy   10 leaving
11 Travelling   12 not walk
13 to get   14 to cycle
15 imagine   16 going
17 having   18 to get
19 getting   20 to see

Unit 5 Fitting in

Listening Part 3: Multiple matching page 43

1
1 E   2 H   3 D   4 A   5 F
(B, C, G not used)

Language focus 1: Time linkers with past tenses page 43

1a
1 for
2 Whenever
3 until, for
4 When
5 before
6 By
7 At
8 for, eventually, after
9 soon
10 While

2
1 *They'd all been working*   past perfect continuous
2 *someone had*   past simple
they would all go out   would + infinitive without *to*
3 *It wasn't*   past simple
I'd been   past perfect simple
I began to feel   past simple, infinitive with *to*
I was   past simple
4 *my dad got*   past simple
we had to move   past simple, infinitive with *to*
5 *It wasn't*   past simple
I'd settled in   past perfect simple
6 *I'd got in with*   past perfect simple
7 *it used to get me down*   used to + infinitive
8 *I stuck with it*   past simple
I left   past simple
my mum and dad had bought   past perfect simple
9 *I'd moved in*   past perfect simple
I made   past simple
10 *I was sleeping*   past continuous
someone broke into   past simple

3
1 Not long ~~time~~ after I …
2 It wasn't until I **had** been studying …
3 … before ~~of~~ leaving the house …
4 … attention **while/when** I was reading …
5 As soon as I **(had) got** up
6 … my friends **for** over half an hour …

7 … an hour after ~~that~~ I'd gone …
8 … but **in the end/eventually** I decided …

Reading and Use of English Part 5: Multiple choice page 44

3
1 A   2 B   3 D   4 C   5 D
6 B

Word formation: Nouns 1 page 46

1
1 inhabitants
2 investigation, distance
3 innovations, electricity
4 homelessness
5 living

2
appearance, performance
assistant, participant
building, meeting
cyclist, scientist
prediction, reduction
tiredness, weakness

3
a
~~patients~~ – patience
b
librarian – library
neighbourhood – neighbour
difficulty – difficult
retirement – retire
friendships – friend
absence – absent
arrival – arrive
replacement – replace
warmth – warm
patience – patient
c
difference, existence
argument, equipment
musician, politician
departure, failure
approval, proposal
length, width
childhood, likelihood
membership, championship

Reading and Use of English Part 3: Word formation page 46

1 survival   2 reliable
3 competition   4 freely
5 comfortably   6 colourful
7 reactions   8 unwelcome

Writing Part 2: Report page 47

1
These words should be crossed out:
1 *look* does not fit grammatically; it requires the preposition *at*.
2 *At first* has the wrong meaning; it is used to talk about the beginning of a situation and to contrast it with what happens later.
3 *during* is a preposition and would be followed by a noun (e.g. *during the lesson*) and not a verb phrase (*students walk into the building*).
4 *to put*; the verb *suggest* is never followed by the infinitive.
5 *for*; *for* **to** *do something* is incorrect when expressing purpose.
6 *However* introduces a contrast with a previous statement and is inappropriate here.
7 *loads of* is informal and does not fit in with the overall style of this report.
8 *themselves* has the wrong meaning.
9 *At last* has the wrong meaning; it indicates very strongly that you have been waiting for something to happen for a long time.
10 *paces* has the wrong meaning.

2
a
would: *a few improvements … would help to create …*
comfortable armchairs would encourage
It would also be a good idea to organise
These could include
I recommend setting up
b Firstly, To begin with, as soon as, when, in order to, so as to, Moreover, In addition, also, so, These (could include), or even, Finally, Lastly, which

3
Sample answer
Introduction
The aim of this report is to consider ways to attract more young people to the library.

Decoration
Firstly, it is important to create the right environment for studying – the reason why most young people come to the library. The white walls could be painted a brighter, more cheerful colour, perhaps with murals designed by the students themselves, and the hard, noisy floor could be covered with carpets.

Cafeteria
Another way to make the library appeal to young people would be to convert the area next to reception into a cafeteria. This would enable students to relax and socialise when they take breaks. Newspapers, magazines and graphic novels could be provided, and each table should have access to a power socket so that students can use laptops, tablets and other devices. Free wifi would, of course, also be available.

Textbook sale
Finally, I recommend letting students use part of the library at the end of each academic year for a second-hand textbook sale. This would be particularly popular with college and university students.

Final comments
I am confident that more young people would use the library as a result of these changes.

Vocabulary: Personality page 48

1
1 reserved = shy, unwilling to talk about or show one's feelings; the others all describe someone who enjoys meeting and talking to people.
2 patient = able to wait for a long time or deal with a difficult situation without becoming angry or upset; the others describe someone who gets angry easily
3 irritable = likely to become easily annoyed or impatient; the others describe a person who can be trusted to do the right thing.
4 sensitive = caring about someone and not wanting to hurt their feelings or likely to become angry or upset easily; the others might be used to describe someone who seeks out and/or is capable of dealing with difficult or dangerous situations.
5 nervous = worried, afraid, not calm; the others describe someone who remains calm and does not easily get upset or angry.
6 tolerant = willing to accept or put up with someone else's behaviour and opinions even if you disagree with them; the others could be used to describe someone who believes in themself and their own abilities and judgements.

Answer key

7 lazy = not willing to work or make an effort; the others describe someone who thinks about other people and wants to help them.
8 practical = making sensible decisions *or* able to do or make useful things; the others are negative and describe someone who is not polite.

Listening Part 1: Multiple choice
page 49
1 A   2 C   3 A   4 B   5 A
6 C   7 B   8 B

Language focus 2: The future
page 49
1
2 an action in progress at a particular moment
3 a possibility
4 an arrangement
5 a personal intention

2
1 going   2 should   3 well
4 are playing   5 has finished
6 likely   7 have been learning
8 hope

Unit 6 News and views

Reading and Use of English Part 6: Gapped text page 50
4
1 B   2 G   3 A   4 E   5 D
6 F   (C not used)

Reading and Use of English Part 1: Multiple-choice cloze page 52
2
b because the article concerns the future of print newspapers and the possibility of losing them.

3
1 C   2 D   3 A   4 C   5 B
6 D   7 D   8 C

Vocabulary: Making decisions
page 53
1
1 account   2 rush, weigh
3 mind, going   4 make, put
5 come, decisive   6 up to
7 rule

Listening Part 4: Multiple choice
page 54
3
1 B   2 A   3 B   4 C   5 C
6 A   7 A

Language focus: Reported speech: Reported statements page 55
1a
1 My mum's in local politics and she's always encouraged me to take an interest in what's going on in the world.
2 Last year, the teacher in charge of the school debating society decided to take a team to the regional meeting.
3 I'll probably go abroad next year to do voluntary work and after that, I want to go to university.

2a
Present simple changes to past simple.
Present perfect changes to past perfect.
Present continuous changes to past continuous.
Past simple changes to past perfect.
Will future changes to *would*.

2b
my → her
me → her
I → she
last year → the previous year
next year → the following year

2c
Direct speech → Reported speech
now → then
today → that day
tomorrow → the following/next day
yesterday → the previous day/the day before
here → there
this → that
can → could
may → might
could, *would*, *should* and *might* do not change.

3
1 My brother told me (that) he needed to go shopping that morning.
2 Mike said (that) they were both going out for a meal the following evening.
3 Helena told me (that) the previous afternoon/the afternoon before she'd/she had been to see the film I'd/I had recommended to her.
4 Elisa said (that) she'd/she had been looking forward to going there.
5 Amy said (that) she knew she should go to the doctor's that day but (that) she'd/she would probably go the following week/the week after instead.

Reported questions page 55
1b
Auxiliary verb *do*, *does*, *did* are not used in reported questions.
Verb tenses change in the same way as in reported statements.
Yes/no questions require the addition of *if* or *whether* when they are reported.
The word order in reported questions is the same as for statements (subject + verb).
Question marks are not used in reported questions.

2
1 He asked Emma what it had been like when she'd got to Barcelona.
2 He asked her if/whether she and her group had shared their solutions with the other committees.
3 He asked her what she thought she had gained from going to Barcelona.
4 He asked her what her plans were for the future.

Reporting verbs page 56
1
1 offered   2 suggested
3 admitted   4 congratulated

2a and b
a infinitive (*to do*)
offer, ask, promise, refuse, threaten
b object + infinitive
invite, advise, ask, encourage, persuade, recommend, remind, tell, warn
c gerund
admit, advise, suggest, deny, recommend
d object + preposition + gerund
advise (somebody against), congratulate (somebody on), accuse (somebody of), blame (somebody for), warn (somebody against)
e (*that*) someone should do something
suggest, insist, recommend

3
1 accused Jim of leaving
2 refused to look
3 (that) he (should) make up
4 asked her/Liz not to
5 for not making/having made
6 insisted on seeing

Writing Part 1: Essay page 56

1
The danger that we might lose our best politicians if they are not paid enough. (Also, that it is rare to find a poor politician.)

2
Paragraph 1: introduction, setting out the main issue
Paragraph 2: arguments against paying politicians more
Paragraph 3: arguments in favour of paying politicians more
Paragraph 4: conclusion, with the writer's opinion
This is a **balanced** essay because the writer considers **both** sides of the argument before giving their own opinion.

3
receive (much lower) salaries, be paid the same amount, make profits, give themselves large salaries, receive income, earn more, are not paid enough, deserve more money, reward

4 a and b
Giving your opinion: *I personally feel that, My personal view is that, I partly/fully agree that*
Introducing one side of the argument: *Some people believe that, On the one hand*
Introducing the other side of the argument: *However, others argue that, On the other hand*
Making additional points: *Besides, What is more, In addition (to this), Moreover, Furthermore*
Concluding: *In conclusion, On balance*

5
Sample answer
Many sportspeople earn extremely high salaries, which most of us can only dream of. While some people accept this as normal, others question whether it is fair or morally acceptable.

On the one hand, the best sportspeople, such as footballers or tennis players, perform to millions of spectators all over the world. Some people feel, therefore, that they should be paid well, in the same way as an author who sells millions of books or an actor whose films are seen in many countries.

On the other hand, the work that professional sportspeople do is just a way of having fun for the rest of us. Although it is true that they have to train hard, they work fewer hours than millions of others who do low-paid physical work. Furthermore, large sums of money can have a negative effect on the way sportspeople behave in public, and they can become poor role models to young people.

On balance, I personally feel that sportspeople should be paid less. The difference between what they earn and the salaries of most normal, hard-working people is too big and very unfair.

Review Units 5 and 6

Reading and Use of English Part 4: Transformations page 58
1 not long after he had/he'd
2 told Jane she was putting
3 if/whether I had/I'd taken
4 unlikely to win
5 its complete failure to
6 take into account/take account of

Reading and Use of English Part 2: Open cloze page 58
1 at 2 be 3 how 4 on
5 why 6 able/ready/willing/prepared 7 whether 8 not/never

Vocabulary page 59
1
1 mannered 2 assured
3 tempered 4 minded
5 going

2
1 **un**sociable   **ir**responsible **un**reliable
2 **un**friendly **im**patient **im**polite
3 thought**less** **in**tolerant **in**sensitive
4 **un**kind **un**caring **im**practical

3
1 e 2 c 3 h 4 a 5 f
6 d 7 b 8 g

Language focus page 59
1
1 am/'m going (to go) or will/'ll be going
2 won't take/doesn't take
3 is coming/'s coming/is going to come/'s going to come/will be coming/'ll be coming
4 gets
5 shall we go (also: can/should we go)
6 am/'m going to stay
7 start/are starting/are going to start
8 will/'ll be revising or am/'m going to revise or am/'m revising
9 'll phone
10 will/'ll be watching
11 to start
12 setting off
13 to be
14 will/'ll probably get or are/'re probably going to get
15 will/'ll give
16 get or have/'ve got

2
He said that he had/'d been expecting to see me on the train but couldn't/hadn't been able to find me.
He asked me if/whether I had/'d gone.
He told me/said (that) it had been amazing.
He told me/said (that) he was sitting there watching the march on TV.
He asked me if/whether I was watching it too.
He told me/said (that) it looked really impressive.
He told me/said (that) it had been a long day so he was going to bed early.
He told me/said (that) he would give me a ring soon.

Unit 7 Survival

Speaking Part 3: Collaborative task page 60
1
Photo 1: books; **Photo 2:** small shops; **Photo 3:** tropical rainforest; **Photo 4:** cinemas; **Photo 5:** board games

Vocabulary 1: Surviving page 60
1
1 get 2 make 3 live
4 stay 5 get

2
b get by with   c live on
d get through the day
e find it hard to make ends meet

Listening Part 1: Multiple choice page 61
1 B 2 B 3 A 4 C 5 A
6 C 7 B 8 A

Answer key

Language focus 1: Countable and uncountable nouns page 62

1
1 hypermarkets [C]
2 tigers [C]
3 schools [C]   money. [U]
4 eBooks [C]
5 damage [U] street [C]
6 trees [C]
7 house [C] roof tiles. [C]
8 knowledge [U] research. [U]
9 journalist [C]   help [U] advice. [U]
10 problems [C]   behaviour. [U]

2

Before [U] nouns	Before plural [C] nouns	Before [U] and plural [C] nouns
a large amount of	many	some
much	a large number of	a lot of
a great deal of	very few several a couple of a few	

3
1 Several, number
2 many, plenty
3 Each, few, little, lot
4 amount, much

Reading and Use of English Part 7: Multiple matching page 62

2
1 D   2 C   3 B   4 C   5 A
6 D   7 B   8 A   9 B   10 C

Vocabulary 2: Prepositions page 64

1a
1 by   2 on   3 in   4 in

2a
1 to   2 for   3 on   4 about
5 at

2b
1 on   2 at   3 by
4 out of   5 in

3
1 charge, fire, risk, danger
2 accident, purpose, pay
3 order, complaining, smiles
4 participated, resulted, agree

Listening Part 2: Sentence completion page 64

2
1 Endurance and Survival
2 five/5
3 January
4 whales
5 bag of onions
6 Japanese
7 round/around the world
8 interactive
9 navigation equipment
10 children under/below 5/five (years old)

Word formation: Adverbs page 65

1a
slowly   carefully
fully   dully

1b
reasonably   gently   truly
wholly   immediately   bravely

1c
happily   noisily

1d
automatically   scientifically
publicly

2a
1 safely   2 eventually
3 specifically   4 enormously
5 extremely   6 Surprisingly
7 Incredibly

Reading and Use of English Part 3: Word formation page 65

1 truly   2 survival
3 exceptionally   4 successfully
5 dramatically   6 Unable
7 decision   8 Amazingly

Language focus 2: Obligation, prohibition, advice and necessity page 66

1a
1 had to   2 mustn't   3 ought
4 have to   5 don't have to
6 need   7 should   8 must

2
1 you aren't allowed/you won't be allowed
2 We had/'d better
3 He made me stay
4 We don't have to wear
5 I needn't have spent
6 had to/have to buy
7 I have to walk
8 no need for you to bring

3a
Possible answers
It might be …
1 … an employee at a petting zoo or a farm speaking to children about the animals.
2 … one child talking to another about the mess they've made at home and their mother's reaction if she sees it.
3 … one pupil talking to another about how a teacher punished him or her.
4 … a bank or shop employee talking to a friend about their dress code at work.
5 … one examination candidate talking to another about the exam.
6 … one person talking to another about a pair of binoculars.
7 … one person talking to another about their car.
8 … one person talking about towels to a friend who is coming to stay.

Writing Part 2: Report page 66

2
1 Introduction
2 Going dancing
3 The sea is free
4 Indoor water fun
5 Conclusion

3
The target reader is the leader of the group of foreign students. The report is written in a formal style.

4a
a **great deal of** money
its **large number of** discos
many (discos)
Most town centre discos
all your students
plenty of amusements
every age group
several water slides

4b
do not **involve spending a great deal of money**
town centre discos are **not cheap**
admission is **inexpensive**
drinks are **affordably priced**
The sea is **free**
There is **no charge for** entry
prices are **reasonable**
there are **generous student discounts**
without having to **spend a fortune**

4c

I would advise students to go to those on the seafront
the beach **(is) a must** for all your students
I would also recommend a visit to the indoor Aqua Park

5

many ... are specifically aimed at under-16s, so are ideally suited to your younger group members.
who will love its fine sand and clean water
which appeal to every age group
it is highly popular with young people

6

Sample answer

Introduction
The aim of this report is to suggest places in town where your students can eat cheap, healthy food during their two-week stay here.

Salad bars
There are two well-known chains of salad bars in the area, 'Lettuce eat' and 'Salad Days', both of which serve excellent quality food. For approximately eight euros, you can choose from a wide variety of salad dishes, and eat as much as you want. I would particularly recommend going to 'Salad Days' next to the town hall, as they play good music and there is free wifi.

Foreign buffet restaurants
There are also a number of buffet restaurants which serve either Indian, Chinese or Japanese food, and which all offer very good value for money. I would advise your students to go to the Indian restaurant 'Taj Mahal', which has several vegetarian options and delicious rice. Although you pay a little more than in some of the others, drinks are included in the price.

Conclusion
Our town is used to welcoming young people who want to eat cheaply and healthily, and your students will have no problem finding suitable restaurants.

Unit 8 Brain games

Vocabulary 1: Memory page 68

1
1 faces 2 figures 3 memory
4 heart 5 memories

Reading and Use of English Part 1: Multiple-choice cloze page 68
1 B 2 B 3 A 4 C 5 B
6 C 7 D 8 B

Listening Part 4: Multiple choice page 69
1 B 2 B 3 A 4 B 5 C
6 C 7 B

Language focus 1: The passive page 71

1
a 2 b 4 c 1 d 3 e 2
f 1 g 2 h 4 i 2

2
b have (often) been asked
c being taken
d were discovered
e had been handed in
f be stored
g will be posted
h to be driven
i are being supervised

Present continuous: are being supervised
Present perfect: have (often) been asked
Past simple: were discovered
Past perfect: had been handed in
Future simple: will be posted
Gerund: being taken
Infinitive with *to*: to be driven
Infinitive without *to*: be stored

3
(to) be, past, by

4
1 b 2 a 3 d 4 c

5
1 *How to Develop a Perfect Memory* was written by Dominic O'Brien in 1993.
2 This artist's work will still be remembered two hundred years from now.
3 We were being given a vocabulary test when the fire alarm went off.
4 Mobile phones must be switched off before the start of the exam.
5 Memory competitions are regularly held all round the world.
6 I have been asked by my neighbour not to play my music so loud.

6
A smartphone has been found in the sports hall. It was discovered by a cleaner early this morning and must have been left there after yesterday's exam. At the moment it is being kept in the head teacher's office. A message about the smartphone will be sent to all those students who were in the sports hall yesterday, asking the owner to go to the head teacher. The owner's parents will then be asked to come to the school to collect their child's smartphone. All students should be reminded that phones are not permitted in exam rooms.

Reading and Use of English Part 5: Multiple choice page 72

3
The following words appear in the text in relation to Shigeru Miyamoto:
*modesty   placid   politeness
respectful   timidity*
In addition, we learn that he is 'not envious of the attention of movie stars' and that 'A Beatles T-shirt and moptop haircut are the only signs of cultural rebellion', from which we can deduce that he is neither *attention-seeking*, nor *vain* nor particularly *rebellious*. The writer speaks of Miyamoto's 'placid temperament' so it is unlikely that he is *moody*, and given the overall impression, and the fact that his games do not include violence, he is probably not *aggressive*.

4
a preserve b reverence
c scarcity d smash
e the limelight f tantrums
g demographic h prosperity

5
1 B 2 C 3 D 4 B 5 B
6 D

Answer key

Language focus 2: Passive of reporting verbs page 74

1
1 to have appeared
2 to be getting
3 to improve
a to be getting   b to improve
c to have appeared

2
It is known that Alfred Hitchcock appeared in most of his films.
It is thought that the human brain is getting bigger.
It is said that memory improves the more often we use it.

3a
1 It is expected that climate change will get much worse over the next few years.
Climate change is expected to get much worse over the next few years.
2 It is said that eating fish improves brain performance.
Eating fish is said to improve brain performance.
3 It is thought that social networking has made people more isolated.
Social networking is thought to have made people more isolated.
4 It is considered that English and Spanish are easy languages to learn.
English and Spanish are considered to be easy languages to learn.
5 It is said that daily life is getting much faster for most of us.
Daily life is said to be getting much faster for most of us.

Vocabulary 2: Arts and culture page 74

2
1 performance: you watch a performance – the others are all places
2 ballerina: this is one person – the others are all groups of people
3 exhibition: this is a group of things – the others are all types of art
4 instrument: this is an object – the others are all people
5 lyrics: these are the words of songs – the others are all types of music
6 sculpture: this is an art form or a work of art – the others are all people
7 stage: this is the place where actors, musicians, etc. perform – the others involve illustrations of some kind

4a
1 stage
2 best-seller
3 graffiti
4 concert hall
5 lyrics

Writing Part 2: Review page 75

2
A
1 c, 2 d, 3 a, 4 b
B
1 c, 2 a, 3 b, 4 d
C
1 d, 2 c, 3 b, 4 a

3
Sample answer
Whether you're a fan of jazz or not, I'd really recommend going to see Jazzamatazza play live.
  Last night was the first of a series of five concerts they'll be performing at the Café Musique in the capital this week – and even though jazz is not my favourite type of music, I absolutely loved it! Jazzamatazza specialise in humorous jazz arrangements of modern pop and rock classics. The concert is a lot of fun, and a must for anyone who wants to have a good laugh.
  There are nine musicians on stage at the same time, with a lead singer who plays keyboards on some of the songs. What made it for me was their version of U2's 'Sweetest Thing', with just the drummer and double bass player accompanying the singer. It was hilarious, and it's worth going just to hear that song.
  Jazzamatazza are on tour for the next four months, so if they play at a venue near you, you really should go and see them. Take your parents as well – they'll enjoy it, and they can pay for you, too!

Review Units 7 and 8

Reading and Use of English Part 4: Transformations page 76

1 not/n't **let** her take
2 **made** him tidy
3 no need for **you** to
4 **must** not be removed by
5 is being **questioned** at
6 is **thought** to be getting

Reading and Use of English Part 2: Open cloze page 76

1 in   2 is   3 every/each
4 which   5 to   6 few
7 Although/Though/While/Whilst
8 the

Vocabulary page 76

1
1 on, for
2 for, at
3 for, at
4 about, at
5 in, at
6 at, by
7 In, in
8 to, on

2
1 get   2 meet   3 brings
4 forgetful   5 limelight
6 modest   7 lyrics
8 performance

Language focus page 77

1
1 each/every, much
2 many, little
3 few, few
4 plenty/lots, couple
5 number/quantity, any
6 some, no/little

2
1 need to
2 needn't/don't have to
3 have to
4 should
5 ought
6 shouldn't/mustn't
7 shouldn't/mustn't
8 needn't/don't have to

3
1 The celebrity was photographed by two members of the paparazzi as he was leaving his house this morning.
2 These tablets should be taken with food.
3 Memory is said to get worse with age.
4 The writer was being interviewed by television presenter Mervyn Bagg when the lights suddenly went out in the studio.
5 Pat had been chosen to join the orchestra, so he was celebrating last night.
6 The decorating must be finished before we go on holiday.

7 The play has been given positive reviews by most critics.
8 The elections will be held on 20 June.

Unit 9 A slave to routine

Reading and Use of English Part 5: Multiple choice page 78

2
Possible answer
Iryna could be Tania and Robbie's elder sister, Polly's sister or perhaps the family's live-in au pair.

3
a fish out   b lash out
c turn up   d draw up
e cram into f burrow   g surge
h grind   i flip   j slumber

4
1 B   2 B   3 D   4 C   5 B
6 A

Language focus: Conditionals page 80

1
b future simple (passive), present simple
c would + infinitive (without *to*), past simple
d past perfect, would + have + past participle (or would + perfect infinitive without *to*)
e past perfect, might not + infinitive (without *to*)

2
1 d   2 e   3 c   4 a   5 b

3
a you get good marks
b you get good marks

4
or

5
1 if we are/'re late
2 I'd hate it *or* if I have to work
3 would have walked
4 unless you study *or* if you don't study
5 as long as you look after them
6 If we'd taken

6
1 did not/didn't have, would/'d go
2 will/'ll make
3 had/'d known, would not/wouldn't have brought
4 will/'ll change, shows
5 had/'d had, would not/wouldn't be
6 would/'d stay, were/was

Vocabulary: Time page 81

1a
1 to   2 on   3 in

1b
1 minute   2 fast   3 left

1c
Possible meanings
1 she is unable to put up with/tolerate it any longer
2 the time on her watch is always five minutes later than the correct time
3 there are only forty-eight seconds remaining for them

2
a from time to time
b at all times
c Time after time   d at a time
e at the time   f By the time

3a
2 make   3 have   4 find
5 set   6 spend/waste
7 waste/spend   8 pass

Listening Part 2: Sentence completion page 82

1 Take it slowly
2 check the time
3 speed
4 enjoy life
5 wear a watch
6 standing up
7 (eating) a meal
8 fair
9 fifty/50
10 traditional

Word formation: Nouns 2 page 82

1
1 behaviour/behavior   2 advice
3 belief   4 thought   5 network

2
1 sale   2 loss   3 flight   4 gift
5 laughter

3a
1 weight   2 height   3 heat
4 timetable   5 knowledge
6 choice   7 proof   8 sight

Listening Part 3: Multiple matching page 84

1

2 *Possible answers*
Noise, stress, worry, exam nerves, using electronic devices with screens before bedtime, eating too late, exercising too late, drinks with caffeine, irregular sleep patterns (e.g. because of shift work), too much light, uncomfortable mattress, sleeping in unfamiliar surroundings, old age

3 *Possible answers*
Avoid those things in 2 which cause you to sleep badly, go to bed and get up at the same time every day, read before bedtime, take regular exercise, practise relaxation techniques (e.g. deep breathing), drink herbal tea

2
1 C   2 G   3 B   4 H   5 E
(A, D, F not used)

Reading and Use of English Part 2: Open cloze page 84

3
1 each/every   2 to   3 few
4 be   5 which/that   6 on
7 front   8 as

Writing Part 2: Letter and email page 85

2
Content: No. A brief general opening paragraph would be appropriate, but a large portion of the first paragraph is devoted to information which is irrelevant to the question.
Organisation: Yes, although a list of numbered points, whilst acceptable, does not enable the writer to use a range of effective linking devices. In addition, the first paragraph, if it were relevant, would be better as two.
Cohesion: No. There is very little evidence of linking in this answer. The first paragraph is a sequence of short sentences and this is followed by a list of imperatives.

Range: Yes. There is some evidence of a range of structures and vocabulary, e.g. [you're] looking forward to your holiday, it must be terrible for you, If it doesn't work, you should go to the doctor's. There is, however, also some repetition (I'm going to, looking forward to, I'm sure, I went), which could be avoided.
Accuracy: Yes. The answer is sufficiently accurate at *Cambridge: First*. There are some spelling mistakes (see exercise 3), but no grammatical errors.
Register: Yes. The letter is consistently informal to neutral throughout.
Format: No. It is not clear that this is a letter. The beginning and ending in particular are not appropriate.
Target reader: Yes, possibly, although it is not clear for example how much exercise Robin should do or when he should do it, what Helena means by 'too late', or which herbal infusions are recommended.

3
I'm **really** looking forward
You're probably looking forward
it will be **beautiful**
a nice **break**
you are finding it **difficult**
I would be very **nervous**
Don't eat **too** late
I hope my **advice** is useful

4
Sample answer
Hi Robin,
Sorry to hear you're having trouble sleeping. Exams used to have that effect on me, but since I started following my doctor's advice, I haven't had any problems.
  The most important thing she told me to do is to take regular exercise. I go jogging every day, but it doesn't matter what the exercise is – just make sure you do something. If you don't like running, you could try swimming, or even just going for long walks. It's best to do this in the morning or afternoon – exercising too late in the day will also prevent you sleeping.
  Another thing that works for me is reading before I go to bed – it really helps me switch off. I don't think it's a good idea to study late at night and you certainly shouldn't work on your computer or look at any kind of screen just before you turn the light out.
  One final piece of advice – never drink coffee after 5 o'clock. If you want a hot drink in the evening, have a herbal tea or warm milk.
  I hope that's useful. All the best in your exams!
David

Unit 10 Getting on

Vocabulary 1: Relationships
page 86

1
1 get, get
2 fell, fell
3 took, took
4 keep, keep
5 broke, break

Reading and Use of English Part 6: Gapped text page 87

3
1 E   2 A   3 C   4 G   5 D
6 F   (B not used)

Writing Part 2: Article page 88

3
1 at, to   2 on, down   3 in
4 by   5 with, up   6 on, of

4
2 reliable   3 knowledgeable
4 humorous   5 tolerant
6 considerate

6
Sample answer
Have you ever had a friend who likes the sound of their own voice and never stops talking? They wouldn't be a friend of mine. The number one quality I look for in a friend is the ability to listen.
  Why is that so important to me? Because friendship for me is all about sharing – and that means sharing the bad things as well as the good. So if I have a problem, I want someone I can turn to, someone who will listen to me and help me try to solve that problem.
  A good sense of humour is another important quality. I don't feel comfortable with people who take life – and themselves – too seriously and never laugh about things. Life isn't always easy, so I'd rather be surrounded by people who make me feel happy, not miserable.
  Last but not least, a good friend has to be comfortable with silence. Sometimes I like to listen to my own thoughts, or the sounds of nature around me. How can I do that if someone is talking all the time?

Listening Part 3: Multiple matching page 89

2
1 C   2 G   3 B   4 A   5 E
(D, F, H not used)

4
1 through   2 of   3 of   4 out
5 to

Language focus 1: *Wish, if only* and *hope* page 90

2
2 d could, 3 c would, 4 a past perfect

3
In sentence **1** the speaker would like it to stop raining but considers it unlikely, whereas in sentence **2** the speaker is simply expressing a wish for the future.

4
1 I wish I **could get** or **I got** higher marks
2 We all wish it **were/was** warmer today
3 I hope Jack **wins** his race
4 If only I **had asked** you to help
5 Claire wishes they **would** stop building
6 If only I **didn't get** carsick

5
Possible answers
1 I wish I had/'d listened to my parents when I was a teenager.
2 I wish I were/was old enough to take my driving test
3 I wish I could come to your birthday party on Saturday.
4 I wish my parents would let me go abroad with my friends this summer.
5 I wish I hadn't been (so) horrible to my brother when I was younger.
6 I wish I didn't have to go to school early for an exam tomorrow.

Should have/ought to have page 90

1
Possible answers
I ought to/should have asked you to help when I had that problem with my car yesterday.

I ought to/should have listened to my parents when I was a teenager.
I ought not to/shouldn't have been (so) horrible to my brother when I was younger.

Vocabulary 2: Age page 91

1
Possible answers
A middle-aged
 in their forties/fifties
 getting on in years
B toddler
 youngster
C newborn
 in their twenties/thirties
D senior citizen
 elderly
 retired
 in their seventies/eighties
 getting on in years
E preteen
 youngster
F teenager
 youngster
 adolescent

Listening Part 4: Multiple choice page 92

2
1 C 2 B 3 A 4 A 5 B
6 C 7 C

Language focus 2: have/get something done page 92

1
1 b 2 a

2
My gran got her house broken into recently, so she's going to get a burglar alarm installed.

3
1 have, checked
2 had, redecorated
3 has, serviced
4 had, stolen
5 having, restyled

Reading and Use of English Part 1: Multiple-choice cloze page 93

3
1 A 2 B 3 C 4 A 5 C
6 D 7 D 8 C

Review Units 9 and 10

Reading and Use of English Part 4: Transformations page 94
1 **wish** they had not/hadn't gone
2 would **get** in
3 **should** not have stopped taking
4 only we could **afford** to
5 have/get his/the operation **performed**
6 had **turned** up on

Reading and Use of English Part 3: Word formation page 94
1 pressures 2 traditional
3 introduction 4 loss
5 behaviour/behavior 6 stressful
7 Supporters 8 encourage

Vocabulary page 95

1
1 takes 2 most 3 all
4 after 5 at 6 fast 7 get
8 through

2a
1 d 2 g 3 a 4 f
5 b 6 h 7 e 8 c

Language focus page 95

1
1 If Rachel's dad hadn't given her a lift, she wouldn't have got to the station on time. *or* Rachel wouldn't have got to the station on time if her dad hadn't given her a lift.
2 I wouldn't know so much about Slow Food if I hadn't read an article about it. *or* If I hadn't read an article about Slow Food, I wouldn't know so much about it.
3 Richard wouldn't have played football last Saturday if the usual goalkeeper hadn't had flu. *or* If the usual goalkeeper hadn't had flu, Richard wouldn't have played football last Saturday.
4 If I'd realised it was Jackie's birthday, I would have bought her a present. *or* I would have bought Jackie a present if I'd realised it was her birthday.
5 You wouldn't have wet feet if you'd worn the right kind of shoes. *or* If you'd worn the right kind of shoes, you wouldn't have wet feet.

2
1 would, on
2 had/got, on
3 have, on
4 have/get, in
5 could, at

Macmillan Education Limited
4 Crinan Street
London N1 9XW

Companies and representatives throughout the world

ISBN 978-0-230-49561-6 (with Answers)
ISBN 978-0-230-49562-3 (without Answers)

Text © Roy Norris 2016

Design and illustration © Macmillan Education Limited 2016

The author has asserted their right to be identified as the author of this work in accordance with the Copyright, Designs and Patents Act 1988.

First published 2016

All rights reserved. No part of this publication may be reproduced, stored in a retrieval system, or transmitted in any form or by any means, electronic, mechanical, photocopying, recording, or otherwise, without the prior written permission of the publishers.

Original design by Macmillan Education Ltd
Page make-up by emc design ltd
Illustrated by Montserrat Batet (Lemonade Illustration) pp25, 80; Atsushi Hara (Dutch Uncle) pp58, 59, 83, 95; Debbie Powell (The Artworks) pp23, 33, 49, 71, 93.

Cover design by Macmillan Education Ltd
Cover photographs by Getty Images/Gregor Schuster, Getty Images/WIN-Initiative

Picture research by Thomas Bonsu-Dartnall

Author's acknowledgements
Roy Norris would like to thank the editor, Jane Coates, for doing such a great job. It was a pleasure to work with you, Jane.

The publishers would like to thank Mark Harrison, Berenika Rewicka, David Toy, Fiona Way and Lynda Edwards.

The author and publishers would like to thank the following for permission to reproduce their photographs:

Alamy/Ableimages p24(r), Alamy/Ace Stock p98(r), Alamy/AF Archive p19, Alamy/Age Fotostock p28(m), Alamy/Agencja Fotograficzna Caro p67(r), Alamy/Apex News and Pictures Agency p6(D), Alamy/Bhandol p74(l), Alamy/Blend Images p10(br), Alamy/Cultura Creative p89(t), Alamy/Cultura RM p24(c), Alamy/Design Pics Inc pp14(t),18, Alamy/Robert Harding World Imagery p81(bl), Alamy/Tom Harradine p50(bl), Alamy/Juergen Hasenkopf p20, Alamy/Hero Images Inc p32(l), Alamy/Ian Kenny pp60(t), 63(b), Alamy/Kuttig - People p32(m), Alamy/Loop Images Ltd p37, Alamy/Laurentiu Iordache pp38–39(2), Alamy/MBI p91(D), Alamy/Paulasphotos p22, Alamy/Royal Geographical Society p64, Alamy/Rubberball p85, Alamy/Edd Westmacott p60(1), Alamy/Adrian Sherratt p90(A), Alamy/WENN ltd p68(b), Alamy/YAY Media AS pp78, 82;
Ardea/Jagdeep Rajput p46;
Brand X Pictures p29;
Cittaslow International p82(logo);
Comstock p52(l);
Corbis/Greg Hinsdale p86(b), Corbis/Catherine Karnow p70(4), Corbis/William Manning pp66–67, Corbis/Eric P p81(tl), Corbis/Radius Images p28(br), Corbis/Andrew Ross p96(1), Corbis/Christine Schneider pp68(t), 75, Corbis/Buck Stucio p87, Corbis/LWA/Dann Tardif/Blend Images p12, Corbis/Topic Photo Agency p81(bl), Corbis/Zero Creatives p35(b);
emc design ltd p24(t);
European Youth Parliament/Janne Vanhemmens p54(l);
Getty Images/Altrendo Images p42(r), Getty Images/Doug Armand pp44–45, Getty/Anzeletti p89(b), Getty Images/Ezra Bailey p86(t), Getty Images/Gareth Cattermole p30(b), Getty Images/Cultura RM/Zero Creatives p48(b), Getty Images/Cultura Travel/Daniel Fox p48(cb), Getty Images/Cultura Travel/Seb Oliver p70(3), Getty Images/James Darrell p36, Getty Images/Christian Deutscher p35(c), Getty Images/Kevork Djansezian p72, Getty Images/Dorling Kindersley p90(B), Getty Images/John Elder p61(4), Getty Images/Sean Gallager p93, Getty Images/Gallo Images – LKIS p79, Getty Images/Davis Gilardini p48(ct), Getty Images/Jamie Grill p6(C), Getty Images/Hero Images p6(A), Getty Images/Yu Yu Hoi pp6(t), 13(tl), Getty Images/Massoud Hossaini/AFP p28(t), Getty Images/Image Source p91(F), Getty Images/Jed Jacobsohn p6(B), Getty Images/Vincent Jary p44(l), Getty Images/Jupiter Images pp42(l), 77, Getty Images/Izett Keribar p60(2), Getty Images/Gerard Launet p53, Getty Images/MoMo Productions p86(b), Getty Images/Simply Mui p35(t), Getty Images/Michael Nagle/Bloomberg p61(5), Getty Images/Lane Oatley/Blue Jean Images p15(tr), Getty Images/Lisa Peardon p98(l), Getty Images/Peopleimages.com p10(tr), Getty Images/Popperfoto p94, Getty Images/Jeff Rotman p48(t), Getty Images/Adrian Samson p15(br), Getty Images/Danil Semyonov/AFP p10(tl), Getty Images/Mike Theiss pp32(t), 38(1), Getty Images/Universal Images Group p91(E), Getty Images/Wayne Walton p97(3);
Glow/Imagebroker p81(tr);
Robert Harding/James Morgan p61(3);
ImageSource p41;
Macmillan p65;
Michael Parker/aquarterof.co.uk p16(cr);
Photodisc pp42(t), 48(cm);
Photolibrary p52(r);
Photoshot p28(tl), Photoshot/Collection Christophel p31, Photoshot/Xinhua p50(tr);
Plainpicture/Cultura p70(2), Plainpicture/Jean-François Gratton p100(t), Plainpicture/Maskot p70(1);
Press Association/Pedro Benavente / Demotix pp50(t), 54(r), Press Association/Primate Research Institute, Kyoto/Tetsuro Matsuzawa p69;
Rex/Jeff Blackler p13(bl), Rex/Cultura p6(E), Rex/Walt Disney/Everett p26, Rex/Jiri Hubatka/imageBroker p24(l), Rex Features/HZ/Pixathlon/SIPA p57, Rex/IFC Films/Everett p74(r), Rex/New Line/Everett p8, Rex/Jeremy Piper/Newspix p50(br), Rex Shutterstock p50(tl), Rex/West End 61 p32(r);
Robert Harding/James Morgan p61(3);
Science Photo Library/B. Boissonnet/BSIP p34;
Shutterstock p16(background), Shutterstock/Phoric p63(t);
Superstock/Ashley Gill/OJO Images p91(C), Superstock/Imagesource p96(2);
Thinkstock pp86(t), 88(tl), 88(tr), 100(b), Thinkstock/Highwaystarz-Photography p92, Thinkstock/John Kasawa p81(bl)

The author and publishers are grateful to reprint the following copyright material:

p84 Adapted material from 'Why bedtime really matters' by Tanya Brown. Originally published in The Times on 6 February 2010. © Times Newspapers Limited, 2010. Reprinted with permission. Available at www.thetimes.co.uk

pp26–27 Adapted material 'Pixar: The real toon army' by Guy Adams. Originally published in The Independent on 23 October 2011. © The Independent, 2011. Reprinted with permission. www.independent.co.uk

p33 Extract from 'Holidaymaker ends up in wrong country' by Jamie Grierson. Originally published in The Independent on 22 October 2011 © Press Association, 2011. Reprinted with permission. www.pressassociation.com

pp44–45 Extract from 'Strange island: Pacific tribesmen come to study Britain' by Guy Adams. Originally published in The Independent on 17 September 2011 © The Independent, 2011. Reprinted with permission. www.independent.co.uk

pp72–73 Extract from 'Nintendo's biggest brain' by Tim Ingham. Originally published in The Independent on 23 October 2011 © The Independent, 2011. Reprinted with permission. www.independent.co.uk

pp78–79 Extract from 'Hearts and Minds' by Amanda Craig. © in the UK, EU & Commonwealth Little Brown Book Group, 2009. © in the USA & Canada Curtis Brown Ltd., 2009. Reprinted with permission.

pp16–17 Adapted material from 'How I made it: Michael Parker, founder of A Quarter Of' by Rachel Bridge. Originally published in The Times on 6 September 2009. © Time Newspapers Limited, 2009. Reprinted with permission. Available at www.thetimes.co.uk

p87 Adapted material from 'The cost of friendship gains new meaning when you can rent a friend' by Caroline Jowett. Originally published in the Express on 8 July 2014 © Northern and Shell Media Publications, 2014. Reprinted with permission. Available at www.express.co.uk

p77 Adapted material from 'California Driving: A Survival Guide' by Hamish Reid. © Hamish Reid, 2015. Reprinted with permission. Available at www.californiadriving.com

These materials may contain links for third party websites. We have no control over, and are not responsible for, the contents of such third party websites. Please use care when accessing them.

Printed and bound in Spain

2028 2027 2026 2025 2024
48 47 46 45 44 43 42